PERFORMANCE-BASED EARNED VALUE®

IEEE
computer
society
60th anniversary

PERFORMANCE-BASED
EARNED VALUE®

Paul J. Solomon, PMP

Ralph R. Young, DBA

A JOHN WILEY & SONS, INC., PUBLICATION

Published by John Wiley & Sons, Inc., Hoboken, New Jersey.
Published simultaneously in Canada.

For general information on our other products and services please contact our Customer Care Department within the U.S. at 877-762-2974, outside the U.S. at 317-572-3993 or fax 317-572-4002.

Wiley also publishes its books in a variety of electronic formats. Some content that appears in print, however, may not be available in electronic format.

Library of Congress Cataloging-in-Publication Data is available.

ISBN-13 978-0-471-72188-8
ISBN-10 0-471-72188-3

Table of Contents

Foreword

Earned value management is now nearing the 40 year mark of its existence. At various points throughout these years, EVM has evolved, stagnated, adapted, and stagnated again, while trying to meet the needs of modern project management. EVM practitioners have been accused at varying times of being myopic and unwilling to see beyond the established set of guidelines that "have stood the test of time". However, at certain times throughout the history of EVM, certain individuals have come forward to advance new applications and new methods of adapting EVM to the evolving needs of project managers. Once in a great while, these new ideas challenge our status quo and encourage us to seize the opportunity to make quantum improvements in our profession.

Paul Solomon and Ralph Young have accomplished this feat through the development of Performance-Based Earned Value (PBEV). Solomon and Young make the strong case that EVM has not kept pace with the increasing emphasis on systems engineering, product quality, risk management, and cycle time reduction that all project managers now face. Indeed, while EVM has always claimed that it integrates work scope, schedule, and budget into the so-called "iron triangle", experience shows us that true integration of product scope and achieving the desired product quality have not been fully integrated with EVM.

It is a paradox that EVM relies so heavily on the measure of "work performed"; indeed, this measure sets EVM apart from other project control techniques. However, the surprises that continue to surface at the end of many projects attest to the fact that perhaps we are not as smart as we would like to believe in measuring work performed. We continue to rely on hastily developed metrics, subjective metrics, or poorly defined milestones to measure our project's performance, even though these measures are the basis of our EVM principles. EVM practitioners ask the perpetual question—How can we get our project managers and engineers to be more engaged with EVM? This is the paradox and current state of EVM.

Solomon and Young propose a new approach that relies on system engineering standards and maturity models. This approach enhances the value of EVM through more objective assessment of true work performance and product quality. Their approach has been tested thoroughly on some of the most demanding projects to date: U.S. military software development. It was found to be a sound technique that yields exceptional results over that of traditional EVM.

It is hoped that PBEV will be thoroughly studied, discussed, and applied as an enhancement to traditional EVM. This book is a thoughtful treatise, carefully researched and replete with many examples. It is my belief that this will lead to major advancements in the understanding and advancement of EVM within both the technical and EVM communities, and be a major evolutionary force in improving EVM practice. Solomon and Young have not only advanced the practice of EVM; they have achieved what many have only dreamed of: proving the worth of EVM to the technical community.

Eleanor Haupt
Past President, Project Management Institute—College of
Performance Management
August 2006

Preface

Performance-Based Earned Value (PBEV) enhances project management by providing an unwavering focus on the customer requirements during all phases of product development. It supplements the Earned Value Management Systems industry standard (EVMS) with guidelines for true integration of project cost, schedule, and technical performance.

PBEV is based on standards and capability and maturity models for systems engineering, software engineering, and project management. It was designed to overcome EVMS's shortcomings in measuring progress toward achieving the product requirements. The use of EVMS has often failed to provide adequate early warning of pending failure to meet project objectives. Reported earned value often overstated technical progress and maturity, overstated the efficiency of project resources, and understated the estimates of the final project cost and completion date.

PBEV adds quality to earned value management by integrating the product or technical baseline with the performance measurement baseline.

If you are measuring the wrong things or not measuring the right way, than EVM may be more costly to administer and may provide less management value. PBEV provides reliable and valid information because:

1. **The right base measures of technical performance are selected,**
2. **Progress is objectively assessed, and**
3. **The indicated quality of the evolving product is measured.**

PBEV evolved from lessons learned in the development of large defense and commercial systems and from reviewing the best practices used in the U.S. defense industry and the commercial software industry in India. Its development was nourished by the authors' zeal for process improvement. We teamed to write this book to leverage our complementary experiences and achievements in earned value management and requirements management. The principles and guidelines of PBEV provide a framework for process improvement.

Acknowledgments

Performance-Based Earned Value happened because of the authors' zeal and shared vision. We are teachers and process improvers that enjoy stimulating the project management community to do better. Paul saw an opportunity to build upon Ralph's expertise in requirements engineering and requirements processes, as well as his publishing success. Ralph shared Paul's zeal to transform earned value management (EVM) from a work-based to a requirements-based project management tool and recognized the synergistic possibilities.

Many others joined our team and must be thanked. Paul's acknowledgements come first. I was inspired by a few great teachers and evangelists of EVM including Wayne Abba, Gary Christle, Quentin Fleming, Eleanor Haupt, and Fred Manzer. I also remember when Darrell Baker patiently tutored me on that strange concept, earned value, after I moved from overhead management to project management. My friend, Ralph Kellogg, joined me on numerous subcontractor surveillance reviews and urged me to publish. I also am indebted to my wife, Adriana, for prodding me to write the book and then showing patience and encouragement throughout the writing process. My son, Thomas, provided support, advice, and a great literary environment. I wrote Appendix A, Fundamentals of EVM, at his home in the sunny Tuscan Hills with pleasant interruptions by my granddaughter, Natalie.

Ralph owes continuing thanks to his wife, Judy, for her understanding of his passion to share ideas and try to help projects, organizations, and industry become ever better. His work colleagues at Northrop Grumman Defense group are a constant source of energy, commitment, and refreshing ideas. Concerning this book, Terry Bartholomew has provided examples and other help that made a big difference.

We are indebted to Fred Manzer and his colleague, Bill Flury, for their time-consuming and valuable critiques of the first draft. Their discovery of logical inconsistencies, oversights, and writing errors, as well as their insightful recommendations, resulted in radical improvements to the content and quality of this book.

We also thank Deborah Plummer, our publisher, for her constant encouragement and support and for getting us back on the same track when we had artistic or technical differences, or just ran out of gas.

Chapter 1

Overview of PBEV

INTRODUCTION

This chapter describes the current state of Earned Value Management
(EVM) and explains the need for a new generation of earned value
techniques. Both major stakeholders, customer and supplier, need a
project management tool that truly integrates a project's cost, schedule, and technical performance objectives, can be tailored to enterprise
and project needs, can be utilized at the lowest possible cost, and supports shorter project cycle times. The characteristics and limitations of
traditional EVM are examined. The characteristics and advantages of
Performance-Based Earned Value (PBEV) are introduced. These will
be amplified and clarified in the remainder of the book and applied to
a typical systems development project.

WHAT IS PBEV?

Performance-Based Earned Value (PBEV) is an enhancement to
the Earned Value Management Systems (EVMS) national standard.
PBEV supplements EVMS with principles and guidelines for true
integration of project cost, schedule, and *technical* performance. It is
derived from standards and capability and maturity models for systems
engineering and project management. PBEV overcomes several
limitations of EVMS with regard to customer satisfaction and risk
management.

PBEV addresses customer satisfaction by incorporating product
requirements and planned quality into the Performance Measurement
Baseline (PMB). EVMS addresses only the *quantity of work* completed.

The customer is satisfied when all *product requirements* have been met, including the expected *quality*. However, EVMS states that the *quality* and *technical content* of the work performed are controlled by *other means*. Consequently, a supplier's application of EVMS may be compliant with the EVMS guidelines but fail to report deviations from the plan to meet the product requirements. PBEV enables true integration of technical performance with cost and schedule performance by linking work packages to milestones for meeting the product requirements. PBEV includes milestones that have documented success criteria and objective measurement of progress toward those milestones.

PBEV also incorporates the outcomes of risk management into revised plans and the Estimate at Completion (EAC). Although EVMS is called a risk management tool, it is silent on the topic of risk management.

PBEV supports agile systems development because it is scalable to match the project risk and is responsive to changing product requirements. PBEV evolved from lessons learned in both the U.S. defense industry and the commercial software industry in India. It is a cost-effective method. The principles and guidelines of PBEV provide a framework for process improvement.

PBEV CHARACTERISTICS

PBEV is a set of principles and guidelines that specify the most effective measures of cost, schedule, and technical performance. It has several characteristics that distinguish it from traditional EVMS:

1. **The plan is driven by product requirements, not work requirements.**
2. **Earned value is based on technical maturity and quality, in addition to work completed.**
3. **Technical performance is determined by meeting success criteria of technical reviews.**
4. **The approach:**
   a. **Adheres to standards and models for systems engineering, software engineering, and project management.**
   b. **Provides smart work package planning.**
   c. **Enables insightful variance analysis.**
   d. **Ensures a lean and cost-effective approach.**
   e. **Enables scalable scope and complexity of management control, depending on risk.**
   f. **Integrates risk management activities with the PMB.**
   g. **Incorporates quantified risk assessment into the EAC.**
   h. **Is applicable to all development models and methods, including agile methods.**

PBEV enables quantitative project management with a high degree of confidence in the reliability and validity of the earned value information. It contributes to project success by signaling early warnings of deviations from systems engineering and other technical plans. PBEV evolved by responding to lessons learned from projects that used legacy EVMS but experienced shortcomings in management visibility and control.

Advice on how to apply PBEV in practice is given in subsequent chapters. To help the reader appreciate the advantages of PBEV, we will first examine the reputation of EVM.

REPUTATION OF EARNED VALUE MANAGEMENT

EVM is defined as a project management tool that effectively integrates the project scope of work with cost, schedule, and performance elements for project planning and control [1]. The Project Management Institute (PMI) states that EVM has proven itself to be one of the most effective performance measurement and feedback tools for managing projects [2]. The PMI standard, Project Management Body of Knowledge (PMBOK® Guide), describes earned value analysis as the most commonly used method of performance measurement [3].

If properly implemented, EVM enables quantitative project management with a high degree of confidence in the reliability and validity of the earned value information. A project manager (PM) can know how efficiently resources are being managed and can use standard mathematical formulae for estimating the project's final costs. EVM contributes to project success by signaling early warnings of deviations from cost and schedule plans. The early warnings allow the PM to take prompt corrective actions to bring the project under control. By using EVM, the PM and the customer expect to understand the status of the project and the most likely outcome at project completion. They hope to avoid unpleasant surprises.

LESSONS LEARNED

Unfortunately, we have observed many PMs and customers who used EVM but were unable to avoid unpleasant surprises. It later turned out that the previous earned value information had reported work progress but failed to account for technical performance that was behind schedule. Consequently, the information overstated the efficiency of project resources and understated the estimates of the final project cost and completion date. Furthermore, the projects incurred significant costs just in administering the EVM processes and reporting EVM status.

As employees of a major corporation that uses EVM on large federal and defense contracts and as taxpayers who pay for the contracts, we want EVM to be a useful project management tool that enables project success. Yet, many stakeholders (including us) have asked:

> Why was the previous earned value information misleading and invalid?
>
> Why are we spending so much money on EVM and not receiving adequate business value?
>
> How can we use EVM more effectively?

Some of the lessons learned by examining the root causes of the unpleasant surprises follow.

Inadequate Early Warning

The use of EVMS has often failed to provide adequate early warning of significant future deviations from project objectives. The customer sometimes has received unpleasant surprises. As discussed above, post mortems and lessons learned disclosed that the previously reported earned value information had overstated technical progress and maturity and understated the impacts on completion objectives.

Poor Implementation of EVMS

Some project surprises are the result of poor implementation of EVMS. There may have been insufficient training, a lack of involvement and urgency by top management, and failure to used the earned value data to detect and control variances. PBEV will not prevent or overcome such lapses in management and discipline.

Reliable, Valid Information

EVM data will be reliable and valid only if:

1. **The right base measures of technical performance are selected.**
2. **Progress is objectively assessed.**
3. **The indicated quality of the evolving product is measured.**

Product Requirements and Quality

Earned value taken should reflect progress toward meeting the product requirements and the expected quality of the product that is being developed. A product requirement is a statement that identifies a product operational, functional, or design characteristic or constraint, which is unambiguous, testable or measurable, and necessary for product or process acceptability (by consumers or internal quality assurance guidelines). Quality is the degree to which a set of inherent characteristics of a product or product component fulfills requirements of customers.

Processes
EVM's effectiveness as a measure of performance depends on the capability and maturity with which the organization performs the related processes for systems engineering (SE) (including software engineering) and project management. The most pertinent SE processes for PBEV are requirements development, requirements management, and performance-based progress measurement.

Measures
Finally, if you are measuring the wrong things or not measuring the right way, then EVM may be more costly to administer and may provide less management value [4].

This book provides a framework and practical guidance for utilizing EVM as a key component of project planning, measurement, and control. The framework is primarily based on actual project experience, and it is also guided by standards and capability models for EVM, systems engineering, software engineering, and project management. The techniques that follow have been used in successful, software-intensive projects and provide the most business value for the money. We call it *Performance-Based Earned Value.*

SNAPSHOT OF EVM
Before EVM, Project Managers (PMs) tracked cost and schedule performance independently of each other. Actual expenditures of resources were compared with planned expenditures through a point in time to determine a so-called cost variance. The actual progress of activities was compared with scheduled activities to determine the schedule variance in measures of time. However, there was no unifying measure that valued the progress of the activities (physical work accomplished) in measures of the resources that were planned for that accomplishment. That measure is earned value (EV).

EVM compares the amount of work that was planned (Planned Value or PV) with what was actually accomplished, EV, to determine whether project cost and schedule performance were achieved as planned. The U.S. standard for EVM includes the following principles:

1. Decompose the program work scope into finite pieces that can be assigned to a responsible person or organization for control of technical, schedule, and cost objectives (control accounts and work packages).
2. Integrate program work scope, schedule, and cost objectives into a performance measurement baseline (PMB) against which accomplishments can be measured.
3. Objectively assess accomplishments at the work performance level.
4. Analyze significant variances from the plan, forecast impacts, and prepare an estimate at completion (EAC) based on performance to date and work to be performed.

EVM uses two performance indices that enable effective analysis and forecasting. The Cost Performance Index (CPI) is the cost efficiency of the resources that were expended. The Schedule Performance Index (SPI) is the ratio of schedule progress against the plan based on budgeted resources, not time. Individually or in combination, the CPI and SPI provide single-point and trend analyses of project performance and statistical forecasts of the EAC that would be attained if the PM failed to make corrective actions to the plan for the remaining work.

A primer on the fundamentals of EVM is provided in Appendices A and B.

EVMS HISTORY AND LIMITATIONS

EVMS History

EVM was used by the U.S. Department of Defense (DoD) to monitor the acquisition of large-scale, high-risk systems. Later, U.S. federal policy for nondefense agencies also required that suppliers use an Earned Value Management System (EVMS). In recent years, EVM has been adapted for use in commercial projects, including software-intensive projects. The EVM standard, EVMS, transformed government contractual requirements into a national standard. However, there are several limitations of the EVMS standard that inhibit its potential to integrate a project's cost, schedule, and technical objectives.

EVMS Limitations

EVM was initially developed to monitor the acquisition of large-scale, high-risk systems. EVMS was the result of transforming government contractual requirements into a national standard. However, EVMS has several shortcomings with regard to best practices in systems engineering and project management.

1. EVMS states that EV is a measurement of the *quantity* of work accomplished. Its discussion states that the quality and technical content of work performed are controlled by *other processes* (EVMS, Section 3.8). A project manager (PM) should ensure that EV also measures the *product quality* and technical maturity of the evolving technical work products instead of just the quantity of work completed.

2. The EVMS principles address the only the *work scope* of a project. They ignore the *product scope* or the product requirements. On the other hand, the systems engineering standards and models address the product requirements and require assessment of progress against requirements, technical performance, design maturity, and the quality of the product being developed. The PMBOK Guide differentiates two components of scope: product scope and project (work) scope. The PMBOK Guide also includes the quality baseline within the product scope and includes the quality baseline as part of the PMB.

3. EVMS encourages but does not require precise, quantifiable measures. It states that objective earned value methods are preferred, but it also states that management assessment (subjective) may be used to determine the percentage of work completed. In contrast, the PMBOK Guide and the capability model cited below provide specific guidance regarding objective measurement.

4. EVM is sometimes described as a risk management tool. However, EVMS provides no guidance on risk management and does not even mention the word "risk." By the time a significant cost or schedule variance exists, it is already an issue that should be addressed. It should not be misclassified as a risk. The variance will remain an issue until it is mitigated or until an effective corrective action plan is in place.

5. EVM is capable of providing powerful measures for measurement, analysis, and control. However, EVMS provides very little guidance for specifying the types of measures that meet management needs and objectives.

6. Finally, measurement costs money. There are significant costs to implement and use EVM. These costs can be reduced if the enterprise has an effective process to determine its information needs and objectives and to specify only those measures that meet those needs and objectives.

In summary, EVMS is a standard that lacks specific guidance on product requirements, quality, and risk management. It does not provide needed guidance for measuring progress toward meeting the customer's requirements. This book supplements EVMS with helpful guidance.

The following guidance will help a PM to understand and implement PBEV as a process improvement, in accordance with standards and models. It will enable EVM to be a more effective component of an integrated management system.

CUSTOMER EXPECTATIONS FOR PERFORMANCE-BASED MANAGEMENT SYSTEMS

Both the U.S. federal government and its military and civilian agencies have policies and acquisition regulations that require performance-based management systems.

U. S. Federal Policy

The U.S. government has acquisition policies and regulations that specify performance-based measurement. The Office of Management and Budget (OMB) requires that all agencies of the government that are subject to Executive Branch review must use a performance-based acquisition management system, based on EVMS, to obtain timely information regarding the progress of capital investments [5]. The system must *measure progress toward milestones* in an independently verifiable basis, in terms of cost, *capability of the investment to meet specified requirements*, timeliness *and quality* (Section 300.5). Both the government and contractors must demonstrate the use of an EVMS for development efforts (Exhibit 300, Part 1 H).

OMB has issued this policy to implement federal statutes, notably the Federal Acquisition Streamlining Act of 1994, Title V (FASA V) and the Information Technology Management Reform Act of 1996 ("Clinger–Cohen"). Federal Acquisition Regulations (FAR) requires the use of an EVMS that complies with the guidelines of ANSI/EIA Standard-748 for major acquisitions for development, in accordance with OMB Circular A-11 and that EVMS requirements will be applied to both prime contractors and subcontractors. One FAR clause requires the Government to conduct Integrated Baseline Reviews to assess the degree to which the management process provides effective and *integrated technical/schedule/cost planning and baseline control*. More information about these topics is in Chapter 14, *Supplier Acquisition Management*, and in Appendix D, *FAR Clauses*.

U.S. Department of Defense Policies

The Department of Defense (DoD) acquisition policy also requires specified suppliers to use performance-based management systems that meet OMB requirements for EVMS. However, DoD also has a policy and guidance regarding the use of systems engineering plans and the integration of systems engineering with EVM. The systems engineering standards that are referenced in the guidance were used as a basis for PBEV.

Integrating Systems Engineering with Earned Value Management

Compliance with the systems engineering standards will support DoD acquisition policy that programs implement systems engineering plans [6]. That policy is a result of DoD analyses that show a definite linkage between escalating costs and the ineffective application of systems engineering [7]. Consequently, the DoD has made the revitalization of systems engineering a priority. Systemic, effective use of systems engineering is a key acquisition management planning and oversight tool.

Regarding requirements, Wynne and Schaeffer add that the earlier in a program's life cycle that requirements are intensively managed by the systems engineering processes, the greater the likelihood that the program's cost and schedule estimates will be on target. Many programs trace their rising costs and lagging schedules to requirements-based problems such as poor program definition, lack of traceable allocations, and incomplete or weak verifications. Key to the successful implementation of systems engineering is the relationship between program management, contract management, and financial management.

Guidance documents that support the DoD policy include a systems engineering chapter in the Defense Acquisition Guidebook (DAG) [8], the Systems Engineering Plan (SEP) Preparation Guide (SEP Guide) [9], Work Breakdown Structure Handbook, MIL-HDBK-881A (WBS) [10], and the Integrated Master Plan and Integrated Master Schedule Preparation and Use Guide (IMP/IMS) [11]. The guides provide discretionary best business practices to complement the policy. Table 1.1 shows pertinent components of the policy and guides.

National Defense Industrial Association

The National Defense Industrial Association (NDIA) Program Management Systems Committee (NDIA PMSC) also recommends integrating SE with EVM, as follows:

> With EVM expanding rapidly across the global project management community, project-based organizations can use EVM effectively to integrate systems engineering, cost estimating, contracting and risk

management for program/project management by government and contractor communities whenever the use of EVM is required. It is recommended for all program management stakeholders . . . The baseline of a program needs to be described in technical terms and requirements (size, weight, capability, performance, etc.). These requirements are determined through the systems engineering process. This process provides a clearer understanding of the program as knowledge of the end product is better defined. [12].

Standards and Capability Models

The following standards and capability models provide the foundation for PBEV principles and guidelines:

TABLE 1.1 DoD SE Policy and Guideines

Policy or Guideline	Policy	DAG	SEP Guide	WBS	IMP/ IMS
Develop Systems Engineering Plan (SEP).	P	4.2.3.2	1.0		
Event-driven timing of technical reviews	P	4.5.1	3.4.4	3.2.3.1	2.3, 3.3.2
Success criteria of technical reviews	P	4.5.1	3.4.4	3.2.3.1	3.3.2
Assess technical maturity in technical reviews.		4.5.1	3.4.4	3.2.3.1	
Integrate SEP with Integrated Master Plan (IMP).		4.5.1	3.4.5		1.2, 2.3
Integrate SEP with Integrated Master Schedule (IMS).		4.5.1	3.4.5		1.2, 2.3
Integrate SEP with Technical Performance Measures (TPM).		4.5.1	3.4.4		1.2, 2.3
Integrate SEP with Earned Value Management (EVM).		4.5.1	3.4.5		1.2, 2.3
Integrate WBS with requirements specification, statement of work (SOW), IMP, IMS, and EVMS.				2.2.3, 3.2.3.3	3.4.3
Use TPMs to compare actual vs. planned technical development and design maturity.		4.5.5	3.4.4		3.3.2
Use TPMs to report degree to which system requirements are met in terms of performance, cost and schedule.		4.5.5	3.4.4		
Use standards and models to apply systems engineering.		4.2.2, 4.2.2.1			
Institute requirements management and traceability.		4.2.3.4			
Use EVM		11.3.1			

1. Earned Value Management Systems (EVMS)
2. Standard for Application and Management of the Systems Engineering Process (IEEE 1220) [13]
3. Processes for Engineering a System (EIA 632) [14]
4. Capability Maturity Model Integration (CMMI) [15]
5. A Guide to the Project Management Body of Knowledge (PMBOK Guide) [3]

The DAG references CMMI, EIA 632, and IEEE 1220 as examples of standards and models. The DAG cites EIA 632 and IEEE 1220 as primary standards that an organization would most likely need to accomplish systems engineering.

CUSTOMER DEMAND FOR EXCELLENT PROCESSES

If an enterprise's processes are consistent with the SE standards, it will support the DoD policy that a program must implement a SEP. The related guidance states that the SEP will address the integration of the technical aspects of the program with the overall program planning, SE activities, and execution tracking to include:

1. The SE processes (from a standard, a capability model, or the contractor's processes)
2. Discussion of metrics [e.g., Technical Performance Measures (TPM) for the technical effort and how these metrics will be used to measure progress]
3. Event-driven timing, conduct, success criteria, and expected products of technical reviews and how technical reviews will be used to assess technical maturity, assess technical risk, and support program decisions

CMMI AS A FRAMEWORK FOR PROCESS IMPROVEMENT

Suppliers to both commercial and government customers have used capability models to improve processes and obtain competitive advantage. The DoD policy cites a capability model as a source of SE processes. In Chapter 15, *Moving Forward*, guidance is provided for using CMMI as a framework for process improvement. PBEV is consistent with informational guidance in CMMI.

CUSTOMER NEEDS FOR REDUCED CYCLE TIME AND EVOLUTIONARY ACQUISITION

Commercial enterprises normally demand short product development cycle times to remain competitive. They must be able to respond to rapidly changing customer requirements.

The DoD has reformed its acquisition policies to encourage reduced cycle times. DoD policy (DoD Directive 5000.1, 2003) [16] states that advanced technology shall be integrated into producible systems and deployed in the shortest time practicable. Evolutionary acquisition strategies are the preferred approach to satisfying operational needs. Spiral development (described below) is the preferred process for executing such strategies.

DoD's guidance (DoD Instruction 5000.2, 2003) [17] for implementation of the policy states that an evolutionary approach delivers capability in increments, recognizing, up front, the need for future capability improvements. The success of the strategy depends on the consistent and continuous definition of requirements and the maturation of technologies that lead to disciplined development and production of systems that provide increasing capability toward a materiel concept. The approaches to achieve evolutionary acquisition include the following:

1. *Spiral Development.* In this process, a desired capability is identified, but the end-state requirements are not known at program initiation. Those requirements are refined through demonstration and risk management; there is continuous user feedback; and each increment provides the user the best possible capability. The requirements for future increments depend on feedback from users and technology maturation.

2. *Incremental Development.* In this process, a desired capability is identified, an end-state requirement is known, and that requirement is met over time by development of several increments, each dependent on available, mature technology.

PBEV supports evolutionary acquisition because of its continual focus on the product requirements baseline, including:

1. Traceability of schedule and cost plans to the known requirements
2. Specific guidance on the requirements development phase, including trade studies
3. Focus on measuring progress toward implementing the requirements
4. Guidance stating that changes to the product requirements baseline drive changes to the performance measurement baseline

INCREASING UTILIZATION OF EVM

There is increasing interest in the utilization of earned value to control commercial systems development projects. For example, two conferences on project management were held in India in 2004 and 2005. The attendees were primarily members of the commercial software industry. Representatives from Infosys, Alcatel, Satyam Computer Services, and Wipro submitted papers on the use of EVMS.

Guidance on PBEV was presented in Bangalore, Delhi, and Hyderabad by Paul Solomon. The software industry in India intends to improve its project management processes to achieve competitive advantage, just as it did with its software engineering processes. Leading-edge Indian companies are beginning to use EVM as part of their tool set.

PBEV AND AGILE METHODS

The need for reduced cycle time and evolutionary acquisition has been a catalyst for project managers to consider using agile development methods. Agile methods are discussed in Chapter 11.

PBEV can support agile systems development. Because it uses requirements-based planning and performance-based measurement, it enables innovation, flexibility, and focus on outcomes instead of non-value-adding processes. Also, PBEV Guidelines 4.1 and 4.2 support agility by tailoring the application of PBEV. Discrete measurement may be applied only to the higher-risk components of the WBS and may be deferred until the initial requirements have been developed.

ENTERPRISE DEMAND FOR COST-EFFECTIVE PROCESSES

As noted above, measurement costs money and an enterprise must incur significant implementation and sustaining costs in order to utilize EVM. These costs can be reduced if the enterprise utilizes an effective process to determine what needs to be measured and limits the measurements to those that meet its information needs and objectives. PBEV incorporates guidance for selecting measures from the standards and models discussed above. Consequently, PBEV can cost less than traditional EVM if the number of measures is reduced. Furthermore, management can control the project more effectively if it focuses on fewer but more critical measures.

EVOLUTION OF PBEV

PBEV was developed incrementally. It began with a series of process improvements within a sector of the Northrop Grumman Corporation. The improvements were initially driven by the need to provide performance measurement of software development at the Northrop

Grumman Corporation Integrated Systems Sector. One of the authors (Solomon) teamed with program management and with the software engineering process group to develop new practices. The first set of improvements used Practical Software and Systems Measurement (PSM) [18] as a framework for process improvement. PSM has principles for identifying, collecting, and tracking project measures that produce work products. Examples of performance-based measures for earned value include functional requirements status, component status, test status, and increment content-function.

These changes paid off during upgrades of the B-2 weapon system. The new metrics helped to make it a very successful program. The PBEV methodology was used to ensure that the warfighter received the most functionality from software development efforts. "The B-2 Spirit Stealth Bomber Program implemented several innovative process improvements using EVM. These include integrating earned value with systems engineering processes, defining improved software engineering metrics to support EVM, and developing a leaner, more effective methodology called performance-based earned value (PBEV)" [19]. A description of these early process improvements and the resultant practices is provided in Solomon, "Practical Software Measurement, Performance-Based Earned Value" [20].

The next evolution incorporated practices from Capability Maturity Model Integration (CMMI), especially those concerning requirements management and measurement. While teaching the use of EVM at the Software Engineering Process Group Conference in India, Paul Solomon was questioned about the relationship between the EVMS guidelines and CMMI. Many of the software companies in India were achieving high levels of CMMI capability. Concurrently, many defense companies in the U.S. were starting to use the CMMI model to improve their capabilities. Solomon, working with the Software Engineering Institute (SEI), published a paper that provides guidance for using CMMI as a framework for improving EVM processes and includes tables that map CMMI practices and information needs to EVMS guidelines [21].

The systems engineering standards cited earlier provide additional guidance for meeting customer requirements including coverage of technical performance measurement (TPM) and success criteria for technical reviews. Finally, the principal tenets of PBEV included guidance from the PMBOK Guide regarding risk management and TPM.

Process improvement at the Northrop Grumman Integrated Systems Sector is ongoing, with the primary frameworks for improvement being

Institute of Electrical and Electronic Engineers (IEEE)-1220, CMMI, and ISO/IEC 15288.

A second visit to India by Paul Solomon provided ideas for adapting PBEV to incorporate some objectives of agile methods. While teaching EVM during the first International Project Management Leadership Conference (Bangalore, 2004), he and students discussed ways to tailor PBEV so that it could support the goals of agile development methods. Some of these ideas are incorporated into PBEV Guidelines 4.1 and 4.2.

COMPARISON OF PBEV WITH EVMS

The principles of EVMS are a foundation for PBEV. However, PBEV adds four principles that enable more effective project management. A comparison of the principles of EVMS and PBEV is shown in Table 1.2.

TABLE 1.2 EVMS and PBEV Principles

Principle (E) = EVMS (P) = PBEV	EVMS	PBEV
(E) Plan all work scope to completion.	Y	Y
(P) Integrate product requirements and quality into the project plan.	N	Y
(E) Break down work scope into finite pieces that can be assigned to a responsible person or organization for control of technical, schedule, and cost objectives.	Y	Y
(E) Integrate project work scope, schedule, and cost objectives into a performance measurement baseline (PMB) against which accomplishments may be measured. Control changes to the baseline.	Y	Y
(P) Specify performance toward meeting product requirements, including planned quality, as a base measure of earned value (EV).	N	Y
(E) Use actual costs incurred and recorded in accomplishing the work performed.	Y	Y
(E) Objectively assess accomplishments at the work performance level.	Y	Y
(E) Analyze significant variances from the plan, forecast impacts, and prepare an estimate at completion based on performance to date and work to be performed.	Y	Y
(E) Use EVMS information in the company's management process.	Y	Y
(P) Integrate risk management with earned value management (EVM).	N	Y
(P) Tailor the application of EVM according to the risk.	N	Y

EVMS Process Flow

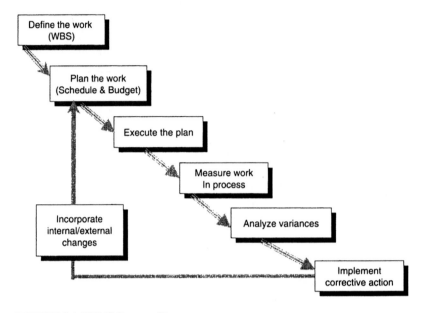

FIGURE 1.1 EVMS Process Flow.

PBEV PROCESS FLOW

The PBEV process flow is consistent with the EVMS process flow but has additional processes regarding the product requirements and risk management. Figures 1.1 and 1.2 show the EVMS process flow (Figure 1.1) and the PBEV process flow (Figure 1.2).

The PBEV processes and guidelines that supplement EVMS are highlighted in Figure 1.2. PBEV includes three processes that supplement EVMS and that address the product requirements:

  1. **Define the product (also called the technical baseline).**
  2. **Integrate product requirements and quality with the plan.**
  3. **Measure progress toward meeting product requirements and quality.**

An additional PBEV process addresses risk management:

  4. **Integrate risk management with the plan.**

ABOUT THIS BOOK

The following chapters provide guidance and examples to illustrate improved practices that follow the guidelines of PBEV. When appro-

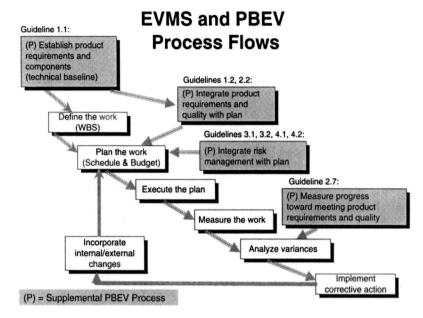

FIGURE 1.2 PBEV Process Flow.

priate, the guidance in this book will cite and display the references from the standards and models that are a foundation of PBEV. A complex engineering development project is introduced in Chapter 4. That project demonstrates the importance of managing requirements with effective systems engineering processes. Examples from the project are continued in subsequent chapters when additional PBEV guidelines are applied.

This book augments legacy or traditional EVMS. The authors assume that the readers understand the principles, guidelines, and practices of traditional EVMS. However, for readers who are new to EVM and for those who need to understand EVMS to meet educational or professional certification requirements, the fundamentals of traditional EVMS are covered in Appendices A and B.

A real, nontechnical project is described, planned, and measured to reflect the role of the Project Manager.

The chapters and appendices include examples of best practices that are instructional and that can be used as templates for using EVM on your project. Appendices C, C-1, and D include useful information and references for customers and suppliers that must comply with the EVMS guidelines. Appendices E through I include guidance and examples for managing technical performance and the technical baseline.

Chapter 14, *Supplier Acquisition Management*, will help the customer to ensure that its suppliers use EVM effectively. All other chapters are intended to benefit both customers and suppliers. We hope that you will consider applying the PBEV guidelines to your project and that both parties will reap the benefits of high customer satisfaction.

SUMMARY

This chapter has reviewed the current state of EVM. The authors assert that there is a need for a new generation of earned value techniques: Performance-Based Earned Value (PBEV). Customers and suppliers need a project management tool that fully integrates a project's cost, schedule, and technical performance objectives; can be tailored to enterprise and project needs; can be utilized at the lowest possible cost; and supports shorter project cycle times. The characteristics and short-comings of traditional EVM were examined. The characteristics and advantages of PBEV were introduced. A comparison of PBEV with EVMS was provided. PBEV adds four principles that enable more effective project management.

REFERENCES

[1] U.S. Federal Acquisition Regulations, Appendix D, paragraph 2.101.

[2] Project Management Institute. *Practice Standard for Earned Value Management.* Upper Darby, PA: Project Management Institute, 2004.

[3] Project Management Institute. *A Guide to the Project Management Body of Knowledge (PMBOK® Guide)*, 3rd ed. Upper Darby, PA: Project Management Institue, 2004 (ANSI/PMI 99-001-2004).

[4] Solomon, Paul. "Integrating Systems Engineering with Earned Value Management." *Defense Acquisition, Technology, & Logistics Magazine*, May 2004 (see www.dau.mil/pubs/damtoc.asp).

[5] Executive Office of the President. OMB Circular No. A-11, Part 7, Section 300.5, *Planning, Budgeting, Acquisition and Management of Capital Assets*, July 2004 (see www.whitehouse.gov/omb/circulars/all/cpgtoc.html).

[6] Wynne, Michael [Acting Undersecretary of Defense, Acquisition, Technology and Logistics (AT&L). Memorandum, *Policy for Systems Engineering in DoD*, February 20, 2004.

[7] Wynne, Michael and Schaeffer, Mark. "Revitalization of Systems Engineering in DoD." *Defense Acquisition, Technology, & Logistics Magazine*, March/April 2005 (see www.dau.mil/pubs/damtoc.asp).

[8] DoD. *Defense Acquisition Guidebook.* http://akss.dau.mil/dag/.

[9] Office of the Under Secretary of Defense for Acquisition, Technology, and Logistics Defense Systems, Systems Engineering, Enterprise Development (OUSD(AT&L)DS/SE/ED). *Systems Engineering Plan (SEP) Preparation Guide.* Version 1.0, November 15, 2005. see http://www.acq.osd.mil/ds/se/publications/pig/sep_prepguide_v1.pdf.

[10] DoD Handbook Work Breakdown Structure. See https://acc.dau.mil/CommunityBrowser.aspx?id=17642

[11] DoD. *Integrated Master Plan and Integrated Master Schedule Preparation and Use Guide.* See https://acc.dau.mil/CommunityBrowser.aspx?id=19559.

[12] National Defense Industrial Association (NDIA) Program Management Systems Committee (PMSC). ANSI/EIA-748-A, *Standard for Earned Value Management Systems Application Guide.* Working Release for User Comment, Arlington, VA, 2005.

[13] Institute of Electrical and Electronics Engineers (IEEE). IEEE Std 1220™-2005, *IEEE Standard for Application and Management of the Systems Engineering Process.* New York, 2005.

[14] Electronic Industries Alliance (EIA). ANSI/EIA 632, *Processes for Engineering a System.* Arlington, VA: EIA, 1998.

[15] Software Engineering Institute (SEI). *Capability Maturity Model Integration*, Version 1.1. Pittsburgh, PA: SEI, Carnegie Mellon University, March 2002.

[16] U.S. Department of Defense (DoD). DoD Directive 5000.1, *The Defense Acquisition System.* May 12, 2003.

[17] U.S. Department of Defense (DoD). DoD Instruction 5000.2, *Operation of the Defense Acquisition System.* May 12, 2003.

[18] U.S. Department of Defense (DoD) and U.S. Army. *Practical Software and Systems Measurement.* See www.psmsc.com.

[19] Solomon, Paul. "B-2 Bomber Team's EVM Innovations Make Program Soar." *Agile Acquisition, the Air Force Acquisition Newsletter* (formerly *Aerospace Acquisition*). January–February 2000.

[20] Solomon, Paul. "Practical Software Measurement, Performance-Based Earned Value." *CrossTalk: The Journal of Defense Software Engineering.* September 2001, pp. 28–29. See www.stsc.hill.af.mil/crosstalk/2001/09/index,html.

[21] Solomon, Paul. "Using CMMI to Improve Earned Value Management" (CMU/SEI-2002-TN-016). Carnegie Mellon University/SEI, October 2002. See www.sei.cmu.edu/pub/documents/02.reports/pdf/02tn016.pdf.

Chapter 2

Principles and Guidelines of PBEV

INTRODUCTION

Chapter 1 described Performance-Based Earned Value (PBEV) as an enhancement to the EVMS standard and introduced the four principles of PBEV. In this chapter, the PBEV guidelines are introduced. These principles and guidelines augment those of EVMS. The majority of the underlying guidelines are derived from industry standards and models. Their sources are cited below. Several PBEV guidelines evolved from the authors' lessons learned and process improvements and therefore are based on practical experience. In subsequent chapters, a typical project will be used to illustrate and clarify the principles and guidelines of PBEV that will help the reader understand, implement, and use PBEV.

EVMS GUIDELINES

EVMS is based on thirty-two guidelines that support its principles. The principles of EVMS were included in Table 1.2, and the guidelines are provided in Appendix C.

PBEV PRINCIPLES AND GUIDELINES

PBEV augments EVMS with four additional principles and sixteen additional guidelines. They are listed and clarified below.

PBEV Principles

The additional principles of PBEV are:

Performance-Based Earned Value, by Paul J. Solomon and Ralph R. Young
Copyright ©2007 IEEE Computer Society.

1. **Integrate product requirements and quality into the project plan.**
2. **Specify performance toward meeting the product requirements, including planned quality, as a base measure of earned value.**
3. **Integrate risk management with Earned Value Management.**
4. **Tailor the application of PBEV according to the risk.**

PBEV Guidelines

The PBEV guidelines are listed in Table 2.1 with references to their source standards and models, where applicable. The first digit of each guideline corresponds with its principle.

FIRST PRINCIPLE

The first principle of PBEV is:

Integrate product requirements and quality into the project plan.

This principle introduces two control elements that distinguish PBEV from EVMS, *product scope* and *product requirements*. A project manager who applies this principle will focus on what is most important to the customer. The customer will be satisfied when it takes delivery of a *product* that meets its *quality requirements and is delivered* within its cost and schedule objectives.

The project manager and the enterprise that contracts with the customer have business objectives to achieve maximum customer satisfaction and to deliver the product with the best possible cost performance. Both elements, product scope and product requirements, will be defined in the context of earned value management and discussed with regard to performance measurement.

Product Scope

The performance measurement baseline (PMB) in EVMS integrates three objectives: work scope, cost, and schedule. However, EVMS is missing the most important objective for customer satisfaction, the product that is to be delivered to the customer with the expected quality. Three EVMS principles discuss work scope but none discuss the product scope.

The differences between the product scope and the work scope are discussed in Chapter 1.

Product Requirements

The cited standards and models, other than EVMS, have similar guidance regarding the product, technical, or quality requirements. However, there are differences in the terminology used. Table 2.2

TABLE 2.1 Performance-Based Earned Value Guidelines

Performance-Based Earned Value® Guidelines	Source	Section Number
1.1 Establish product requirements and allocate these to product components.	IEEE 1220 EIA 632 CMMI® [1] PMBOK® Guide [2]	4.1 4.5.2 RD SP 2.1, 2.2 8.1.1.3
1.2 Maintain bidirectional traceability of product and product component requirements among the project plans, work packages, planning packages, and work products.	CMMI PMBOK® Guide	REQM SP 1.4 5.5
1.3 Identify changes that need to be made to the project plans, work packages, planning packages, and work products resulting from changes to the product requirements.	CMMI PMBOK® Guide	REQM SP 1.5 4.3, 5
2.1 Define the information need and objective to measure progress toward meeting product requirements.	CMMI IEEE 1220 EIA 632 PMBOK® Guide	MA SP 1.1 6.8.1.5, 6.8.6 4.2.1, 4.2.2 5.2.3.1, 5.5, 8.1.3.5
2.2 Specify work products and performance-based measures of progress for meeting product requirements as base measures of earned value. Examples are: • Results of trade-off analysis • Allocated requirements developed, implemented into design, or tested successfully • Achieving planned TPMs • Meeting entry and success criteria for technical reviews • Other quality objectives achieved.	CMMI CMMI CMMI IEEE 1220 EIA 632 PMBOK® Guide	MA SP 1.2 RD SP 3.3 DAR SP 1.5 6.1.1.13, 6.7.6, 6.8.1.5, 6.8.6 4.2.1, 4.2.2, 4.5.1 5.2.3.1, 8.2.1.4, 8.1.3.5, 10.3.1.5, Glossary
2.3 Specify operational definitions for the base measures of earned value, stated in precise, unambiguous terms that address: Communication: What has been measured, how it was measured, what the units of measure are, and what has been included or excluded. Repeatability: Can the measurement be repeated, given the same definition, to get the same results?	CMMI PMBOK® Guide	MA SP 1.2 8.1.3.2
2.4 Identify event-based, success criteria for technical reviews that include development maturity to date and the product's ability to meet product requirements.	IEEE 1220 EIA 632	3.1.1.6, 4.12, 5.2.4, 5.3.4, 6.4, 6.6, 6.8.1.5 4.2.2

CHAPTER 2 PRINCIPLES AND GUIDELINES OF PBEV 23

TABLE 2.1 *Continued*

Performance-Based Earned Value® Guidelines	Source	Section Number
2.5 Establish time-phased, planned values for measures of progress toward meeting product requirements, dates or frequency for checking progress, and dates when full conformance will be met.	IEEE 1220 EIA 632 PMBOK® Guide	6.8.1.5, 6.8.6 4.2.1, 4.2.2, Glossary 11.6.2.4
2.6 Allocate budget in discrete work packages to measures of progress toward meeting product requirements.	IEEE 1220 EIA 632 PMBOK® Guide	6.8.1.5, 6.8.6 4.2.1 5.2.3.1, 10.3.1.5
2.7 Compare the amount of planned budget and the amount of budget earned for achieving progress toward meeting product requirements.	IEEE 1220 EIA 632 PMBOK® Guide	6.8.1.5, 6.8.6 4.2.2, 6.1.2.6 11.6.2.3
2.8 Use the Level of Effort (LOE) method to plan work that is measurable but is not a measure of progress toward meeting product requirements, final cost objectives, or final schedule objectives.	CMMI LL	MA SP 1.2
2.9 Perform more effective variance analysis by segregating discrete effort from LOE.	LL	
3.1 Identify changes that need to be made to the project plans, work packages, planning packages, and work products resulting from responses to risks.	PMBOK® Guide	11.1.3, 11.6.3.2
3.2 Develop revised estimates of costs at completion based on risk quantification.	PMBOK® Guide	7.3.2.3
4.1 Tailor the application of PBEV to the elements of the work breakdown structure according to the risk.	CMMI LL	MA SP 1.2
4.2 Tailor the application of PBEV to the phases of the system development life cycle according to the risk.	CMMI LL	MA SP 1.2

Key to abbreviations:
RD: Requirements Development Process Area
REQM: Requirements Management Process Area
DAR: Decision Analysis and Resolution Process Area
SP: Specific Practice
MA: Measurement and Analysis Process Area
LL: Author's Lessons Learned and Process Improvements
Copyright© 2005 by Paul Solomon

TABLE 2.2 Sources of the Term "Product Requirement"

Standard or Model	Terms and Usage

EIA 632	4.2.1, Requirement (Req.) 5—Technical Effort Definition
	  a) Identify project requirements to include: agreement requirements; other stakeholder requirements; and enterprise, project, and associated process constraints.
	  d) Define product metrics by which the quality of the products will be evaluated.
	4.3.1, Req. 16—System Technical Requirements
	  b) Define operational requirements to include operational profiles, and for each operational profile the utilization environment, events to which system end products must respond, frequency of use, physical and functional interfaces, and system functional requirements (what system end products must accomplish).
	  c) Define the performance requirement (how well each functional requirement must be accomplished), including identification of critical performance parameters.
	  d) Analyze acquirer and other stakeholder requirements to define human factor effects and concerns, establish capacities and timing, define technology and product design constraints, define enabling product requirements, identify conflicts, and determine criteria for tradeoff analyses to resolve conflicts.

IEEE 1220	3.1.3.3 Requirement: A statement that identifies a product or process operational, functional, or design characteristic or constraint, which is unambiguous, testable or measurable, and necessary for product or process acceptability (by consumers or internal quality assurance guidelines). 3.1.2.7 Measure of effectiveness (MOE): The metrics by which a customer will measure satisfaction with products produced by the technical effort. 3.1.29 Performance requirement: The measurable criterion that identifies a quality attribute of a function, or how well a functional requirement must be accomplished. 6.8.6 Metrics . . . enable the overall system quality . . . evaluation.
CMMI	Glossary: Quality—The ability of a set of inherent characteristics of a product or product component to fulfill requirements of customers.
PMBOK® Guide	8.1.3.2 Quality Metric—an operational definition that describes, in very specific terms, what something is and how the quality control process measures it. 8.1.3.5 The quality baseline reports the quality objectives of the project. The quality baseline is the basis for measuring and reporting quality performance as part of the PMB. 10.3.1.5 The PMB typically integrates scope, schedule, and cost parameters of a project, but may also include technical and quality parameters. Glossary: Quality—The degree to which a set of inherent characteristics fulfills requirements.

Project Management Institute, *A Guide to the Project Management Body of Knowledge (PMBOK® Guide)—Third Edition*, Project Management Institute, Inc. 2004. Copyright and all rights reserved. Material from this publication has been reproduced with the permission of PMI®.

contains the definitions and usage of the terms that are pertinent to product, technical, or quality requirements. The key terms are in **bold face**. PBEV uses *product requirements* in the context of customer acceptance.

In the context of PBEV, the product scope is defined and bounded in terms of product requirements. The product requirements baseline is integrated into the PMB measurement baseline along with work scope, schedule, and cost objectives. We will define and clarify the characteristics of product requirements and the guidelines that support the first principle. That will set the baseline for the second principle, the measurement of performance towards satisfying the product requirements.

Development of Product Requirements

A product requirement may be described as a characteristic of a product that is mandatory in order for the product to meet verified customer needs.

Guideline 1.1

> Establish the product requirements baseline and allocate the product requirements to product components.

The set of product requirements must be defined, validated, and incorporated into a product requirements baseline. The validated product requirements baseline is also called the technical baseline. This involves identifying all mandatory characteristics of each product in order for it to meet validated customer needs. Then, each product requirement must be allocated to a product component.

Guideline 1.2

> Maintain bidirectional traceability of product and product component requirements among the project plans, work packages, planning packages, and work products.

The CMMI defines requirements traceability as the evidence of an association between a requirement and its source requirement, its implementation, and its verification. We need to be able to trace a requirement from its source to a statement of the requirement, to its inclusion in a requirements specification, to design, to system component development, through testing and system documentation. Requirements traceability is maintained from a requirement to its derived requirements as well as to its allocation to functions, objects, people, processes, and work products. The CMMI requires that a requirements traceability matrix be generated and that bidirectional traceability be provided. That is, one must be able to trace from a requirement's source forward through the system development and implementation and also back in the other direction to the source of the requirement. The intent is to maintain bidirectional traceability of requirements for each level of product decomposition. This helps determine that all source requirements have been completely addressed. The traceability should cover both the horizontal and vertical relationships, such as across interfaces.

Chapter 3 includes practical advice for implementing Guideline 1.2.

Guideline 1.3

> Identify changes that need to be made to the project plans, work packages, planning packages, and work products resulting from changes to the product requirements.

It is important to maintain the integrity of the performance measurement baseline (PMB) that is being used to manage and control performance. Guidelines 1.1 and 1.2 address the initial establishment of the product requirements and requirements traceability. These guidelines are then applied to all subsequent changes to the product requirements.

This guideline logically follows its precedents. Normally, when a change to the product requirements is made, it impacts the cost and schedule. Once the change to the product requirements is approved, there should be timely incorporation of changes to the affected plans, work packages, planning packages, and work products. Timely incorporation of changes enables continual performance measurement and management. Maintaining bidirectional traceability of the changes provides evidence that the changes to the baselines are controlled.

Chapter 10 includes practical advice for implementing Guideline 1.3.

SECOND PRINCIPLE

The second principle of PBEV is:

> Specify performance toward meeting the product requirements, including planned quality, as a base measure of earned value.

The first principle addressed integrating product scope and requirements into the PMB. The second principle addresses the measurement of performance and specification of what should be measured to determine earned value.

Performance

Project performance may be measured against cost objectives, schedule objectives, and the product requirements. The validity of schedule performance and cost performance information is dependent on the accurate measurement of progress towards meeting the product requirements.

Project management processes require the measurement and reporting of progress at periodic intervals, no less frequently than monthly. However, progress toward meeting the *product* requirements is not always measurable on a periodic basis. For example, a hardware or software component may require the completion and assembly of many enabling work products, such as drawings or coded software modules, before the integrated set of drawings or software modules may be tested or analyzed to determine whether they will meet the product requirements. So, until that assembly is completed, measurement of progress is normally against the plan to complete enabling work products. Whether an enabling work product, such as a drawing, is complete is determined by the organization's *process* quality procedures and process quality standards. Normally, the organization's technical or quality assurance procedures will define the process and criteria for determining the completeness of those enabling work products against the organization's process quality criteria. Successful peer reviews or testing are often used to determine the completeness of enabling work products against a process quality standard.

Of primary importance for PBEV is the performance towards achieving a combination of:

1. **Schedule objectives for enabling work products that meet process quality objectives**
2. **Event-driven success criteria when the event is meeting a measurable product requirement**

Meeting a product requirement is consistent with IEEE's definition of event-based planning: an approach to establishing engineering plans, tasks, and milestones based on satisfying significant accomplishments associated with key events rather than calendar-oriented milestones (IEEE 3.1.1.6).

Base Measure

The Capability Maturity Model Integration (CMMI) defines a base measure as a distinct property or characteristic of an entity and the method for quantifying it and defines derived measures as data resulting from the mathematical function of two or more base measures.

Earned value is a derived measure. It is a function of the measured, base activity multiplied by the budgeted, resource value such as hours or dollars. Consequently, the business value and validity of earned value data depends on choosing the right base measures of schedule and quality performance.

Guideline 2.1

> Define the information need and objective to measure progress toward meeting product requirements.

It costs money to measure processes and progress. Costs are incurred to set up the PMB, to measure performance, to record and report performance, and to analyze it. Also, management attention is focused on deviations or variances from the plan. If the measurement does not provide information that is needed for project control, than the costs of measurement are wasted and management attention is diverted from the important deviations. As Rear Admiral Dave Antanitus said, "Be careful here—just because you can measure something does not mean it is a useful metric!"[3].

The CMMI provides guidance for determining what should be measured. In the Measurement and Analysis (M&A) process area, SP 1.1, states:

> Establish and maintain measurement objectives that are derived from identified information needs and objectives . . .

Sources of information needs and objectives include:

1. **Established management objectives**
2. **Project plans**
3. **Monitoring of project performance**
4. **External industry benchmarks**

The PMBOK Guide also addresses the measurement of quality. It states that the PMB typically integrates scope (including product scope), schedule, and cost parameters of a project, but may include technical and quality parameters (PMBOK Guide 10.3.1.5) and that the quality baseline is the basis for measuring and reporting quality performance as part of the PMB (PMBOK Guide 8.1.3.5).

Later, Guidelines 4.1 and 4.2 use this guideline to justify excluding some elements of the project from the discipline and expense of earned value measurement.

The industry standards cited in Table 2.1 are the source of Guideline 2.1.

Chapter 5 includes practical advice for implementing Guideline 2.1.

Guideline 2.2

Specify work products and performance-based measures of progress for meeting product requirements as base measures of earned value. Examples are:
1. Results of trade-off analysis
2. Allocated requirements developed, implemented into design, or tested successfully
3. Achieving planned TPMs
4. Meeting entry and success criteria for technical reviews
5. Other quality objectives achieved

Having defined the objective to measure progress toward meeting product requirements, the next step is to specify what will be measured to address the measurement objectives [CMMI Measurement and Analysis process area, Specific Practice (SP) 1.2]. These measures should be work products and performance-based measures of progress for meeting product requirements.

Peter Baxter discusses measuring the status of requirements: "In order to track differences between developed and planned requirements, it is necessary to also measure the status of each requirement as it moves through life cycle activities. A typical requirement status could be: defined, approved, allocated, designed, implemented, tested, and verified."[4].

Baxter goes on to state:

A measure that shows the status of all requirements is essential in monitoring program status and acts as a scorecard to illustrate that requirements are being implemented. Early in the program schedule, ensure that requirements become defined, approved, and allocated as the system architecture is finalized. Near the end of the program schedule, you should see requirements move from implemented status to tested, then to verified status. While valuable in detecting "requirements volatility," this measure also supports monitoring effort, configuration management, and quality.

Guidance for selecting performance-based measures is provided in Table 2.3.

TABLE 2.3 Performance-Based Measures

Standard	Guidance (paraphrased)
EIA 632	**4.2.1, Req. 5, Technical Effort Definition** • Define product metrics of the quality of the products • Define process metrics of the efficiency and effectiveness of the technical effort • Identify and track TPMs to determine the success of the system • It must be possible to project the evolution of the parameter as a function of time toward the desired value at the completion of development. The projection can be based on verification, validation, planning, or historical data. **4.2.2, Req. 10, Progress Against Requirements** Identify product metrics, and their expected values, that will affect the quality of the product and provide information toward satisfying acquirer and other stakeholder requirements, as well as derived requirements.

IEEE 1220	**6.8.1.5.a Performance-Based Progress Measurement:**
	• Evaluate progress and completion of technical tasks
	• Provide progress measurements of:
	  ◦ Design maturity.
	  ◦ Performance risks in satisfying requirements.

PMBOK® Guide	**11.6.2.4** Technical performance measurement compares technical accomplishments during project execution to the project management plan's schedule of technical achievement. Deviation, such as demonstrating more or less functionality than planned at a milestone, can help to forecast the degree of success in achieving the project's scope. **Glossary:** It (TPM) may use key technical parameters of the product produced by the project as a quality metric. The achieved metric values are part of the work performance information.

This guideline is also intended to preclude the unnecessary measurement of activities for which there are no information needs. Activities that are measurable but are not indicators of progress towards satisfying product requirements need not be measured at all. They can be classified as Level of Effort (LOE). Guidance for LOE is provided in Guidelines 2.8 and 2.9.

Chapter 5 includes practical advice for implementing Guideline 2.2.

Guideline 2.3

Specify operational definitions for the base measures of earned value, stated in precise, unambiguous terms that address:

Communication: What has been measured, how was it measured, what the units of measure are, and what has been included or excluded. Repeatability: Can the measurement be repeated, given the same definition, to get the same results?

CMMI SP 1.2, in the Measurement and Analysis process area, is a best practice that applies to all measurements. This guideline simply extends the practice to the base measures of earned value.

Chapter 5 includes practical advice for implementing Guideline 2.3.

Guideline 2.4

> Identify event-based, success criteria for technical reviews that include development maturity to date and the product's ability to meet product requirements.

The systems engineering standards discuss identification of success or exit criteria for technical reviews that include development maturity to date and the product's ability to meet product requirements. These same success criteria, normally included in a systems engineering plan, also become the criteria for taking full earned value in work packages. Development or technical maturity to date should be measured against predefined success criteria and assessed during technical reviews.

The general purposes of technical reviews are shown in Table 2.4. Guidance for technical reviews at the completion of the preliminary design stage and the detailed design stage are shown in Appendix I, Tables I.1 and I.2. Examples of technical reviews to be conducted at the completion of an application of the SEP are shown in Table I.3 and Table I.4.

TABLE 2.4 General Purposes of Technical Reviews

Standard	Technical Reviews for Performance-Based Progress Measurement
EIA 632	4.2.2, Req. 11 • Ensure that all event-based plan criteria have been met • Provide status of design maturity and how well the concepts satisfy requirements • Provide traceability of requirements
IEEE 1220	6.8.1.5.d Conduct technical reviews at the completion of an application of the SEP and/or end of a stage of development to: • Assure that all master schedule success criteria have been met • Assess development maturity to date • Assess the product's ability to satisfy requirements • Assure traceability of requirements and validity of decisions

TABLE 2.5 Guidance for Establishing Time-Phased Planned Values for Measures of Progress

Standard	Guidance (paraphrased)
EIA 632	**4.2.1, Req. 5, Technical Effort Definition** • Identify and track TPMs to determine the success of the system • It must be possible to project the evolution of the parameter as a function of time toward the desired value at the completion of development. The projection can be based on verification, validation, planning, or historical data. **4.2.2, Req. 10, Progress Against Requirements** Identify product metrics, and their expected values, that will affect the quality of the product and provide information toward satisfying acquirer and other stakeholder requirements, as well as derived requirements.
IEEE 1220	**6.8.1.5.d Performance-Based Progress Measurement:** • Assess development maturity to date • Assess product's ability to satisfy requirements
	6.8.6 Track product metrics at pre-established control points to enable . . . comparison of planned goals and targets.

Chapter 5 includes practical advice for implementing Guideline 2.4.

Guideline 2.5

> Establish time-phased, planned values for measures of progress toward meeting product requirements, dates or frequency for checking progress, and dates when full conformance will be met.

During this step in the planning process, the PM establishes the enabling success path towards system acceptance by the customer. Table 2.5 provides guidance for establishing time-phased planned values for measures of progress.

Chapter 7 includes practical advice for implementing Guideline 2.5.

Guideline 2.6

> Allocate budget in discrete work packages to measures of progress towards meeting product requirements.

Table 2.6 provides guidance for allocating budget in discrete work packages.

Chapter 7 includes practical advice for implementing Guideline 2.6.

Guideline 2.7

> Compare the amount of planned budget and the amount of budget earned for achieving progress toward meeting product requirements.

TABLE 2.6 Guidance for Allocating Budget in Discrete Work Packages

Standard	Guidance (paraphrased)
EIA 632	4.2.1, Req. 6, Schedule and Organization Identify resources required to complete the scheduled tasks
IEEE 1220	6.8.1.5.c) Cost and schedule performance measurements assess progress based on actual cost of work performed, the planned cost of the work performed, and the planned cost of the work scheduled.

Previous guidelines establish the need to measure progress toward meeting product requirements and specify measures to meet that need. EVMS requires that schedule variance be performed. This guideline focuses management analysis on deviations from the plan to meet product requirements.

This guideline also repeats guidance in the cited standards to integrate cost and performance measurements with the use of earned value, as shown in Table 2.7.

Chapter 7 includes practical advice for implementing Guideline 2.7.

Guideline 2.8

> Use the Level of Effort (LOE) method to plan work that is measurable but is not a measure of progress towards satisfying product requirements, final cost objectives, or final schedule objectives.

This guideline complements Guidelines 2.1 and 2.2. Its purpose is to preclude measurement of activities for which there are no information needs. It reduces costs.

Many tasks are measurable but are not indicators of technical performance. Examples of these are cost performance reports and technical review meetings. See Chapter 9 for amplification of this guideline and for reasons why these tasks may use the LOE earned value method.

Chapter 9 includes practical advice for implementing Guideline 2.8.

Guideline 2.9

> Perform more effective variance analysis by segregating discrete effort from LOE.

A PM should be careful when analyzing summary earned value information. A summary of only the discrete tasks that measure technical performance should be prepared and analyzed. The performance-based earned value will show schedule and cost variances that are not distorted by LOE content. Also, the related cost performance index will

TABLE 2.7 Guidance to Integrate Cost and Performance Measures with Use of Earned Value

Standard	Guidance (paraphrased)
EIA 632	4.2.2, Req. 10, Progress Against Requirements: The developer shall assess the progress of system development by comparing currently defined system characteristics against requirements ... Compare results against requirements to determine the degree of technical requirement satisfaction, progress toward maturity of the system being engineered, and variations and variances from requirements. 6.1.2.6, Cost collection and reporting Cost and performance measurements are combined using an earned value approach.
IEEE 1220	6.8.1.5.c Performance-Based Progress Measurement: ... Calculated cost and/or schedule variances quantify the effect of problems being experienced. Cost and schedule performance measurements are integrated with TPMs to provide current schedule and performance impacts and to provide an integrated corrective action to variances identified. 6.8.6 Track product and process metrics Metrics are collected, tracked, and reported at pre-established control points ... to enable: • Overall system quality and productivity evaluation • Comparison of planned goals and targets • Early detection of problems • Benchmarking of the SEP
PMBOK® Guide	11.6.2.3 Earned value analysis ... may be used for monitoring overall project performance. Outcomes from these analyses may forecast potential deviation of the project at completion from cost and schedule targets.

be a truer indicator of future costs. LOE should be summarized and analyzed separately. Quentin Fleming calls this "quarantining LOE."

Chapter 8 includes practical advice for implementing Guideline 2.9.

THIRD PRINCIPLE

The third principle of PBEV is:

Integrate risk management with Earned Value Management.

This principle overcomes EVMS' silence regarding risk management. It also fosters unambiguous and candid communication regarding the impact of risk mitigation activities on the project's PMB and

TABLE 2.8 Guidance for Integrating Risk Management with EVM

PMBOK® Guide	Guidance (paraphrased)
	11.1.3 Risk Management Planning: Outputs • Budgeting. Assigns resources and estimates and costs needed for risk management for inclusion in the project cost baseline. **11.6.3.2 Risk Monitoring and Control: Outputs** Implementing contingency plans or workarounds frequently results in a requirement to change the project management plan to respond to risks.

Estimate at Completion (EAC). Risk may be defined as the probability of suffering loss.

Guideline 3.1

> Identify changes that need to be made to the project plans, work packages, planning packages, and work products resulting from responses to risks.

The most straightforward guidance for integrating risk management with EVM is in the PMBOK® Guide (Table 2.8). It is needed to fill the vacuum in EVMS regarding risk management.

Simply stated, new risk management activities should be planned, budgeted, and scheduled if they consume resources. It is especially important to add the risk response activity to the master schedule and to establish a logical link between the risk response activity and its dependent activity on the schedule. The schedule linkage is a useful control whether or not the risk response activity requires resources. The outcome of many risk response activities is information that influences subsequent engineering activities, such as a design or procurement decision. By adding the risk response activity to the PMB and master schedule, its progress can be monitored using earned value and the impact of schedule deviations can be seen.

Chapter 9 includes practical advice for implementing Guideline 3.1.

Guideline 3.2

> Develop revised estimates of costs at completion based on risk quantification.

PMBOK® Guide's guidance is clear and simple; an EAC is a forecast of the most likely total value based on project performance and risk quantification (PMBOK® Guide, Section 7.3.2.3). This guideline may be applied at the control account or work package level. Normally, it is applied at the project level based on the project manager's assessment of overall project performance and consideration of top risks.

Chapter 9 includes practical advice for implementing Guideline 3.2.

FOURTH PRINCIPLE

The fourth principle of PBEV is:

> Tailor the application of PBEV according to the risk.

This principle leverages the value of Guideline 2.1. It gives the PM discretion to apply PBEV to a subset of the work breakdown structure (WBS) or of the systems development life cycle instead of to the whole work scope. It is also a gateway to the selection of agile development methods, as discussed in Chapter 11.

Guideline 4.1

> Tailor the application of PBEV to the elements of the work breakdown structure according to the risk.

Guidelines 4.1 and 4.2 are the only PBEV guidelines that are not compliant with EVMS. Simply stated, there may not be an information need to use earned value on all elements of the WBS. If there is no information need and no contractual requirement to use EVMS that covers the total contract costs, than the PM should consider tailoring the earned value process to cover only the highest risk elements of the WBS.

During the project risk assessment process, some WBS elements may be assessed as having low risks towards achieving their technical, schedule and cost objectives. The PM may apply Guideline 2.1 to conclude that the low-risk WBS elements may be sufficiently managed the old fashioned way (before earned value). It may be sufficient to use effective schedule management and to compare actual costs with the time-phased budget. This approach will minimize administrative costs and focus management attention on the high-risk WBS elements.

Chapter 11 includes practical advice for implementing Guideline 4.1.

Guideline 4.2

> Tailor the application of PBEV to the phases of the system development life cycle according to the risk.

Guideline 4.2 applies the rationale of the previous guideline to the system development life cycles. As you will learn in Chapter 3, effective requirements development is not a linear process. Although it may include risk mitigation activities, such as trade studies, there is usually little technical risk regarding the completion of this cycle because the product itself is not yet being designed. Consequently, the PM may apply Guideline 2.1 to conclude that there is no information need for PBEV until after the completion of requirements development.

A PM may also determine that there is no information need for PBEV in subsequent phases of the system development life cycle for every WBS element. The determination should be based on a risk assessment, by WBS element, of the risk towards achieving the project's cost, schedule, and technical objectives. If there are no significant risks, than the Level of Effort technique may be used for that WBS element in that phase.

Chapter 11 includes practical advice for implementing Guideline 4.2.

SUMMARY

This chapter introduced the guidelines of PBEV. In the remaining chapters, additional information and examples will be provided. The intent is to provide advice concerning how to implement the guidelines into your processes and use them on your projects.

REFERENCES

[1] Software Engineering Institute (SEI). *Capability Maturity Model Integration*, version 1.1. Pittsburgh, PA: SEI, Carnegie Mellon University, March 2002.

[2] Project Management Institute. *A Guide to the Project Management Body of Knowledge (PMBOK® Guide)*, 3rd ed. Upper Darby, PA: Project Management Institute, 2004 (ANSI/PMI 99-001-2004).

[3] Antanitus, Dave. "The Business of Metrics–Measuring the Product of the Plan." *Program Manager (now Defense AT&L)*, March-April, 2003, p. 11.

[4] Baxter, Peter. "Focusing Measurement on Managers' Informational Needs." *CrossTalk: The Journal of Defense Software Engineering.* July 2002, pp. 22–55.

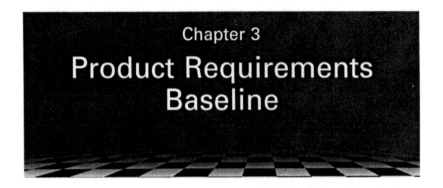

Chapter 3
Product Requirements Baseline

INTRODUCTION

This chapter describes the process of developing the validated product requirements baseline and allocating the requirements to product components and subcomponents. The terms *requirement* and *allocated requirements* are defined. We describe the engineering process of moving from high-level requirements to lower-level requirements and then allocating requirements to components of the system. *Requirements traceability* is a necessary activity of mapping customer needs to the requirements and tracking how the requirements are met throughout the development process—in the design, to system component and subcomponent development, through testing and system documentation, including validation and verification. In Chapter 4, we discuss tracing the same requirements to the work packages.

A case study of a hypothetical project is introduced to assist the reader in understanding and visualizing the process—this project example will be utilized throughout the

PRINCIPLE
Integrate product requirements and quality into the project plan.

GUIDELINE 1.1
Establish the product requirements baseline and allocate the product requirements to product components.

Performance-Based Earned Value, by Paul J. Solomon and Ralph R. Young
Copyright ©2007 IEEE Computer Society.

remainder of the book. The basic approach that we are recommending in this book is that the use of earned value techniques can be much more useful and reliable than typical earned value computations when the earned value computations are based on completion of the real requirements in the system to be delivered to the customer.

WHAT ARE THE REQUIREMENTS BASELINE AND THE TECHNICAL BASELINE?

We previously defined a *requirement* as a statement that identifies a condition, capability, characteristic, or quality factor of a system in order for the system to have value and utility to a user. A *baseline* may be defined as a specification or product that has been formally reviewed and agreed upon and thereafter serves as the basis for further development; it is changed only through formal change control procedures. The *requirements baseline* is the set of requirements associated with a particular release of a product or system. Sometimes we refer to this as the *product requirements baseline* when we use it in the context of a particular product. The U.S. Department of Defense calls this the technical baseline. So, near the beginning of a project, we might create a version of the requirements baseline that is immature—not yet well thought out nor reviewed by stakeholders—and (importantly), it may not yet contain the set of *"real" requirements* for the products of the system. We cannot overstress that spending time and effort to evolve the real requirements ("investing more in the requirements process") is an industry best practice and a key to project success. When we do not invest sufficiently in the requirements process to evolve the real requirements (industry data show that we most often *do not* invest sufficiently in the requirements process), we initiate other engineering work prematurely, creating a need for *rework* (work that must be done over again because it was not done correctly in the first place). Another industry best practice is to write a project vision and scope document to help gain a more informed understanding of the planned system. Note that the worldwide industry average for rework on projects is in the neighborhood of 45%—almost half of what we do! The critically important lesson that urgently requires the attention of PMs is that we need to take advantage of industry experience—be sure to incorporate effective requirements practices throughout your project process [1].

WHAT ARE ALLOCATED REQUIREMENTS?

Once we have evolved the set of real requirements (at least those that are knowable at this phase of the development effort), we can begin design of the system. One of the activities within the system design process is allocating the requirements to the components of the system. So, an *allocated requirement* is a requirement that has been assigned to an element of the system design (e.g., subsystem, component, or part). The allocated requirements are important to the earned value analysis because they become a determinant of earned value, as illustrated in Chapters 5 and 6.

The set of allocated requirements also becomes the technical baseline that is formally reviewed and agreed upon, that serves as the basis for further development, and that can be changed only through formal change control procedures.

HIGH-LEVEL REQUIREMENTS TO LOWER-LEVEL REQUIREMENTS

We recommend the approach of identifying a workable number (say, on the order of 50 to 200) *system-level or high-level requirements* for a large system [2]. We also recommend crafting a *"Project Vision and Scope Document"* [3]. The reason is that the work involved in preparing this document will facilitate deciding that which should and should not be included in the project. It clarifies for all stakeholders the vision of what the system, project, and products are, and it bounds the scope of these as well. The high-level (or system-level) requirements describe the set of real stakeholder needs in terms of the general capabilities that are to be provided by the system and its products.

Once the set of (real) high-level requirements is set, one can create a baseline and initiate the process of identifying the *lower-level requirements*. There are two types of lower-level requirements as discussed and illustrated below in this chapter. When the parent requirement is simply flowed down to a component of the system with little or no modification to the original product level requirement, the component requirement is a *flowdown* requirement. However, when the component requirement is completely new (reflecting capabilities that would not be obvious at the system level), the new component requirement is called a *derived* requirement. Lower-level requirements provide more detail and specifics needed to implement the high-level requirements. Lower-level requirements include derived requirements. A derived requirement may be described as a requirement that is further refined from a primary source requirement or from a higher-level derived requirement, or a requirement that results from choosing a specific implementation or system element.

ENGINEERING APPROACH

The engineering approach recommended in this book is that advocated in Electronics Industries Alliance (EIA)-632, *Processes for Engineering a System* [4], and in the Institute of Electrical and Electronics Engineers (IEEE) *Standard for Application and Management of the Systems Engineering Process*, IEEE STD 1220-2005 [5]. Figures 3.1 through 3.6 are provided here (with permission from EIA and IEEE) from these standards.

Figure 3.1 describes the context within which engineering work is performed.

Note that the external environment, the enterprise environment, and the project environment are characterized and described in Figure 3.1.

Figure 3.2 describes that a system has *end products* that consist of subsystems and *enabling products* that include development products, test products, training products, production products, deployment products, support products, and disposal products.

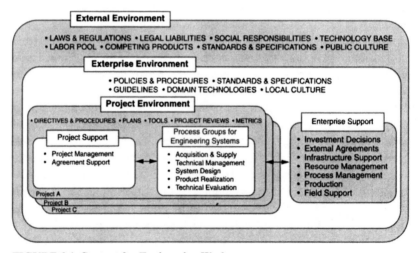

FIGURE 3.1 Context for Engineering Work.

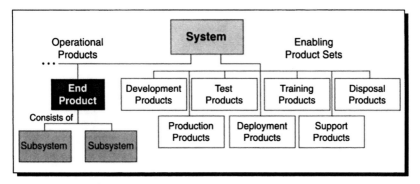

FIGURE 3.2 A System and Its Products.

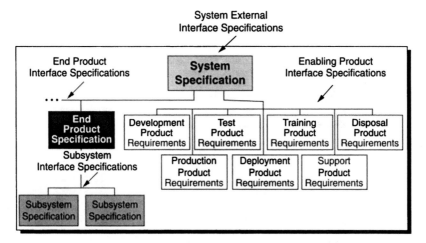

FIGURE 3.3 Types of Requirements Added to the System Specification.

Figure 3.3 shows how the requirements are added to the building block. Figures 3.1, 3.2, and 3.3, and citations in subsequent tables are excerpts from *Processes for Engineering a System* (ANSI/EIA 632), Copyright © (1999), Reaffirmed 2003, Government Electronics and Information Technology Associates, a Sector of the Electronics Industries Alliance. All rights reserved. Reprinted by Permission.

Figure 3.4 provides a flowchart for the requirements analysis process.

Requirements analysis is performed to establish what the system shall be capable of accomplishing; how well system products should perform in quantitative, measurable terms; the environments in which system products operate; the human/system interfaces requirements; the physical/aesthetic characteristics; and constraints that affect design

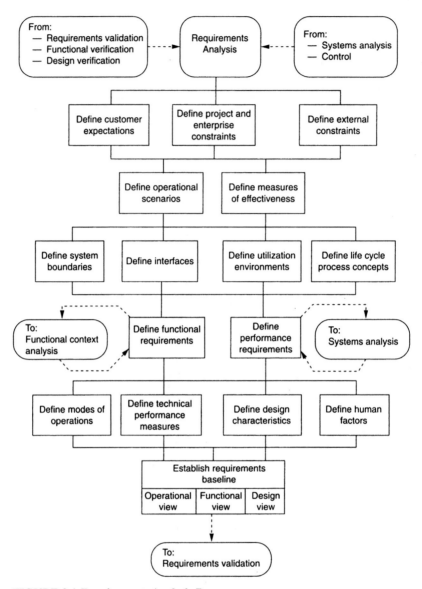

FIGURE 3.4 Requirements Analysis Process.

Figures 3.4, 3.5, and 3.6, and citations in subsequent tables are printed with permission from IEEE Std. 1220™-2005, *IEEE Standard for Application and Management of the Systems Engineering Process*, by IEEE. The IEEE disclaims any responsibility or liability resulting from the placement and use in the described manner.

solutions. As noted above, the results of these activities are documented in a requirements baseline that guides the remaining activities of the systems engineering process. The tasks of the requirements analysis process are shown in Figure 3.4 and described in detail in IEEE 1220.

Note that IEEE 1220 Task 6.1.5 is "Define measures of effectiveness (MOEs)." MOEs are system effectiveness measures that reflect overall customer expectations and satisfaction. Key MOEs may include performance, safety, operability, usability, reliability, maintainability, time and cost to train, workload, human performance requirements, and other factors. Technical performance measures (TPMs) are key indicators of system performance. Selection of TPMs should be limited to critical measures of performance (MOPs) that, if not met, put the project at cost, schedule, or performance risk. Specific TPM activities are integrated into the systems engineering master schedule (SEMS) to periodically determine achievement to date and to measure progress against a planned value profile.

PERFORMANCE REQUIREMENTS

Performance requirements are one of five requirements types that are described by Tom Gilb in his book *Competitive Engineering* [6]. Competitive Engineering and Performance-Based Earned Value have a common objective: focus on results. Gilb states that it is the delivery of the required results from a system that counts and those projects must ensure that their focus is on delivering critical and profitable results.

Performance requirements state the performance levels that the stakeholders want the system to achieve. Gilb describes a performance attribute as a potential effectiveness attribute of a system. It is "how good" a system is, in objectively measurable terms. Performance attributes

1. **Are valued by defined stakeholders**
2. **Are always capable of being specified quantitatively**
3. **Are variable (along a definable scale of measure)**
4. **Can be a complex notion, consisting of many elementary performance attributes**

There are three types of performance attributes: quality, resource saving, and workload capacity. These are described as follows:

QUALITY: A quality attribute describes "how well" a system performs. Examples of qualities are availability, usability, customer satisfaction, staff development, environmental impact and innovation.

RESOURCE SAVING: A resource saving attribute is a measure of "how much" resource is "saved" compared to some reference or benchmark system. Resource savings are measures of performance, which describe system costs in relation to alternative costs. They are a way of viewing relative costs for two systems at once, rather than the absolute costs of one system alone; one system will be the target system, and the other system will either be a past benchmark system or a competitor's system.

Example: A new car has 10% better fuel consumption than the last model.

Other examples of resource savings include:

1. **Operational savings of any resource (such as effort, money, time, materials, and space)**
2. **Capital investment savings (say, for activities such as for launch, training, installation, and acquisition)**

WORKLOAD CAPACITY OR CAPACITY: A workload capacity attribute describes "how much" a system can do. Workload capacity describes the potential workload a system can tolerate. Workload capacity attributes include:

1. **Throughput capacity: how much work can be done**
2. **Storage capacity: how much information can be contained**
3. **Responsiveness: how fast the system responds**

Each performance attribute must be precisely defined by a set of numeric, measurable, testable specifications. Each performance attribute specification will include different specified levels for different conditions (time, place, and event). Unless there is clear communication in terms of numeric requirements, there is every chance of the real requirements not being met; and we have no clear indication of the criteria for success and failure.

Finally, Gilb concludes that performance requirements are the key statements of expected and necessary critical stakeholder benefits for a project. Performance requirements are the main reason why projects are funded at all. So it is critical that they are done well and managed well.

EARLY VALIDATION

The next process after requirements analysis is requirements validation.

Validation should be performed early in the engineering life cycle. The following discussion of early validation is from the Systems and Software Productivity Consortium [7].

Leaving validation until the end of the project severely increases the risk of failure. Validation activities early in the project can reduce that risk. Early validation activities reveal:

1. **Clarifications**
Perhaps the most important purpose of early validation is to clarify the real meaning of requirements. The obvious cases are where requirements are incomplete. However, the riskiest requirements are subjective. These include phrases such as "readable" or "user-friendly" or involve human interfaces in general. Early validation can get a response to various interpretations and provide more specifics in areas such as acceptable size, placement, or motion.

2. **Drivers**
Some requirements are more critical to the customer than others. Some have a larger cost or design impact on the product. With early validation you can uncover the customer's priorities and relate them to the development impact to identify the serious drivers.

3. **Additions**
You can use early validation to discover and coordinate new requirements during the program. An issue is that no spec is totally complete, and it is assumed that the designer has a familiarity with the intended end use environment. Particularly in a new environment with which the designer is not familiar, early validation of requirements can uncover missing requirements. Another use is to coordinate derived requirements with the customer. In this case, the need is often driven by the customer's lack of knowledge of the technologies being applied and their impact on the use of the product.

4. **Hidden expectations**
Discussions with the customer can reveal unstated expectations or assumptions about the design. One hint is extreme detail in the requirements that may be surrogate for "I want it to work like the old or another system."

Early validation of requirements is an effective requirements practice. Techniques for accomplishing this include involving the user, site visits, models and simulations, prototyping, and early delivery.

REQUIREMENTS VALIDATION PROCESS

Figure 3.5 provides a flowchart for the requirements validation process.

Note that the final task in the requirements validation process is to establish the validated requirements baseline. The validated requirements baseline is also called the technical baseline.

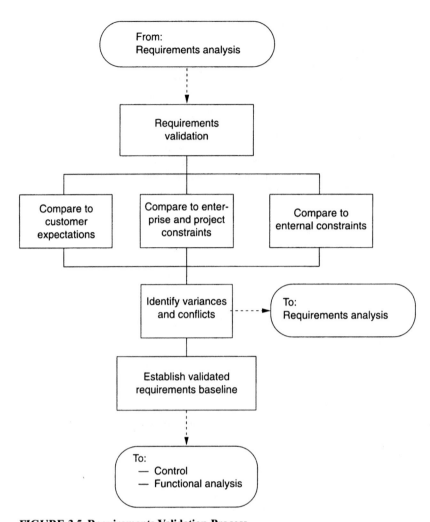

FIGURE 3.5 Requirements Validation Process.

The next process is functional analysis. Functional analysis is performed to describe the problem defined by requirements analysis in clearer detail and to decompose the system functions to lower-level functions that shall be satisfied by elements of the system design (e.g., subsystems, components, or parts).

The validated requirements baseline is used to develop a functional architecture. During this process, performance requirements are directly allocated to functions. Requirements that are not directly allocable, such as range, should be translated into derived performance requirements, such as fuel capacity and engine efficiency, through appropriate engineering techniques and analyses. The enterprise documents the allocation of system performance requirements to functions to provide traceability and to facilitate later changes (6.3 and 6.3.1.3, IEEE 1220-2005) and development of the functional architecture.

The next process is functional verification. Figure 3.6 provides a flowchart for the functional verification process.

The purpose of the functional verification process is to (1) assess the completeness of the functional architecture in satisfying the validated requirements baseline and (2) produce a verified functional architecture for input to synthesis (defining design solutions and identifying subsystems to satisfy the requirements of the verified functional architecture).

REQUIREMENTS TRACEABILITY

Recall Guideline 1.2 (Maintain bidirectional traceability of product and product component requirements among the project plans, work packages, planning packages, and work products). As noted in the introduction to this chapter, requirements traceability is a necessary (not optional) activity of mapping customer needs to the system requirements and tracking how the system requirements are met throughout the development process—in the design, to system component development, through testing and system documentation, including for validation, verification, as well as to the project plans, work packages, planning packages, and work products [8]. The Capability Maturity Model® Integration (CMMI®) (an accepted industry standard) requires bidirectional traceability, that is, it requires that evidence of an association between a requirement and its source requirement, its implementation, and its verification is established from the source requirement to its lower-level requirements, and from the lower-level requirements back to their source [9]. A requirements traceability matrix (RTM) is used to track the requirements. An RTM capability is provided in most industry-strength automated requirements tools, such as CaliberRM™, the Dynamic Object Oriented Requirements System (DOORS), and Requisite-Pro (Req-Pro). Figure 3.7 provides an RTM Template (example of an RTM capability).

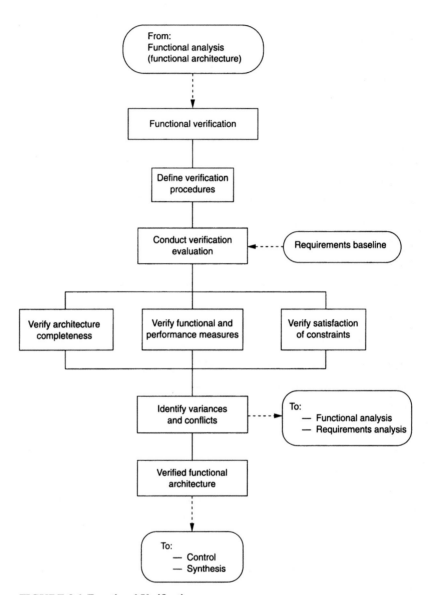

FIGURE 3.6 Functional Verification.

REQUIREMENTS TRACEABILITY MATRIX TEMPLATE

REQT #	REQUIREMENT DESCRIPTION	REQT DATE	REQT STATUS	SOURCE & (PP.;PARA #)	REQT CATEGORY	Reqts Spec Trace (PP.;PARAGRAPH)	SYSTEM COMPONENT	VERIFICATION METHOD	DATE REQT SATISFIED	VERIFIED BY
1	To allow for peak load conditions, the system SHALL be designed to handle a peak hourly load that is twice the number of retrievals from heritage systems per hour (3,503), namely 7,006 system retrievals per hour.	29-Jul-05	ORIGINAL	SOW Par. 1.1	Performance	2.1	SOFTWARE	TEST	15-Sep-05	RY

FIGURE 3.7 RTM Template.

1. **Human, Ergonomic, Environmental:**
   a. Weight: 40 lb.
   b. Waterproof in continuous, driving rain (this will later be translated into derived, testable requirements for design and test. I.e., max. wind speed, duration, gallons per minute per sq. inch? etc.)
   c. Impact resistant: Soldier falls on back, hitting hard surface (derived requirements could include impact pressure of x lb./sq. inch)
   d. Battery life without recharge: 4 hours
2. **Mission/Technical (there will be some trade studies to close in on some of the requirements)**
   e. Used by reconnaissance scout to communicate with and control small, unmanned air vehicle (UAV).
   f. Hardware Components:
      i. COTS Laptop computer, color screen, meeting environmental impact requirements above (operating system not specified)
      ii. Radio transmitter/receiver to UAV (2 frequencies or bandwidths)
      iii. Radio transmitter/receiver to satellite (1 frequency, bandwidth)
      iv. Radio transmitter/receiver to his platoon commander (up to 5 miles away).
      v. Links to computer with wire (USB 2.0 or Ethernet? Not specified) and wireless (not specified whether bluetooth? 802.11 or something else, security addressed later)
   g. Performance functionality (not specified whether the following is accomplished by software or hardware)
      i. UAV can see and transmit up to 2 miles from scout
      ii. Scout can see several screens:
         1. Images from UAV with data such as target coordinates
         2. Mission data received from satellite
         3. Map and coordinates that show himself, UAV's view with target highlighted, and his platoon commander's location.
   h. Encryption:
      i. Log on procedure with passwords
      ii. Data encryption software is customer-furnished
3. **Training and maintenance manuals (no further detail).**

FIGURE 3.8 Statement of Work (SOW). Product: Mobile (backpack) Command and Control Center for Unmanned Reconnaissance Helicopter.

A CASE STUDY

Figure 3.8 introduces a case study—a hypothetical project that will be referred to throughout the remainder of the book.

The intent in the Statement of Work (SOW) is to define and describe what is required to provide the needed functionality in the delivered system. Project engineers would identify lower-level derived requirements from the high-level requirements provided in the SOW. Analysis, simulations, prototypes, and similar techniques would be utilized

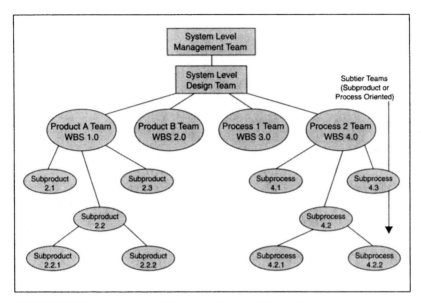

FIGURE 3.9 Enterprise-Level Integrated Product Team Structure.

to capture the vision and the real needs of the stakeholders in increasing levels of detail ("decomposing" higher-level requirements)—for example, two or three different radio frequencies could be required; we might have to refine a GUI screen or provide alternative versions; there might be a requirement to key in information—a set of functional requirements must be developed that can drive the hardware and software.

Let's look at how this might be done in practice, starting with the Statement of Work for the Mobile (backpack) Command and Control Center for Unmanned Reconnaissance Helicopter. The process is typically carried out in three iterative steps (discussed below), ideally by an Integrated Product Team (IPT). The following paragraphs provide information concerning IPTs.

The Department of Defense (DoD) IPT team structure at the enterprise level is shown in Figure 3.9. There is usually a management team and also a design team at the top level. The management team consists of the customer and contractor program managers, the deputy program manager(s), possibly the contractor chief executive officer, the contracting officer, major advisors picked by the program manager, the system design team leader, and other key members of the system design team. The design team usually consists of the first-level subsystem and life cycle integrated team leaders shown as the product and process teams noted below.

Product or process teams comprise the lower levels of the enterprise structure. These teams are responsible for designing system segments (product teams) or designing the supporting or enabling processes (process teams). Teams should be formed only to the lowest level necessary to control the integration.

The Enterprise-Level Integrated Product Team structure shown in Figure 3.9 is a hierarchy that provides for continuous vertical communication. This is achieved primarily by having the team leaders, and, if appropriate, other key members, be team members of the next highest team. In this manner the decisions of the higher team are immediately distributed and explained to the next team level, and the decisions of the lower teams are presented to the higher team on a regular basis. Through this method, decisions of lower-level teams follow the decision making of higher teams, and the higher-level teams' decisions incorporate the concerns of lower-level teams—as a result, project communication is enhanced.

The three iterative steps that the IPT will perform are:

1. **Conversion of customer needs, problems, and requirements to product requirements**
2. **Allocation of product requirements to product component requirements**
3. **Development of the product component requirements**

CONVERSION OF CUSTOMER NEEDS, PROBLEMS, AND REQUIREMENTS TO PRODUCT REQUIREMENTS

The first step is to convert statements of customer needs, problems, and requirements to product requirements. Product requirements are statements of external behavior that meet the customer's requirements and needs and solve (or at least alleviate) the problem. The conversion process consists of taking each customer requirement, problem, or needs statement and writing one or more statements from the viewpoint of the system that states how the system will solve the problem. These statements (both customer requirements and product requirements) are then captured in a requirements repository, most often the commercial requirements management tool mentioned above, and linked to each other to create a Requirements Traceability Matrix (RTM). Each requirement type, that is, customer, product, and one type for each product component requirement (described in the third step) is set up in the requirements repository with the RTM template.

Customer Requirements	Product Requirements
Customer001	PROD001
Customer002	PROD002
•	•
•	•
•	•
Customer00n	PROD00n

FIGURE 3.10 Preliminary Requirements Traceability Matrix.

This conversion process is one of the most important aspects of Requirements Engineering. The best guidance available is IEEE Standard 1233-1998, *Guide for Developing System Requirements Specifications* [10], in which the process for writing "well formed requirements from raw requirements" is described. Other good sources for this conversion process can be found in *Principles of Software Engineering Management* [11] and many books on Quality Function Deployment (QFD) that discuss the translation of customer desires into technical parameters in the First House of Quality such as *Step-by-Step QFD: Customer-Driven Product Design* [12].

The most important point to remember is that product requirements are developed from customer requirements through an engineering process that starts with statements of customer needs and desires and results in statements of product capabilities that meet those needs and desires. It's important to emphasize that product requirements do not come from the technology to be used; they come from the customer's environment and needs. At the end of this direct conversion, the Requirements Traceability Matrix looks like the preliminary matrix shown in Figure 3.10.

Although the product requirements will be modified and improved during subsequent processing steps, there are several qualities each product requirement should have after conversion from a statement of customer need—among those qualities are the following [13]:

1. **Abstract: Each product requirement should be implementation independent.**
2. **Unambiguous: Each product requirement should be stated in such a way so that it can be interpreted in only one way.**
3. **Traceable: Each product requirement should be able to be related back to one or more specific documented customer statement(s) of need.** (Note that this is straight forward when product requirements are created by conversion from customer needs in the first place.)

Customer Requirements	Product Requirements	Product Component A	Product Component B	Product Component C
Customer001	PROD001	X	X	
Customer002	PROD002	X		X
• • •	• • •			
Customer00n	PROD00n		X	X

FIGURE 3.11 Product Requirements Allocated to Product Components.

4. **Validatable: Each product requirement should have the means to prove that the system satisfies the customer requirements.** (This is usually accomplished through a qualitative or quantitative attribute that becomes part of the product requirement. The quality of this attribute usually improves greatly with subsequent processing steps).

ALLOCATION OF PRODUCT REQUIREMENTS TO PRODUCT COMPONENT REQUIREMENTS

The second step is to allocate the product requirements to one or more product components. The allocation process is iterative and usually uncovers inconsistencies in both customer requirements and the product component definition. At this stage, product architects and designers must become involved with the requirements process to ensure that the requirements and product definition form a cohesive whole and that each is consistent with the other. The result of this allocation is the traceability of each product requirement to one or more product component such as seen in the matrix shown in Figure 3.11.

This is an important step. It is here that customer requirements, product requirements, and product component requirements are related to each other. It is here that detecting errors and inconsistencies is most effective and cost efficient. It is not necessary that each and every product requirement be allocated to product components. Some product requirements can only be satisfied at the product level.

DEVELOPMENT OF THE PRODUCT COMPONENT REQUIREMENTS

The third step is to develop product component requirements for each allocation made in the previous step. Product component requirements

Customer Requirements	Product Requirements	Product Component A Requirements	Product Component B Requirements	Product Component C Requirements
Customer001	PROD001	CompA001	CompB001	
Customer002	PROD002	CompA002		CompC001
• • •	• • •			
Customer00n	PROD00n		CompB002	CompC002

FIGURE 3.12 Requirements Traceability Matrix for Product Component Requirements.

can be seen as "children" to the "parent" product requirement. All child requirements must be satisfied before a parent requirement can be considered satisfied.

As noted above, there are two types of product component requirements, depending on the relationship to the parent product requirement. When the parent product requirement is simply flowed down to the product component with little or no modification to the original product-level requirement, the product component requirement is a "flow down" requirement. However, when the product component requirement is completely new to reflect product component capabilities that would not be obvious at the system level, this new product component requirement is a "derived" requirement. Systems engineers are responsible for identifying all necessary derived requirements. The result of the flowdown and derivation step is a fully detailed requirements traceability matrix as seen in Figure 3.12.

The third step completes the requirements traceability matrix (RTM) for the requirements phase. This matrix usually takes the form of the customer requirements on the left with the product and product component requirements on the right. The RTM provides horizontal (customer requirements to product requirements) traceability and vertical (product requirements down through product component requirements) traceability. Subsequent phases will add lower-level design information to the RTM to trace design decisions all the way back to customer requirements.

Figure 3.13 shows an example of the RTM through the third step of the requirements phase described above. The figure contains the first four customer requirements from the SOW, and each customer requirement is converted to one or, in the case of the impact requirement, two product requirements. The weight product requirement is for the whole product and is not allocated to any of the product components, but the

Customer Requirement	Product Requirement	Enclosure Component Requirement	Radio Transmitter Component Requirement	Battery Component Requirement	Control Component Requirement	Software Component Requirement
RQMT 001 Weight: no greater than 40lb.	PROD001 The overall weight of the Mobile C2 Center shall not exceed 40lbs.					
RQMT 002 Waterproof in continuous, driving rain	PROD002 The Mobile C2 Center shall be waterproof in continuous (up to 2 hours) driving rain with a wind speed of up to 65 miles per hour and rainfall of up to 4 inches per hour.	ENCL002 The Mobile C2 Center shall be waterproof in continuous (up to 2 hours) driving rain with a wind speed of up to 65 miles per hour and rainfall of up to 4 inches per hour.				

FIGURE 3.13 RTM for the Mobile (backpack) Command and Control Center for Unmanned Reconnaissance Helicopter, Showing the Three Steps of Requirement Conversion, Allocation, and Development of the Product Component Requirements.

RQMT 003	PROD003	ENCL003	PROD004	ENCL004	RADIO002	BATT002	CONT002
Impact resistant: Soldier falls on back, hitting hard surface	The Mobile C2 Center shall show no damage after at least 3 successive impacts with a hard, abrasive surface of up to 15 lbs./sq. in.	The Mobile C2 Center shall show no damage after at least 3 impacts with a hard, abrasive surface of up to 15 lbs./sq. in.	The Mobile C2 Center shall retain full operational capability after at least 3 impacts with a hard, abrasive surface of up to 30 lbs./sq. in.	The Mobile C2 Center Enclosure component shall retain full operational capability after at least 3 successive impacts with a hard, abrasive surface of up to 30 lbs./sq. in.	The Mobile C2 Center Radio component shall retain full operational capability after at least 3 successive impacts with a hard, abrasive surface of up to 30 lbs./sq. in.	The Mobile C2 Center Battery Component shall retain full operational capability after at least 3 successive impacts with a hard, abrasive surface of up to 30 lbs./sq. in.	The Mobile C2 Center Control component shall retain full operational capability after at least 3 successive impacts with a hard, abrasive surface of up to 30 lbs./sq. in.

FIGURE 3.13 Continued

Customer Requirement	Product Requirement	Enclosure Component Requirement	Radio Transmitter Component Requirement	Battery Component Requirement	Control Component Requirement	Software Component Requirement
RQMT 0004 Battery life without recharge: 4 hours	PROD005 The Mobile C2 Center shall operate on a single charge for at least 4 continuous hours.			BATT003 The battery shall have a fully charged capacity of at least 60 Wh.		
RQMT 005 Encryption is required.	PROD006 The Mobile C2 center shall use encryption for all transmissions.					FUNC001 The Mobile C2 center shall support up to 256-bit cipher strength encryption at a minimum.
						FUNC002 The Mobile C2 center shall at a minimum use the Data Encryption Standard (DES) in accordance with FIPS Pub 46-3 (Triple DES).

FIGURE 3.13 *Continued*

RQMT 006 Up to three drone helicopters will be controlled in a given area of operations at the same time.	**PROD007** The Mobile C2 center shall allow the user to select up to three sets of channels to control three helicopters simultaneously.				**FUNC003** The Mobile C2 center shall incorporate digital signatures using public key encryption technology.
					FUNC004 The Mobile C2 center shall support up to three sets of channels simultaneously.
					FUNC005 The Mobile C2 center shall have five channels per channel set, one for each helicopter being controlled.
					FUNC006 The Mobile C2 center shall have a separation of 10kHz (kilohertz) between channels.

FIGURE 3.13 *Continued*

Customer Requirement	Product Requirement	Enclosure Component Requirement	Radio Transmitter Component Requirement	Battery Component Requirement	Control Component Requirement	Software Component Requirement
RQMT 007 Capable of selecting multiple sensing devices	PROD008 The Mobile C2 center shall allow the user to select from multiple sensing devices for imaging on screen.					FUNC007 The Mobile C2 center shall allow the user to select a visible image of the terrain being surveilled.
						FUNC008 The Mobile C2 center shall allow the user to select an infrared image of the terrain being surveilled.
						FUNC009 The Mobile C2 center shall allow the user to select either a high-pass or a low-pass filter to enhance the visible image of the terrain being surveilled.

FIGURE 3.13 *Continued*

rest are allocated to one or more product components. With the exception of the battery component requirement for battery life, all product component requirements are "flow down" requirements because the information contained in them is also contained in the parent product requirement. The battery component requirement is a "derived" requirement because it contains new information not already contained in the product requirement.

When requirement types (customer, product, and product component) are set up in the requirements repository according to the RTM template described above, several matrices can be designed, each showing different types of information as needed. For example, one matrix can show testing information on a requirement-by-requirement basis while another can show requirement status by category, and yet another can show the system component (or components) where the requirement is realized.

DEFINING THE TECHNICAL PERFORMANCE MEASURES

After attending several of the IPTs and talking to her design team, the project manager determined that two particular requirements held the most potential risk for a successful completion of the Mobil C2 Center Project: the requirements for the waterproof enclosure (the backpack itself) and the capability to control three drones simultaneously.

The Measure of Effectiveness (MOE) for the waterproof backpack was ambiguous, but the IPT determined that the customer expected it to be waterproof up to at least a tropical storm force wind and rain level. Thus the Measure of Performance (MOP) was set to 2 hours of continuous driving rain at 65 miles per hour. An implied but unstated requirement for the backpack was that the design should account for extended normal wear of the fabric. This implied requirement eliminated various fabric waterproofing treatments and suggested that some sort of layered membrane technology would be necessary. The project manager consulted with the test team and determined that a Technical Performance Measure (TPM) could be derived that would successfully test that the backpack would meet the MOP design and thus satisfy the MOE. This TPM is shown in the first row of Figure 3.14.

The risk associated with controlling three helicopter drones simultaneously was not so easily mitigated, however. The project manager realized that the risk in this case was not related to the technology used. The radio transmitter and control unit could easily handle three simultaneous sets of control channels with five channels for each set. The risk in this case was related to the user interface. The project manager

MOE (What the customer wants)	MOP (What the engineer will design to)	TPM (How the performance will be determined)
RQMT002 Waterproof in continuous, driving rain	ENCL002 The Mobile C2 Center shall be waterproof in continuous (up to 2 hours) driving rain with a wind speed of up to 65 miles per hour and rainfall of up to 4 inches per hour.	1. Subject the backpack (empty) to 25 wash/dry cycles to simulate fabric wear. 2. Insert calibrated moisture meter probe into main body of backpack (meter accurate to 0.5% over 0 to 35% moisture range). 3. Perform a 120-minute liquid integrity (shower) test in wind tunnel conditions of 65 miles per hour. Expected Results: The moisture content according to the probe shall not increase by more than 5% during the duration of the test.
RQMT 006 Up to three drone helicopters will be controlled in a given area of operations at the same time.	FUNC004 The Mobile C2 center shall support up to three sets of channels simultaneously.	Essential Efficiency (EE) EE = 100 * Number of essential steps divided by the number of enacted steps. Task Concordance (TC) TC = 100 * Number of pairs of tasks ranked in correct order divided by the total number of task pairs. Task Visibility (TV) TV = 100 * Sum of feature visibilities (either 0 or 1 for each feature) of each enacted step divided by the total number of enacted steps to complete the use cases. Expected Results: The user interface design that maximizes the values of EE, TC, and TV simultaneously is considered the most useable interface.

FIGURE 3.14 Mobile C2 Center Critical MOPs and Related TPMs.

decided to institute a suite of usability metrics [14] that would indicate how easy the user interface was to use.

The Project Manager asked the IPT to create "Essential Use Cases" for the use of the Mobile C2 Center. The IPT had already created "Concrete Use Cases" that described interactions between a user and a given or assumed user interface over a set of likely scenarios. An "Essential Use Case" is a simplified, abstract use case defined in terms of user intentions and system responsibilities without any unnecessary restrictions or assumptions regarding specific implementation details. The essential use cases form the basis for three usability metrics by which the user interface may be evaluated, as follows:

1. **Essential Efficiency.** Essential Efficiency (EE) is a simple ratio of the ideal length of the steps in the essential use case to the enacted length of the steps actually performed. EE has a possible range of 0—100%, with a higher percentage being the more efficient.

2. **Task Concordance.** Task Concordance (TC) is an index of how well the distribution of task difficulty with a particular interface design fits with the expected frequency of the various tasks. Task concordance is computed from the correlation between tasks in the essential use case ranked by anticipated frequency in use and by enacted difficulty. TC has a possible range of −100 to +100%, with a perfect score of +100%.

3. **Task Visibility.** Task Visibility (TV) measures the fit between the visibility of features and the capabilities needed to complete a given task or set of tasks. TV reaches a maximum of 100% when everything needed for a step is visible directly on the user interface as seen by the user at that step. TV actually should approach 0% in some exceptional circumstances such as a high-security interface for remote access where only authorized users know what the exact information is and in what order it is to be entered.

After consulting with the test team, the project manager determined that the usability metrics TPM would show that the Mobil C2 Center MOP design is met and satisfies the MOE. The usability metric is shown in the second row of Figure 3.14.

SUMMARY

This chapter has described the process of developing the validated product requirements baseline. We defined a requirement, a baseline, a requirements baseline, the product requirements baseline, real requirements, stated requirements, rework, allocated requirements, flowdown requirements, and a derived requirement. We stressed that spending time and effort to evolve the real requirements (investing more in the requirements process) is an industry best practice and a key to project success. We recommended development of a "Project Vision and Scope Document" and the approach of identifying a workable number of system-level or high-level requirements for a system. We described the engineering process and approach of moving from high-level requirements to lower-level requirements and then allocating requirements to components of the system. We described the context within which engineering work is performed, end products, enabling products, and the types of requirements in the system specification. We provided flowcharts for the requirements analysis process, the requirements validation process, and the functional verification process, noting how MOEs, TPMs, and MOPs help us verify customer requirements, thus ensuring customer satisfaction and also facilitating us in meeting cost, schedule, and system performance objectives.

We noted that bidirectional traceability is required. We defined integrated product teams and described their role in this process to perform three iterative steps; conversion of customer requirements to product requirements; allocation of product requirements to product component requirements; and development of the product component requirements. We defined requirements traceability and stressed its importance and the use of a requirements traceability matrix. We provided a template for an RTM, and also a statement of work for a case study (a hypothetical project) that will be used throughout the remainder of the book—the Mobile (backpack) Command and Control Center for an Unmanned Reconnaissance Helicopter. We will call it Project X in subsequent chapters.

We emphasized that the basic approach we are recommending in this book is that the use of earned value techniques can be much more useful and reliable when based on completion of the real requirements in the system to be delivered to the customer.

REFERENCES

[1] Young, Ralph R. *Effective Requirements Practices*. Boston, MA: Addison-Wesley, 2001. This book provides a set of recommended requirements practices based on a comprehensive review of industry literature and practical experience (see also www.ralphyoung.net).

[2] The determination of the appropriate number of system-level requirements is a function of the complexity of the system being developed. A requirement density of one requirement per thousand lines of code of a planned system is the approximate order of magnitude to capture the vision of the stakeholders and to estimate the cost and schedule to build the system.

[3] Young, Ralph R. *Project Requirements: A Guide to Best Practices*. Vienna, VA: Management Concepts, 2006. A sample Project Vision and Scope Document template is provided in Appendix C.

[4] Electronic Industries Alliance (EIA). ANSI/EIA 632, *Processes for Engineering a System*, Arlington, VA: EIA, 1998.

[5] Institute of Electrical and Electronics Engineers (IEEE). IEEE Std 1220™-2005, *IEEE Standard for Application and Management of the Systems Engineering Process*. New York, 2005.

[6] Gilb, Tom. *Competitive Engineering*. Burlington, MA: Elsevier Butterworth-Heinemann, 2005.

[7] Systems and Software Consortium, Verification and Validation Website, Topic: Validation. http://www.software.org/PUB/VNV/. Special permission to reproduce material from the Systems and Software Consortium (SSCI) website is granted by SSCI.

[8] See Young, Ralph R. *Project Requirements: A Guide to Best Practices*. Guidance concerning requirements traceability is provided in Appendix A.

[9] Refer to Specific Practice (SP) 1.4 of the Requirements Management (REQM) Process Area (PA) of the CMMI. See *Capability Maturity Model Integration*, version 1.1. Pittsburgh, PA: Software Engineering Institute, Carnegie Mellon University, March 2002.

[10] IEEE. IEEE Standard 1233-1998, *Guide for Developing System Requirements Specifications*. New York: IEEE, 1998.

[11] Gilb, Tom. *Principles of Software Engineering Management*. Harlow, UK: Addison-Wesley, 1988.

[12] Terninko, John. *Step-By-Step QFD: Customer-Driven Product Design*. Boca Raton, FL: St. Lucie Press, 1997.

[13] See Young, Ralph R. *The Requirements Engineering Handbook*. Boston, MA: Artech House, 2004, p. 8, for a discussion of these criteria.

[14] See Constantine, Larry L. and Lockwood, Lucy A. D. *Software For Use: A Practical Guide to the Models and Methods of Usage-Centered Design*. ACM Press, 1999.

Chapter 4
Maintain Bidirectional Traceability

INTRODUCTION

In Chapter 3, we discussed the principle of integrating product scope and requirements into the performance measurement baseline and, more specifically, Guideline 1.1, establishing product requirements and allocating them to product components. This chapter identifies some of the work products in the systems engineering process. We described the importance of establishing the project requirements baseline and how it is established and noted the need to maintain traceability between requirements. Guideline 1.2 establishes the need for bidirectional traceability from the product requirements to the project plans, activities, and work products. The purposes of this guideline are to ensure that all product requirements are captured in the project plan and in the elements of that plan. The successful execution of the plan will result in delivery of a product that meets those requirements and satisfies the customer.

PROJECT PLANS AND THE PERFORMANCE MEASUREMENT BASELINE

The discussion of Guideline 1.1 in Chapter 3 included the need to maintain bidirectional traceability of requirements for each level of product decomposition. Project planning should ensure that all products and

Performance-Based Earned Value, by Paul J. Solomon and Ralph R. Young
Copyright ©2007 IEEE Computer Society.

product components are included in the project scope. The project scope is the work that needs to be accomplished to deliver a product with the specified features and functions (PMBOK Guide, 5.5) [1]. The plans to accomplish that work include the engineering or technical plans, work packages, planning packages, and work products. The time-phased budget for the work and planning packages is the Performance Measurement Baseline (PMB).

INTEGRATION OF PRODUCT SCOPE AND PROJECT SCOPE

Before the PMB is established, the schedule is developed. Before the activities are scheduled, the completion milestones are identified. To ensure that the project delivers the product that is expected by the customer, the end product and its milestone should be established with completion criteria that address the product requirements. Specification of the right interim milestones and completion criteria is critical to integrating the project scope with the product scope. The milestones should indicate the completion of significant activities and their work products. Integration of product and project scope is necessary to ensure that the work of the project will result in the delivery of the specified product scope (PMBOK Guide, 5.5).

Work packages and planning packages are budgeted activities within the PMB. See Appendices A and B for examples of how they are used. The completion of a work product is a condition for completing a work package and earning all the value that was budgeted to it.

WORK PRODUCTS

The project's end product is the result of developing and integrating many subcomponents and enabling work products. A work product is an artifact that is the output of a work package. It need not be engineered or part of the end product. It may have attributes that are stated as project planning parameters and should have clearly stated criteria for evaluation. Examples of work products are:

1. **Drawings**
2. **Prototypes**
3. **Software modules**
4. **Reports that complete trade studies**
5. **Revised procedures and tools that are needed to implement cost reduction initiatives**
6. **Updated database that contains the requirements baseline**

A project has many categories of work products. Some are the outcomes of major systems development life cycle stages and are high-level manifestations of the system requirements or design. Others are low-level artifacts that are not directly traceable to specific product requirements or physical components but are necessary for compliance with the organization's engineering or business processes. Some work products are enabling work products that are traceable to the product requirements and mandatory for completion of the product.

All work products should be the output of scheduled activities and of the work and planning packages that are the financial representation of those activities.

We will discuss the importance of maintaining traceability between the product requirement baseline and the enabling work products. The sample project will continue to be used to provide examples and practical templates.

The systems engineering standards and models cited previously describe typical work products. Some of the work products that should be incorporated into the PMB, during the various stages of the engineering life cycle, are discussed below.

Two sets of higher-level work products that are outcomes of the systems engineering process are shown in Table 4.1.

Establishing a PMB that is consistent with the product requirement baseline is an iterative process because the product requirement baseline is not known until the completion of the systems definition stage. Consequently, the first iteration of the PMB will cover the total project work scope, but only those activities needed to develop the initial product requirement baseline will be detail planned into work packages. All other activities will be in planning packages.

TABLE 4.1 Work Products Involved in Establishing the PMB

IEEE 1220 [2] 4.1 SE Process Work Products (Figure 4)	EIA-632 [3] Work Products Req. #—Description
• Requirements Baseline	16—System Technical Requirements
• Validated Requirements Baseline	17—Logical Solution Representations
• Functional Architecture	18—Physical Solution Representations
• Verified Functional Architecture	19—Specified Requirements
• Physical Architecture	28—Validated System Technical Requirements
• Verified Physical Architecture	29—Validated Logical Solution Representations
	30—Verified Design Solution

The product requirement baseline includes the verified physical architecture of the system and many interface requirements. It includes the product requirements and the product component requirements. However, the products and product components that will be the design solution to meet those requirements are work products that will not exist until the completion of the design stage.

SYSTEM DEFINITION STAGE

The activities and work products involved in the system definition, per IEEE 1220, are listed in Table 4.2.

EIA 632 ENGINEERING LIFE CYCLE PHASE WORK PRODUCTS

Per EIA 632, there are engineering phases during which significant work products are generated. These work products should also be included in integrated planning and measured with earned value. The process products of EIA 632 are also listed in Table 4.3.

EIA 632 also contains requirements for processes used in engineering a system that are applicable for the engineering of the end products that make up a system, as well as the development of enabling products required to provide life cycle support to system end products. Table 4.4 includes systems definition work products in EIA 632.

DESIGN STAGE

Work Products and Work Packages

To ensure traceability of the product requirements to the work tasks or work products, the planning process should focus on identifying those work products and intermediate work products that are on the path toward satisfying the product requirements and to incorporate these work products into scheduled activities and work packages.

Typically, iterative replanning of the scheduled activities, work packages, and planning packages is performed during the system definition stage. There usually is a major replanning and decomposition of activities at the start of the design phase. The results of that planning iteration include a set of scheduled work products and a PMB that are consistent with the product requirements baseline. Some of these work products should be traceable to the product requirements. Some significant planning activities in the design stage follow:

TABLE 4.2 Activities and Work Products Involved in the System Definition

IEEE 1220 System Definition Stage: Activities	Work Products
5.1 Define the system with focus on system products required to satisfy operational requirements.	

Establish system definition
• Select system concept.
• Establish project and technical plans.
 	
• Identify subsystems and subsystem interface requirements.
 	
• Identify human/system interface requirements.
• Mitigate system risks using simulation, scale-model tests, prototype tests.
• Assess subsystem risks.
• Define life cycle quality factors and allocate to products and subsystems.
	• System concept
	• Initial engineering plans including activity accomplishment criteria for determining system definition progress assessment
	• Subsystems and subsystem interfaces
	  ○ Functional and performance requirements allocated to subsystems
	• Performance, workloads, design constraints, usability
	• Project Risk Register that provides evidence of mitigated risks and assessed subsystem risks
	
	• Description of life cycle quality factors
	  ○ Producibility
	  ○ Test
	  ○ Ease of distribution
	  ○ Usability
	  ○ Supportability
	  ○ Trainability
	  ○ Disposability
	  ○ Total ownership costs

• Complete specifications (specs).	• System and product interface specifications
	• System and product specifications
	  ○ Functional requirements
	  ○ Performance requirements
	  ○ Design characteristics
	  ○ Design constraints
	  ○ System qualification requirements
	  ○ Allocation of requirements to each product
	  ○ Product qualification requirements
	  ○ Methods used to confirm satisfaction of requirements
	• Subsystem interface specifications

TABLE 4.2 *Continued*

IEEE 1220 System Definition Stage: Activities	Work Products
	• Preliminary subsystem specifications • Preliminary human/system interface specifications • Preliminary manpower, personnel, and training specifications
• Establish configuration baselines.	• System baseline • Subsystem design-to baseline
• Complete technical reviews. • Alternate concept review.	• Selected concepts
• System definition review	• Trade-study data • Analysis, test, and/or technical data to support decisions

TABLE 4.3 Engineering Phases and Associated Work Products

EIA 632 Life Cycle Phase	Work Products
System Definition	• Specified requirements for the end products • Initial specifications, including interface specifications, for subsystems of each end product • Enabling product requirements to enable an end product to meet functionality requirements during development, production, test, deployment, training, support, and disposal, as applicable
Subsystem Design	• Same as above but applied to building blocks at the second-layer subsystems
Detailed Design	• Same as above but applied to building blocks at the third and lower layers of the project • Detailed drawings or documents, as appropriate, for the end products

1. Identify the products, product components, and work products.
2. Trace the product requirements to the products, product components, and work products.
3. Develop, decompose, and schedule the activities needed to produce the products, product components, and work products.
4. Establish the milestones that indicate the end of those activities and the completion criteria for the resultant work product.
5. Develop a preliminary Integrated Master Schedule (IMS).
6. Determine the resources (budget) necessary to complete the scheduled activities.
7. Develop the time-phased budget for each activity.
8. Reiterate above steps until a realistic PMB is approved.

TABLE 4.4 System Definition Work Products

EIA 632 Requirement	Work Product

16—System Technical Requirements	• Required transformation rules, priorities, inputs, outputs, states, modes, and configurations
	• Operational requirements, events to which system end products must respond, frequency of use, physical and functional interfaces, and system functional requirements
	• Performance requirements
	  ○ Performance expectations for functional requirements
	  ○ Measures of performance (MOP)
	  ○ TPMs that will be key indicators of end product or system performance
	  ○ Functional and performance testability approach for each requirement statement

17—Logical Solution Representations	• Abstract definition of the solution with functional analysis, object-oriented analysis, or other techniques • System technical requirements assigned to subfunctions, groups of subfunctions, objects, etc. • Derived technical requirements statements
18—Physical Solution Representations	• Sets of functions, objects, behaviors, derived technical requirements assigned to physical entities (e.g., sensor, engine, power source that will make up a physical solution) • Physical interfaces • Assessed physical solution options • Preferred physical solution representation

Synthesis

Synthesis is performed to define design solutions and to identify subsystems to satisfy the product requirements (IEEE 1220, 6.5). The tasks performed during synthesis are shown in Table 4.5. Some work products from IEEE 1220 that are outputs of synthesis are shown in Table 4.5.

A similar set of design solution work products in EIA 632 follows.

EIA 632, Req. 19—Fully characterized design solution

1. Hardware drawings and schematics
2. Software design documents
3. Parts lists
4. Interface descriptions
5. Procedural manuals

CMMI [4] provides guidance for specifying significant work products, called typical work products (TWP). For organizations that use

TABLE 4.5 Tasks Performed During Synthesis

IEEE Section	Work Products
6.5.2	• **Functional and performance requirements allocated to design elements** • **Design solution alternatives**
6.5.11	• **Models and prototypes** • **Failure modes and effects analyses (FMEA)**
6.5.17	Integrated data package • **Drawings, schematics, software documentation, manual procedures, etc.**
6.5.18	Design architecture • **Requirements traceability and allocation matrices** • **Trade-off analysis results**

the CMMI, a subset of TWPs during the design solution stage is shown in the Technical Solution Process Area in Appendix E, Table E-1. Guidance for improving earned value management processes within the framework of CMMI is provided in [5]. That guidance includes a set of typical work products within each of the CMMI process aeas.

Design Verification

Design verification is performed to ensure that:

1. **Requirements of the lowest level of the design architecture, including derived requirements, are traceable to the verified functional architecture**

2. **The design architecture satisfies the validated requirements baseline (IEEE 1220, 6.6)**

The completion of design verification indicates the end of the detailed definition stage. Often, the customer conducts a technical review at this point. This review is sometimes called a Critical Design Review (CDR). The CDR is discussed further in Chapter 5, Guideline 2.4 (Event-based success criteria).

Some work products from IEEE 1220 that are outputs during design verification are shown in Table 4.6.

Comparable design verification work products in EIA 632 are within Requirements 30 and 31, Design Solution Verification and End Product Verification. A partial set follows:

1. **Method for design solution and end product verification**
2. **Verification procedures and success criteria**
3. **Verification outcomes**

TABLE 4.6 Work Products of Design Verification

IEEE Section	Work Products
6.6.1.1	Inspection, analysis, demonstration, or test requirements • **Verification method** • **Verification matrix** • **Models or prototypes to be used**
6.6.1.2	Verification procedures
6.6.1.3	Verification environment • **Facilities, tools, simulations, measuring devices, personnel, climatic conditions**
6.6.2	Evaluation results
6.6.7	Specification and configuration baselines

Most verification work products that will be used during the test stage are developed during the earlier stages of the software development life cycle (SDLC). These include:

1. Lists of work products selected for verification
2. Verification methods for each selected work product
3. Verification procedures
4. Verification criteria
5. Entry and exit criteria for peer review of work products

TEST STAGE

During the test stage, the CMMI TWPs include the verification results and the analysis report.

SUMMARY

This chapter has described Guideline 1.2: Maintain bidirectional traceability of product and product component requirements among the project plans, work packages, planning packages, and work products. The work products in the systems engineering process were discussed. Synthesis is performed to define design solutions and to identify subsystems to satisfy the product requirements. Design verification is performed to ensure that requirements of the lowest level of the design architecture, including derived requirements, are traceable to the verified functional architecture and that the design architecture satisfies the validated requirements baseline.

REFERENCES

[1] Project Management Institute. *A Guide to the Project Management Body of Knowledge* (*PMBOK Guide*), 3rd. Ed. Upper Darby, PA: Project Management Institute, 2004.

[2] Institute of Electrical and Electronics Engineers (IEEE). IEEE Std 1220™–2005, *IEEE Standard for Application and Management of the Systems Engineering Process*. New York: IEEE, 2005.

[3] Electronic Industries Alliance (EIA). *ANSI/EIA 632, Processes for Engineering a System*. Arlington, VA: EIA, 1998.

[4] Software Engineering Institute (SEI). *Capability Maturity Model Integration, version 1.1*. Pittsburgh, PA: SEI, Carnegie Mellon University, March 2002.

[5] Solomon, Paul. "Using CMMI to Improve Earned Value Management." (CMU/SEI-2002-TN-016). Carnegie Mellon University/SEI, October 2002 (see www.sei.cmu.edu/pub/documents/02.reports/pdf/02tn016.pdf).

Chapter 5
Progress Toward Meeting Product Requirements

INTRODUCTION

We have covered the first principle of Performance Based Earned Value (PBEV). We know how to ensure that the product scope and product requirements are integrated into the Performance Measurement Baseline (PMB). This chapter covers performance measurement. It includes the second principle of PBEV and its first four guidelines. Now we will learn how to specify the base measures of earned value.

The second principle of PBEV is: Specify performance toward meeting product requirements as a base measure of earned value.

This principle involves quantifying the progression of requirements from concept to formulation to design to test. Peter Baxter discusses assessing these requirements to ensure that your product contains all required functionality. Baxter's advice addresses software requirements but is also applicable to the system requirements.

It is advisable to measure the number of requirements that each software process generates or accepts. Measure the number of system or top-level software requirements (i.e., features or capabilities) as well as

---

Performance-Based Earned Value, by Paul J. Solomon and Ralph R. Young
Copyright ©2007 IEEE Computer Society.

the decomposition of system requirements into more detailed requirements. To track differences between developed and planned requirements, it is necessary to also measure the status of each requirement as it moves through life cycle activities. A typical requirement status could be: defined, approved, allocated, designed, implemented, tested, and verified. A measure that shows the status of all requirements is essential in monitoring program status and acts as a scorecard to illustrate that requirements are being implemented. Early in the program schedule, ensure that requirements become defined, approved, and allocated as the system architecture is finalized. Near the end of the program schedule, you should see requirements move from implemented status, to tested, then to verified status [1].

We believe that measuring the status of each requirement as it moves through life cycle activities is an essential control tool. It deserves its own chapter in this book, Chapter 12, *Requirements and Earned Value.*

GUIDELINE 2.1

Einstein observed, "Not everything that counts can be counted, and not everything that can be counted counts 2000 [2]. Applying Einstein's wisdom to project management, "If you are measuring the wrong things or not measuring the right way, than EVM may be more costly to administer and may provide less management value" [3].

To minimize the costs of measurement and focus management's attention on the most important variances, the project stakeholders should agree on important information needs and objectives regarding project progress. Some of the information may be contractually required. Most information is required for internal control. The enterprise processes and project plan should define an information need and objective to measure progress toward satisfying product requirements. Conversely, the PM should be thrifty and be sure that activities or processes are not measured unless the measurements provide useful information for awareness and decision-making.

This guidance is not intended to limit the measurement of work products to those that are directly related to product requirements. Information is also needed concerning the schedule progress of many other enabling work products that cannot be tested for their ability to meet a product requirement. Organizational processes, including quality assurance processes, determine the completion criteria of enabling work products. Examples of lower-level, enabling work products are design drawings or interface control documents. These normally should be measured by the percent complete or milestone method. Guidance for measuring enabling work products that cannot be tested for their ability to meet a product requirement is given in Appendix A.

Normally, these lower-level, enabling work products are first assembled or integrated into a design of a subcomponent or component. That design can be analyzed or tested for its ability to meet product requirements. Often models, simulations, analysis, or prototypes are used to estimate the component's ability to meet product requirements. With traditional EV, the completion of the enabling work products is measured without considering whether or not the product requirements are being achieved.

An example of enabling work products from Project X is in Appendix E, Example E.2.

PBEV uses a combination of measuring the "untestable," lower-level, enabling work products (testable against organizational process and quality assurance requirements but not against product requirements) and periodic analysis or testing of the integrated/assembled subcomponent/component design to determine progress vs. plan toward satisfying the product requirements, usually as percent complete. PBEV also implies that, if there is no information need or objective to measure an activity, don't measure it.

This guideline has two objectives regarding lean, cost-effective EV practices:

1. **Establish a policy that there is an information need and objective to measure progress toward satisfying product requirements.**
2. **Reduce the wasteful measurement of activities and work products that, although measurable, do not satisfy any information needs and objectives.**

When Product Requirements Are Not Measurable

As discussed in *Effective Requirements Practices* [4], during the system definition stage, and with the evolutionary acquisition approach, the real product requirements are not yet known. Consequently, activity accomplishment criteria should be established to determine progress assessment until the early product requirements have been determined.

What If Measurement Is Not Needed?

Dick Kitterman, of the Northrop Grumman Corporation, published an innovative and useful set of tests to use for determining whether a measure is truly needed. Kitterman asks a series of questions to take a more structured approach to generating, evaluating, and using metrics. A key factor is to view metrics as existing only to give an objective basis for decisions. The *only* value of a metric is in giving *an objective basis for a decision*, then seeing the results of the actions flowing from that decision translated into changes in the direction desired.

Tests that can be used to evaluate the goodness of the metrics for use in a decision process include the following key questions:

1. **If the metric result were not where one wants it to be, would anyone get sincerely emotional about it?** Observably, there are a lot of metrics, many of them interesting, but not all of them are ones that that would create worry or delight when the results came in. If a metric doesn't "grab the gut," it's not a good metric.

2. **Would the metric drive a decision to take action?** If the person receiving the information from a metric isn't going to use the information to help make a decision, the metric has no value.

3. **Were action taken, would that indeed create a change?** Trivial as this question may seem, it is in fact rather powerful: There are many occasions when action is taken that do not map back to the causative factors that are giving a particular result.

4. **If the change occurs, will it show up in a future value of the metric?** This is just a test that the loop does close, which sometimes does happen. Related to that is asking whether the change could affect any other metrics [5].

These tests, although subjective, are easy to apply. We recommend using them when specifying the base measures of EV. Conversely, those measurable activities that do not pass these tests should be classified as Level of Effort, as discussed in Guideline 2.8.

Having defined the need to measure progress toward meeting product requirements, Guidelines 2.2 through 2.5, 2.8, 4.1, and 4.2 are helpful for specifying the base measures of EV. Next in this chapter, Guidelines 2.2 through 2.4 will be clarified. Examples or case studies will be introduced in some of the guidelines and continued in subsequent chapters and guidelines. This teaching technique will enable the reader to follow the development of the PMB from specification of the work products through allocating the budget to measures of progress.

GUIDELINE 2.2

Having established the information need and objective to measure progress toward meeting product requirements, the next planning steps are to specify the work products and then the measures of progress that will meet that need and objective. This guideline quantifies the progression of requirements from concept to formulation to design to test.

Work Products

A project has many categories of work products. Some are the outcomes of major systems development life cycle stages and are high-level manifestations of the system requirements or design. Others are low-level artifacts or enabling products that are not directly traceable to specific product requirements.

Systems Engineering Process Work Products

The systems engineering process generates significant work products that should be included in integrated planning and measured with earned value. The primary systems engineering process work products of IEEE 1220 and EIA-632 are listed in Chapter 4, Tables 4.1 through 4.6. These work products should be included in the master schedule and be the output of work packages.

CMMI also includes guidance and typical work products (TWPs) for controlling and documenting the systems engineering process, especially those needed for requirements management and traceability. The key TWPs are shown in Table 5.1. These processes and TWPs are important enough to deserve a separate chapter. Chapter 4, *Maintain Bidirectional Traceability*, provides techniques that we recommend highly.

TABLE 5.1 CMMI TWPs—Requirements Management and Traceability

CMMI Process Area	Typical Work Products for Requirements Management and Traceability
Requirements Management	Requirements traceability matrix
Validation	Validation results
Verification	• Exit and entry criteria for work products • Verification results

Additional examples of work products and measures of progress for meeting product requirements follow. They are grouped in the following categories and are discussed further in their respective appendices:

1. **Trade study data to substantiate that system requirements are achievable** (Appendix F).
2. **Allocated requirements developed, implemented into design, or tested successfully** (Appendix G).
3. **Technical Performance Measures (TPMs) and evidence that planned values have been achieved** (Appendix H).
4. **Entry and success criteria for technical reviews and evidence that they were met** (Appendix I).

A comprehensive list of typical work products in CMMI is provided in Appendix E, Table E.1.

Measures of Progress

Project management processes require measuring and reporting at periodic intervals, normally monthly. However, progress toward achieving product requirements is not always measurable on a periodic basis. For example, a hardware or software component may require the completion and assembly of many enabling work products, such as drawings or coded software modules, before the integrated set of work products may be measured against product quality objectives. Consequently, interim progress measurement is normally against the scheduled completion of enabling work products.

The completion criteria for an enabling work product, such as a drawing or a related set of drawings, are determined by the organization's *process* quality procedures and standards. Successful peer reviews or testing are often used to determine the completeness of interim work products against process quality procedures.

PBEV provides guidance to measure performance toward achieving a combination of:

1. **Schedule objectives for enabling work products that meet process quality objectives**
2. **Event-driven quality objectives when the event is the achievement of measurable product requirements.**

The achievement of significant performance requirements may not be measurable at the component or subcomponent level but may depend on achieving planned TPM values or other quality objectives that are measurable at higher levels of the system architecture. Consequently, earned value at the work package level may be quantitatively linked to the performance of integrated components at a higher level of the work breakdown structure.

For example, the project technical plan may prescribe the use of analytical techniques, models, or simulation to determine whether planned TPM values are achieved for a component. The component, at that stage of technical maturity, is the result of many enabling work products and work packages. The work packages may include hardware and software components. With traditional EVM, one of those work packages, such as the set of drawings that define a component, may be assessed as complete when all the drawings have been completed. If the organization's process quality procedures and standards had been applied to the set of drawings, then one hundred percent of earned value would be taken. The project would appear to be on schedule. If subsequent measurements determined that the planned TPM values had not been achieved, the rework of those drawings would traditionally be planned and measured in a separate work package. Even worse, some organizations fail to budget or measure this type of rework at all but just run up costs against a higher Estimate at Completion (EAC). The importance of establishing rework in a separate work package from the initial development is discussed more thoroughly in Chapter 6 in the section on planning for rework.

In contrast, this guideline requires that, when a work package includes a TPM, one of its completion criteria be that the planned value to be achieved was achieved. For example, during the early stages of drawing development, it may be too early to measure TPMs. Consequently, earned value would be based only on completing drawings per the organization's process quality procedures and standards. Later, TPM achievement is taken into account. If ninety percent of the work package budget had been allocated to completing the drawings and ten percent to achieving planned TPMs, then the work package would be held at ninety percent complete until all TPM success criteria were met.

GUIDELINE 2.3

This guideline is the same as a specific practice in the Measurement and Analysis process area of CMMI. Its purpose is to ensure that reported earned value is based on objective measurement and that all stakeholders may understand and rely on the validity of the information. It is especially important that the operational definitions address:

1. **The completion criteria of a work package**
2. **The criteria for measuring interim progress and taking partial earned value for a work package**

Some examples of operational definitions that are precise and unambiguous follow:

1. **All initial drawings complete per functional and QA procedures, approved, and in database.**
2. **Software module unit tested and peer reviewed and includes baseline functionality or requirements.**
3. **Technical data package for design:**
   a. **Completed per functional and QA procedures.**
   b. **Meets all allocated requirements and planned TPMs.**
4. **All lesson modules complete per functional and QA procedures and include all requirements.**
5. **Test procedure complete and approved, and includes all requirements.**
6. **Trade study results accepted by IPT management.**

GUIDELINE 2.4

Event-based planning is an approach to establishing engineering plans, tasks, and milestones based on satisfying significant *accomplishments* associated with key events rather than calendar-oriented milestones (IEEE 3.1.1.16). Technical reviews are scheduled and often have a name that reflects significant life cycle gates or events, such as a preliminary design review or a detailed design review. The milestone for that review, and the work packages that support that milestone, will not be shown as complete unless the planned success criteria have been met.

Success Criteria

The standards discuss the importance of holding technical reviews at various stages of development to ensure that all success criteria have been met. The success criteria should include verification that the planned development or technical maturity has been achieved and that the product being developed is on schedule toward satisfying the product requirements of the end product.

IEEE 1220 is especially helpful in providing success criteria. For example, some of the criteria for completion of a system-level review of the preliminary design are:

1. **Prior completion of subsystem reviews.**
2. **Each detailed component definition is sufficiently mature to meet measure of effectiveness/measure of performance (MOE/MOP) criteria.**
3. **Component specifications are reasonable and provide a sound component concept.**

4. Component and related life cycle process risks have been mitigated to a level to support fabrication, assembly, integration, and test.

5. Trade study data are adequate to substantiate that detailed component requirements are achievable.

6. Decisions made in arriving at the detailed component configuration are well supported by analysis and technical data.

Appendix I includes examples of success criteria, including entrance and exit criteria, as follows:

1. Guidance and success criteria from IEEE 1220 for completion of technical reviews at several phases of engineering development (Tables I.1 through I.4)

2. Excerpts from entrance and exit criteria for a Critical Design Review (CDR) (Example I.1)

3. An example from Project X of success criteria for the completion of detailed design (Example I.2)

4. Excerpts of success criteria and technical baselines from the Defense Acquisition Guide (DAG) (Example I.3 and Table I.5)

The success criteria for major life cycle events should be defined in a plan document. The customer should review these plans with the supplier and reach agreement on the validity and sufficiency of the success criteria to be used at major technical reviews.

SUMMARY

In this chapter, we have discussed initiating the planning for performance measurement. We have established the need to measure progress toward satisfying product requirements and have specified significant, needed work products and measures. We learned that measurement must be objective and that the base measures of earned value must be defined precisely and unambiguously. Then we discussed the identification of success criteria for technical reviews that focus on the evolving product's planned maturity and indicated ability to eventually meet product requirements.

In the following chapters, we will establish the PMB and the actual performance-based objectives that must be achieved to take earned value.

REFERENCES

[1] Baxter, Peter. "Focusing Measurement on Managers' Information Needs." *CrossTalk: The Journal of Defense Software Engineering*. July 2002, pp. 22–25.

[2] Calaprice, Alice. *The Expanded Quotable Einstein*. Princeton, NJ: Princeton University Press, 2000.

[3] Solomon, Paul. "Integrating Systems Engineering with Earned Value Management." *Defense Acquisition, Technology, & Logistics Magazine*, May/June 2004 (see www.dau.mil/pubs/damtoc.asp).

[4] Young, Ralph R. *Effective Requirements Practices.* Boston, MA: Addison-Wesley, 2001.

[5] Kitterman, Dick. "A Structured Method for Generating, Evaluating and Using Metrics." *Proceedings of the International Symposium of the International Council on Systems Engineering*, July 2005.

Chapter 6
Establish Planned Values and Allocate Budget

INTRODUCTION

On the basis of previous guidelines, the work products and measures of progress toward meeting product requirements were established (Guideline 2.2) as well as the success criteria for technical reviews (Guideline 2.4). Guideline 2.5 provides for establishing the planned values to be achieved when measuring progress and declaring success. Guideline 2.5 is the key enabler of quantitative project management because the planned "performance" values for Performance-Based Earned Value (PBEV) are quantified and scheduled. As a result of applying Guideline 2.6, the budget for a work package is allocated to the measures of progress. This guideline enables the recording and reporting of earned value that is directly related to the progress.

This chapter explains how to establish milestones for achieving the number of requirements to be met or the planned technical performance and to allocate budget to those milestones. Several examples that were developed in previous chapters are continued and new examples are introduced. Guidance for planning rework is introduced in this chapter.

Performance-Based Earned Value, by Paul J. Solomon and Ralph R. Young
Copyright ©2007 IEEE Computer Society.

GUIDELINES 2.5 AND 2.6

During these steps in the project planning process, the Project Manager and the Control Account Managers (CAM) establish the interim planned values for achieving the product requirements and the dates or frequency of the measurement activities. Then, the CAM allocates the total work package budget to the measurement events.

The categories of work products and measures of progress for meeting product requirements that were used for Guideline 2.2 are:

1. **Trade studies**
2. **Allocated requirements**
3. **TPMs**

In the remainder of this chapter, Guidelines 2.5 and 2.6 will be applied to examples within these categories. The types of examples and clarification of the guidelines are described in this chapter. The actual examples are in the appendices.

Some of the examples will illustrate several approaches for planning and measuring rework, as discussed in a subsequent section.

TRADE STUDIES

An example of allocating budget to trade study activities is in Appendix F. The study is being performed to select the best design approach to meet a set of requirements. The objective of this trade study is to evaluate five candidates and select one.

Example F.2, Evaluate Trade Study Candidates, illustrates the application of this chapter's guidelines to the following trade study activities:

1. **Establish interim and completion milestones for evaluating each of five candidates.**
2. **Establish a milestone for selection of two candidates for subsequent evaluation.**
3. **Establish a milestone for selection of the recommended alternative.**
4. **Allocate budget to interim and final milestones.**

Additional guidance for trade studies is provided in Appendix F.

ALLOCATED REQUIREMENTS

The next series of examples show how to base earned value on progress toward meeting the allocated product requirements.

Additional examples show how to take earned value based on the sum of two measures:

1. **Progress toward completing the set of enabling work products**
2. **Progress toward meeting the product requirements**

Other examples will show how to set up work packages in two scenarios with regard to rework:

1. **Rework is not planned in a separate work package from the initial development.**
2. **Rework is planned in a separate work package from the initial development.**

Allocated Requirements with Rework Examples

In the following examples, the Statement of Work (SOW) calls for initial development of a set of drawings of a component design and the rework of those drawings until they meet the allocated product requirements.

G.1 **Requirements Development**

G.2 **Design EV Based on Completion of Drawings and Meeting Requirements**

G.3 **Negative EV If Enabling Work Products Must Be Reworked**

G.4 **Test Organization EV Based on Executing Tests and Meeting Requirements**

Four rework examples are provided in Appendix G (G.1, G.3, G.4, and G.5). The examples are summarized below. Their topical differences are highlighted in **bold type** to enable you to quickly locate the topic of your interest.

Example G.1: Rework Is Not Planned in a Separate Work Package (Project X). An example from Project X of utilizing Guidelines 2.5 and 2.6 when establishing a work package that is based on allocated requirements is given in Appendix G, Example G.1.

Example G.3: Rework Is Not Planned in a Separate Work Package. Earned value is taken for each drawing based on the organization's engineering process but without regard to meeting the allocated product requirements. There is another work package for analyzing the drawings to determine whether they will meet product requirements, such as a weight constraint. The analysis is scheduled to begin when the drawings are planned to be 80 percent complete. Negative earned value is taken if a previously completed drawing is now incomplete and must be reworked.

Example G.4: Rework Is Planned in a Separate Work Package as Part Level of Effort (LOE) and Part Completion Milestone. The initial set of drawings is developed in one work package. Each drawing is complete based on the organization's engineering process but without regard to meeting the allocated product requirements. *A separate work package is established for planned rework* of the drawings until the product requirements are met. The *rework work package* is part LOE and part completion milestone.

Additional discussion of how and when to use the LOE technique is provided in Chapter 8 and in Appendix B.

Example G.5: Rework Is Planned in a Separate Work Package with no LOE. In this example, there is *no* LOE. EV is based on the number of weighted requirements met.

TECHNICAL PERFORMANCE MEASUREMENT

The preceding examples addressed the allocated product requirements. The allocated requirements include both functional and performance requirements. The following guidance and examples address just the performance requirements. Technical Performance Measures (TPMs) are defined and evaluated to assess how well a system is achieving its performance requirements. These requirements are normally technical, but they may address other system requirements such as life cycle costs and maintainability. TPMs are used to plan and measure the evolving product's ability to meet those requirements.

Technical parameter values to be achieved are documented as planned performance profiles. Achieved values for these parameters are compared with the planned values. Technical performance measurement uses actual or predicted values from engineering measurements, tests, experiments, models, simulations, or prototypes.

The concept of using a TPM planned performance profile that also shows achieved values and a tolerance band is illustrated in Figure 6.1. In this graph, the vertical axis is expressed as a percentage of the required TPM and the horizontal axis is the timeline. The vertical axis may also be expressed in absolute terms.

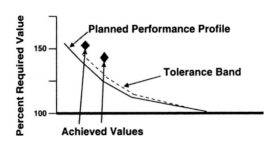

FIGURE 6.1 TPM Plan and Performance.

If we use this technique to control weight, assume that the product requirement is that the system, component, or subcomponent has a specified, maximum weight of 300 pounds. The required weight should be 300 pounds at the time of the detailed design review. Consequently, 300 pounds is 100 percent of the required value. During project planning, establish milestones for interim progress. For example, milestones may be established that a maximum weight of 360 pounds be achieved at the time of the preliminary design review (120% of the required value) and 330 pounds at the time of the detailed design review. Relating this example to Guideline 2.4, the success criteria for the preliminary design review to be successful may include:

1. **The achieved value is no more than 360 pounds.**
2. **There is a corrective action plan that will result in a weight of 300 pounds by a specified date.**

Some customers and suppliers classify technical performance measurement as a risk management technique and do not integrate the planned performance profile into the schedules and work packages. Later, if the achieved values for these parameters fall short of the expected values, neither the schedules nor the earned value will have shown a behind-schedule condition. PBEV Guideline 2.5 and its source standards provide guidance for using EVM to monitor TPM progress and to provide an early warning if the evolving product is failing to meet customer requirements.

IEEE 1220, EIA 632, and the PMBOK Guide provide similar guidance for TPM planning and measurement and for integrating TPMs with EVM. TPM guidance in the systems engineering standards is illustrated in Table 6.1.

The PMBOK Guide also provides guidance for TPMs. It defines TPMs as a performance measurement technique that compares technical accomplishments during project execution to the project management plan's schedule of planned technical achievements. It also states that work performance information used in Quality Control includes TPMs (Section 4.4.3.7).

Finally, the International Council on Systems Engineering (INCOSE) warns, in its SE Handbook [1] that, without TPMs, a project manager could fall into the trap of relying on cost and schedule status alone. This can lead to a product developed on schedule and within cost that does *not meet* all key *requirements*. The INCOSE Handbook states that periodic recording of the status of each TPM provides continuing verification of the degree of anticipated and actual achievement of technical parameters.

TABLE 6.1 TPM Guidance in Systems Engineering Standards

Standard	Section	Guideline
IEEE 1220	6.8.1.5: Performance-based progress measurement	a. TPMs are key to progressively assessing technical progress. Track relative to time with dates established for when: • Progress will be checked • Full conformance will be met Use to assess conformance to requirements. c. Cost and schedule performance measurements integrated with TPMs to: • Provide current schedule and performance impacts • Provide an integrated corrective action to variances identified.
EIA 632	4.2.1: Planning Process Requirement 5: Technical Effort Definition	f. Identify TPMs that will be used to determine the success of the system, or portion thereof, and that will receive management focus and be tracked.

EIA 632	Glossary: TPM	• Predict future value of key technical parameters of the end system based on current assessments.
		• Planned Value Profile is time-phased achievement projected.
		  ○ Achievement to date
		  ○ Technical milestone where TPM evaluation is reported

TPM Flowdown Procedure

The procedure for allocating EV for a subcomponent or component that contributes to TPM objectives at a higher Work Breakdown Structure (WBS) level follows.

1. Examine the requirements traceability matrix (RTM) to identify all components and subcomponents that are traceable to the allocated functional and performance requirements.

2. Examine the WBS to identify the work products that support the development of those subcomponents or components.

3. Trace those work products to their respective work packages.

4. Allocate a portion of the total work package Budget At Completion (BAC) to achieving all planned TPMs, including a TPM that may be allocated to the work product at the work package level and any TPMs that are allocated to higher-level work products.

5. Distribute the budget allocations for TPM achievement in the time periods when TPM measurements are scheduled.
6. Either take negative EV for failing to achieve the TPM planned value, or take EV for achieving the TPM planned value, depending on how the PMB and the EV techniques were established.

Evidence of Achieving Planned TPM Values

Several examples of applying the guidelines discussed in this Chapter with TPMs are provided in Appendix H, *Technical Performance Measures*:

Example H.1: Budget Is Allocated to Achieving TPM Planned Value for Weight

Example H.2: Negative EV If TPM Planned Value Is Not Achieved

Example H.3: Partial EV If TPM Is Within Tolerance of Planned Value

Example H.4: EV When TPM Is at a Higher WBS Level

Example H.5: Waterproofness—Project X

Example H.6: TPM of Software Quality—Project X

PLANNING FOR REWORK

Rework occurs when, subsequent to the completion of the initial development of the enabling work products, it is discovered that one or more of those work products no longer meet the requirements. It is desirable to plan rework in a separate work package from the initial development of the enabling work products. A separate work package for rework enables improved planning, control, and analysis because:

1. The initial development of the work product has a distinct, baseline completion date.
2. Progress can be tracked toward meeting that date.
3. Slips and impacts can be shown on the Integrated Master Schedule (IMS) and in the Estimate to Complete (ETC).
4. Variance analyses for the initial development and for rework are based on separate and distinct performance data.

Rework should be planned with a discrete earned value technique. A time-phased plan should be developed with milestones for planned values of the number of requirements to be met or for TPM planned values to be achieved at specified dates. The rework budget should be allocated to those milestones and earned based on performance. Additional guidance for rework is provided in Appendices A, B, and G.

SUMMARY

This chapter has presented how to establish time-phased, planned values for measures of progress toward meeting product requirements, dates or frequency for checking progress, and dates when full conformance will be met. Also, it has described how to allocate budget in discrete work packages to measures of progress toward meeting product requirements.

Important distinctions for the recommended PBEV approach as contrasted with traditional EV are:

> 1. **Earned value is taken only when a work product meets its requirements.**
> 2. **Early warning is provided if the evolving product is failing to meet requirements.**

In Chapter 7, we describe how to control the project by analyzing the PBEV data and estimating the remaining costs and time until the product requirements have been met.

REFERENCES

[1] International Council on Systems Engineering (INCOSE). *INCOSE Systems Engineering Handbook*, Version 3, June 2006, p. 7.11. See www.incose.org.

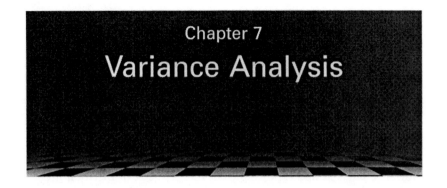

Chapter 7

Variance Analysis

<table>
<tr><td>

GUIDELINE 2.7

Compare the amount of planned budget and the amount of budget earned for achieving progress toward meeting product requirements.

</td></tr>
</table>

INTRODUCTION

Previous guidelines established the need to measure progress toward meeting product requirements and to specify measures to meet that need. This guideline focuses management analysis on deviations from the plan to meet the product requirements. The importance of relating schedule, technical, and cost performance is stressed.

Fundamental earned value analysis, including analysis of cost variances and the use of the Cost Performance Index (CPI), are discussed in Appendix A. The most useful guidance we have seen for variance analysis regarding the product requirements is EIA 632, Requirement 10 [1], paraphrased as follows:

> Assess the progress of system development by comparing currently defined system characteristics against requirements and by comparing results against requirements to determine the degree of technical requirement satisfaction, progress toward maturity of the system being engineered, and variations and variances from requirements.

Earned value variance analysis supports this requirement if the base measures of earned value measure the degree of technical requirement satisfaction and progress toward maturity of the system.

In this chapter, lessons learned will be discussed regarding the validity of mathematical Estimates at Completion (EACs) when there are

---

Performance-Based Earned Value, by Paul J. Solomon and Ralph R. Young
Copyright ©2007 IEEE Computer Society.

significant technical problems in meeting the product requirements and the importance of measuring requirements achieved during integration testing and rework.

The chapter concludes with an approach to adjusting earned value when the deliverable from each activity or Work Breakdown Structure (WBS) component does not meet a quality standard that is critical to project success.

VARIANCE ANALYSIS

Variance analysis and reporting is an integral part of the total project management control process. Schedule variance analysis includes a thorough assessment of the following:

1. **Cause of the variance**—Include a clear and concise explanation of the problem, what caused the performance to deviate from the plan, and whether it is recurring or nonrecurring in nature. Address related variances that have a common cause, such as a schedule variance and a related variance from achieving Technical Performance Measurement (TPM) planned values.

2. **Program impact (cost, schedule, and quality)**—Include a narrative of the real and potential impact of the schedule variance on project cost and schedule objectives as well as the schedule impact on other activities. If appropriate, discuss the possibility of a trade study to investigate trade-offs between cost, schedule, and product quality objectives. Include a revised EAC, if appropriate.

3. **Corrective actions**—Include a description of the planned corrective actions. If the corrective actions were described earlier, discuss their status.

4. **Recovery date**—Include the anticipated recovery date.

SCENARIOS

One purpose of this chapter is to provide examples of effective analysis when the project gets behind schedule in meeting the product requirements. Several scenarios will be developed and analyzed. For some scenarios, several alternative root causes will be postulated, with their respective impact analyses and corrective action plans. The scenarios follow.

Scenario 1: Sudden behind-schedule condition when TPM planned value was not achieved.

Scenario 2: Software integration test results disclose a consistent, adverse trend. The schedule variance becomes worse each reporting period. The number of requirements tested successfully is lower than the plan.

Scenario 3: The systems engineering group is behind schedule in completing requirements management and traceability operations.

Scenario 4: A trade study to select a new sealant is behind schedule. None of the original candidates is capable of meeting requirements.

Scenario 1: TPM Schedule Variance

Background. A control console in a cockpit requires a maximum surrounding temperature that does not exceed 100 degrees Fahrenheit for more than 30 seconds and never exceeds 120 degrees. The designs of the control console and its nearby equipment, the thermal analyses of the heat emitted by each device, and the design for air circulation and other cooling methods have been developed on schedule and have met individual TPM requirements at the lower levels. However, when tests were conducted on a model of the complete, integrated cockpit environment, the results showed that the planned TPMs were not achieved.

Earned Value. Before the TPM milestone was reached, there had been no significant schedule variances. If the TPM planned value had been achieved, there would be no decrement to earned value. However, because of the TPM actual values, the cumulative earned value in appropriate work packages is decremented by an arbitrary but significant amount, the equivalent of one month of budget. How should this be described in variance analysis? It depends on the root cause of the problem and even whether the root cause is known.

Variance Analysis 1

Cause. The problem is caused by insufficient space between components of the integrated equipment. Consequently, there is insufficient airflow to cool the equipment. Going to the root cause, the systems engineers who wrote the requirements failed to specify maximum dimensions for cables and connecting devices that resided in the airflow space.

Impact. Subsequent activities will be delayed a minimum of 4 weeks until a design solution that meets the requirements is completed. The cost of redesign, including the costs of subcontractors and internal labor waiting to resume planned activities, is an increase of $50,000.

Corrective action plan. Rework the requirements and design. Rerun the test of the model.

Variance Analysis 2

Cause. One of the components in proximity to the control console generates much more heat than anticipated. The prior testing and thermal analysis had failed to detect the deficiency in meeting requirements.

Corrective action plan and impact. The redesign of the component will delay the project by a minimum of 8 weeks and result in a cost increase of at least $100,000.

Lesson Learned Regarding Variance Analysis and EAC. Before proceeding to the next scenario, there is an important lesson to be learned by looking at the variations in the impacts, cost, and schedule, depending on the cause of the variance. The adverse impact of the problem in Variance Analysis 2 was twice that of Variance Analysis 1. The most likely EAC was determined by developing a plan for the remaining activities.

Many users of EVM, including the customer and the supplier, develop mathematical EACs that are based on projections of past cost and/or schedule performance, such as the Cost Performance Index (CPI). However, when there is a significant technical issue, only detailed planning of the remaining work can result in a valid EAC. In the above scenario, the CPI was the same for Variance Analysis 1 and Variance Analysis 2 at the time of the failure, yet the future costs of the two variants were very different from each other and were not logically related to the past cost performance.

The lesson learned is: Be wary of using mathematical projections of final cost and schedule when the project has significant technical problems.

Scenario 2: Software Behind Schedule in Meeting Requirements

Background. The development of code through unit testing was on schedule. The first build was turned over to test with all baselined requirements. The number of defects that were found and included in problem reports fluctuated greatly from period to period. The burn down or disposition of defects, both those due to requirements and those due to code, is at the planned rate because of the availability of planned resources for rework.

Earned Value. The earned value is based on the number of requirements that are tested successfully. Consequently, it does not fluctuate based on the number of open defects or problem reports at any time. Some fluctuations in earned value occur because a requirement may have been tested successfully in one period and failed during regression testing in a subsequent period when new conditions were encountered or new, planned defects were inserted.

Root Causes. The primary cause is insufficient peer review of code and unit tests because the average skill level of the team was lower than planned. The same lack of skills is jeopardizing the project during rework.

Impact and Corrective Action. There is a significant adverse impact on the project's final cost and schedule for several reasons. First, the problems found were related to the functionality and requirements that were planned to date. These were only 25% of the total project requirements. In fact, the control account manager cannot even determine a credible EAC until an executable plan is developed to acquire more highly skilled people and, possibly, to improve the peer review process.

Lesson Learned Regarding Software Integration Testing and Rework. The primary base measure of earned value during integration testing and rework is the number of requirements planned to be achieved each period. When the schedule variance was detected and tracked, it indicated that significant corrective actions must be taken. Had the earned value been based on defects, problem reports, or LOE, the severity of the problem might not have been quickly understood.

Scenario 3: Systems Engineering Behind Schedule in Requirements Management

This scenario is based on the SOW and measurements described in Chapter 6. The severe impacts to the project from falling behind schedule were also discussed there.

The cause of a schedule variance in the early stages is almost always not having the right people, or enough of the right people, committed to defining and validating the requirements. This includes the customer's commitment.

The corrective action plan, in this situation, is to quickly assign the right people to the tasks and to give it the highest priority.

If the requirements definitions are dependent on the completion of trade studies, then all stakeholders should assess the trade study process to determine whether it can be improved.

Scenario 4: Trade Study Behind Schedule

The trade study to select a new sealant is behind schedule. None of the original candidates is capable of meeting requirements.

The cause of the variance is the unique technical requirements. A sealant that meets the technical requirements for the width of the gap and all environmental requirements has not been developed before. This situation was identified previously as a risk with both high probability and high impact.

The corrective action is to perform a new trade study to seek another engineering solution. Management Reserve includes contingent budget for this risk. It now needs to be transferred to the Performance Measurement Baseline. There is no schedule impact to other project activities because the selection of the sealant was planned far ahead of its need date. However, if an acceptable alternative is not found by a certain date, then fabrication of the test item will fall behind schedule.

VARIANCE FROM CRITICAL-TO-QUALITY PARAMETERS

In Chapter 1, we discussed the shortcomings of the legacy EVMS principles. One shortcoming is their failure to address the product requirements and the quality of the product being developed. A novel approach to analyzing variances from the product requirements was presented by Mr. Lakshminarayana Kompella at the PMI Pearl City Chapter (PMIPCC)—Asia Pacific Conference in Hyderabad, India [2] (copyright permission to use excerpts from this paper has been obtained from the PMIPCC).

His paper states that the available methods of EV calculation make assumptions in arriving at the EV that do not capture the quality of the deliverable delivered from the activity or WBS component. The deliverable from each activity or WBS component should meet the respective quality standard so that the project can meet its agreed goals and objectives. These goals and objectives are primarily defined to focus on the parameters that are critical to the project's success. He refers to these parameters as Critical-To-Quality (CTQ).

With the CTQ approach, EV (as measured by one of the legacy methods) is adjusted downward when a product metric (such as a TPM or a software quality metric) deviates from the norm. When this occurs, additional effort as compared to the plan will be required to correct the deviation. This effort is unplanned and will be treated as a failure cost. There should be a negative correction to EV, called EV_{corr}. The formula for the correct EV is:

$$EV_{actual} = EV - EV_{corr},$$

where EV_{corr} represents the correction required toward the deviation of the project's CTQs from the norms.

An example of a CTQ is acceptance or field errors. If the number of defects is more than 0.15 defects/1000 lines of code (KLOC), the additional effort to correct the deviation will be captured as EV_{corr}.

Mr. Kompella concludes that it is primarily important that the CTQs are agreed on with all the stakeholders, at the beginning of the project, and the effort is calculated for both value-added and non-value-added activities. These activities determine the correction to earned value. Corrective or preventive actions could be initiated to minimize non-value-added activities, thereby enabling the project to meet its CTQs.

SUMMARY

We now know the importance of understanding the causes of variances from the plan to achieve the product requirements, to determine the impacts on project objectives, and to develop and monitor corrective actions.

Several examples of variances were presented. Finally, we discussed a novel approach to correct the earned value when there are deviations from the planned product requirements.

REFERENCES

[1] Electronic Industries Alliance (EIA). *ANSI/EIA 632, Processes for Engineering a System.* Arlington, VA, EIA, 1998.

[2] Kompella, Lakshminarayana. "Earned Value Management for Software Products: An Approach." *Souvenir of the PMIPCC–Asia Pacific Conference*, April 2005.

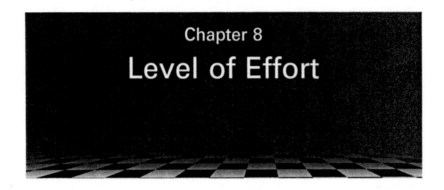

Chapter 8

Level of Effort

INTRODUCTION

In the previous chapters, we discussed discrete tasks that should be planned and measured. In this chapter, guidance is provided for determining whether a work package should be measured with a discrete EV method or should use the level of effort (LOE) technique.

Also, in this chapter we recommend a method for performing effective variance analysis when summary level information includes both LOE and discrete work packages.

A detailed discussion of LOE is included in Appendix B.

GUIDELINE 2.8
Measurable but Not Practicable to Measure

Many tasks are measurable but their performance is not an indicator of the project's capability to meet product requirements. Examples are the completion of a technical assessment meeting or the issuance of a recurring report such as a contract performance report (CPR). If a CPR is delivered late, there is no schedule impact on a subsequent activity. The report is usually issued shortly after it was due, and the organization usually tightens up the process to prevent recurrence of the

Performance-Based Earned Value, by Paul J. Solomon and Ralph R. Young
Copyright ©2007 IEEE Computer Society.

deviation. Also, there is no impact on final costs. So why incur the costs to measure CPRs with a discrete earned value method or to analyze resultant schedule variances?

The same is true for technical assessment reviews such as technical interchange meetings (TIM), preliminary design reviews (PDR), and final or critical design reviews. Per IEEE 1220 and EIA 632, a purpose of the reviews is to *assess* progress and the project's development maturity. However, it is common practice to base earned value on the completion of the meeting or review (people met, talked, and reviewed data) instead of on the quantified assessment of progress and technical maturity.

If discrete earned values were taken because the review *occurred* and the review was held on schedule, then the work packages that had completion criteria tied to *holding* the review would appear to be on schedule. However, if during the review, the team assessed that the design maturity did not meet the *success criteria* that were planned for that *event*, then earned value might mask a behind-schedule condition. Likewise, the master schedule would be misleading if the review milestone were shown as complete despite a shortfall in technical performance or maturity.

We recommend that many measurable but nontechnical tasks be classified as LOE. As a result, there would be lower measurement costs and earned value performance would more closely track technical performance. Furthermore, management would not have to spend time to address non-technical schedule variances. Management would have more time to monitor the schedule performance of technical activities.

A decision not to measure non-technical tasks is also consistent with the CMMI specific practice that is cited in Guideline 2.1. If there is no information need or objective to measure non-technical tasks, don't measure them.

The EVMS standard states, "Only that effort which is unmeasurable or for which measurement is *impracticable* to measure may be classified as LOE." When trying to determine whether a work package should be discrete or LOE, remember that the only value of a metric is in giving an objective basis for a decision and use the tests for evaluating the goodness of metrics (Chapter 5). We believe that many non-technical tasks are impracticable to measure and should be classified as LOE.

Exception to Guideline 2.8: Planned Process Improvements

There are exceptions to this guideline. A project manager may choose to discretely measure some activities that do not affect technical performance but will affect cost or schedule performance.

Process improvements are often planned to enable the achievement of the project's final cost objectives or final schedule objectives. However, progress toward cost or schedule reduction initiatives is not a measure of progress toward satisfying product requirements. The tasks to develop these process improvements should be monitored with discrete earned value techniques.

An example is a cost-reduction initiative that must be implemented in order to reduce future costs. The SOW might be development of a new, more efficient process flow or acquisition and implementation of a software productivity tool. Normally, the completion of the cost-reduction initiative is the predecessor for the planned reduction of recurring costs. The impact of late implementation will cause future costs to be higher than plan. If the cost reduction initiative were planned and measured with discrete earned value, than an unfavorable schedule variance would be an early indicator of downstream failure and resultant cost increases over the plan.

A planned process improvement to increase production rates or to achieve other schedule objectives should also be planned discretely, not as LOE. Any significant schedule slip to the process improvement plan would appear as a schedule variance and trigger corrective action.

Arbitrary Limits to LOE

Many PMs expect that the percentage of LOE budget should not exceed a specified level. We believe that setting an arbitrary maximum threshold for LOE can increase contract costs and cause management to waste time by focusing on the wrong things. As discussed with Guideline 2.1, it costs money to measure progress, but the measurement may not be useful.

GUIDELINE 2.9

All levels of management perform variance analysis. Cost and schedule performance information is available and used at the work package level and at all reporting levels above that level.

Commingling LOE with Discrete Work Packages

This guidance is simple. When reviewing performance information, segregate or quarantine the performance of the LOE work packages so that it is not summarized or commingled with the performance of the discrete work packages.

If the LOE performance is not quarantined, the summary performance data will be distorted. If the discrete components of the summary are behind schedule, the inclusion of LOE will diminish the magnitude of the schedule variance.

The following example will illustrate the problem that is created by commingling both discrete and LOE work packages. Assume that a control account is comprised of two work packages. One is discrete and the other is LOE. The planning and performance information is shown in Table 8.1.

Let's do some schedule variance analysis. At the end of February, the discrete work has a cumulative, budget-based schedule variance of −100. If we convert this to a time-based or duration variance, it is equivalent to 1 month behind schedule.

Now, let's look at cumulative summary data at the control account level. The schedule variance is the same (−100). That is expected because LOE work never has a schedule variance. Earned value equals the Budgeted Cost of Work Scheduled (BCWS). However, the more important schedule variance for management control is the time-based variance.

TABLE 8.1 Commingled LOE

	January	February
Discrete Work Package:		
BCWS current (cur.)	100	100
EV current (cur.)	50	50
BCWS cumulative (cum.)	100	200
EV cum.	50	100
AC	60	120
CPI cum.	0.83	0.42
Schedule variance (SV) current	−50	−50
SV cumulative (cum.)	−50	−100
SV cum. (duration)	0.5 month	1.0 month
LOE Work Package:		
BCWS	40	40
EV	40	40
AC	40	40
CPI	1	1
SV current	0	0
Total Control Account:		
BCWS current (cur.)	140	140
EV current (cur.)	90	90
BCWS cumulative (cum.)	140	280
EV cum.	90	180
AC cum.	100	200
CPI cum.	0.9	0.9
SV current	−50	−50
SV cumulative (cum.)	−50	−100
SV cum. (duration)	0.36 month	0.71 month

The time-based Schedule Variance (SV) of the discrete work is 1 month. We are truly one month behind schedule. However, the time-based SV at the summary level is only 0.71 month behind schedule. The LOE component of the summary data has masked or distorted the magnitude of the schedule variance.

Solution: Quarantine LOE Performance

Quentin Fleming and Joel Koppelman first warned about this deception in an article that was aptly named "The Curse of EVM, LOE—Always Quantify and Quarantine LOE" [1]. They observed that LOE would often mask serious problems in project performance because LOE performance will offset negative discrete results.

They recommend that LOE always be quarantined. Keep all of the LOE work in a separate bucket, and never commingle LOE work with discretely measured work when you summarize all roll-up data. You need to keep the legitimate discrete work separate to allow for the accurate measurement of performance to your baseline.

SUMMARY

This chapter on LOE has two unrelated guidelines. The first guideline steers some potentially discrete effort to the LOE method. This reduces administrative costs, provides a more accurate summary of technical performance, and focuses management attention on the most important tasks for maintaining schedule control.

The second guideline reinforces the value of the first by enabling accurate, undistorted measurement of technical performance.

By implementing both guidelines in your processes, you will have much better control of technical performance with regard to schedule and more time to focus on the important variances.

REFERENCE

[1] Fleming, Quentin and Koppelman, Joe. "The Curse of EVM, LOE—Always Quantify and Quarantine LOE." *The Measurable News*, June 2002.

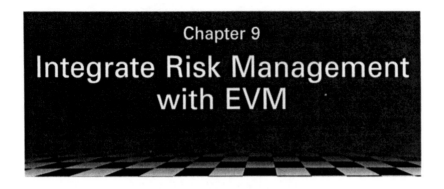

Chapter 9

Integrate Risk Management with EVM

INTRODUCTION

The third principle of PBEV is:

Integrate risk management with Earned Value Management (EVM). This principle fosters unambiguous and candid communication regarding changes to the project work scope that should be made to incorporate risk mitigation activities that are identified after project initiation. The risk mitigation activities may affect the project's performance measurement baseline (PMB) and estimate at completion (EAC).

> **GUIDELINE 3.1**
>
> Identify changes that need to be made to the project plans, work packages, planning packages, and work products resulting from responses to risks.

> **GUIDELINE 3.2**
>
> Develop revised estimates of costs at completion based on risk quantification.

Users of earned value management are aware that the EVMS standard has no guideline concerning risk management. However, a separate document, the NDIA PMSC ANSI/ EIA-748-A *Standard for Earned Value Management Systems Application Guide* [1], recommends that EACs should consider all emerging risks that will impact the integrated master schedule and resource plan for the remainder of the work. Excerpts from this guide are included in Appendix C-1.

The following PBEV guidelines supplement the standard. They provide practical guidance for integrating risk management with EVM.

Performance-Based Earned Value, by Paul J. Solomon and Ralph R. Young
Copyright ©2007 IEEE Computer Society.

GUIDELINE 3.1

Simply stated, the output of risk response planning inserts resources and activities into the budget, schedule, and project management plan, as needed (PMBOK Guide, Section 11.5). It is especially important to add the new activities to the master schedule, to define exit criteria for the disposition of the risk, and to establish a logical link between the risk response activity and a dependent activity on the schedule. The new activities are then measured with earned value.

Some risk management activities do not require additional resources. For example, if skilled engineers are not available when planned, the project will become behind schedule. Assume that management has identified a risk that the hiring and training program may not meet its goals. One risk response may require no change to the plan and, therefore, have no affect on the PMB, as follows:

> Monitor the planned hiring and training rates for three months. Do not commit any additional resources unless there are significant deviations from the plan.

Another risk response may require additional activities and resources that are considered beyond the baseline work scope, as follows:

> Develop a detailed plan to hire an additional recruiter for six months, to engage an employment agency that works on commission, and to advertise job openings in Sunday newspapers.
>
> If these activities are charged directly to the project, they will require additional budget. New hiring and training activities and milestones should be established on the master schedule and work packages should be established to track progress with earned value. The completion milestones should have success criteria that include the staffing level needed at the future time. The completion milestones will be linked with the activities that require the resources.

Next, we will look at alternatives for responding to risks where the responses are technical activities, not administrative.

Assume that a system includes a requirement that hydraulic devices operate some of its components. The requirement is that the hydraulic subsystem achieves and maintains hydraulic pressure of 3000 pounds per square inch (psi). The team has identified a risk that the selected design approach will not work because it will not meet structural and weight requirements for the tubing. An alternative approach had been evaluated in a trade study but had been rejected because of the higher cost. The probability of failure and the impact on project cost and schedule objectives were high.

After discussing the trade study recommendations, the team developed a risk mitigation plan. It involved developing and testing a prototype of an alternate design solution to meeting the requirements. The cost was high, $250,000. On the other hand, the potential cost to the project if the baseline design failed was higher. If the baseline design failed, the impact on the project costs would be from $500,000 to $1,000,000. If the team were to declare failure early in project development, the cost impact would be less than if the decision came later.

There was also a significant schedule constraint to the risk mitigation plan. The systems engineering plan for the baseline design included using models, simulations, and Technical Performance Measures (TPMs) to determine whether the design would meet the requirements. The TPM plan included a milestone that the simulated system would achieve a planned value of 3200 psi at the end of the tenth month of development.

The team decided that the risk mitigation plan would have to be completed at the same time as the TPM milestone for achieving the planned value of 3200 psi. The master schedule included an activity to decide whether or not to continue the baseline design. Accordingly, the completion of the risk mitigation plan had to be logically linked to the same decision milestone.

The risk mitigation plan was discussed with the customer and was approved by all stakeholders, including the budget to be transferred from Management Reserve (MR). The risk mitigation activities and milestones were added to the master schedule. Discrete work packages were budgeted and became part of the PMB. The EAC was also increased.

The team proceeded to execute the risk mitigation plan. It used earned value to manage the plan.

GUIDELINE 3.2

This guideline is based on the PMBOK® Guide. It is clear and simple. An EAC is a forecast of the most likely total value based on project performance and risk quantification.

This guideline may be applied at the control account level or at the work package level. It is also applied at the project level based on the project manager's assessment of overall project performance and consideration of top risks.

Control accounts include statement of work (SOW) and budget for authorized, budgeted work. Consequently, the EAC at the control account level may only be related to the authorized work in its PMB. If risk mitigation plans are budgeted, as discussed above, they become part of the PMB and will have an EAC.

Potential risk mitigation plans that have not been authorized and budgeted are part of MR that is normally held at the PM level. MR is budget that may be transferred to control accounts. The Project Manager (PM) is responsible for assessing the EAC of the budget MR. This is sometimes called MR EAC. The total project EAC equals the EAC at the PMB level plus the MR EAC.

The MR EAC is based on the PM's analysis. It is supported by a set of quantified risk assessments. Only at the project's inception should it be equal to the MR budget. At project inception, it may also include an assessment of undefined or unknown risks. During execution of the project, new risks are normally identified, old risks go away, and the quantified risk assessments change. Consequently, after these events occur, there is no logical relationship between the remaining MR budget and MR EAC and no reason for them to be equal.

Additional discussion of MR EAC is provided in Chapter 14, *Supplier Acquisition Management.*

SUMMARY

Risk management activities should be budgeted and tracked with earned value if they consume resources. The outcome of risk management activities, whether budgeted or not, should be logically linked to a dependent activity on the master schedule. In all cases, the project's EAC should include the results of quantified risk assessments.

REFERENCE

[1] National Defense Industrial Association (NDIA) Program Management Systems Committee (PMSC). NDIA PMSC ANSI/EIA-748-A. *Standard for Earned Value Management Systems Application Guide*, 2005.

Chapter 10

Changes to the Performance Masurement Baseline

INTRODUCTION

It is important to maintain the integrity of the performance measurement baseline (PMB) that is being used to manage and control performance. Guidelines 1.1 and 1.2 address the initial establishment of the product requirements and subsequent requirements traceability. Guideline 1.3 applies the preceding guidelines to all subsequent changes to the product requirements.

> **GUIDELINE 1.3**
>
> Identify changes that need to be made to the project plans, work packages, planning packages, and work products resulting from changes to the product requirements.

Normally, when a change to the product requirements is being considered, the impacts on the cost and schedule plans are assessed. Once the change to the product requirements is approved, there should be timely incorporation of changes to the affected plans, work packages, planning packages, and work products. Timely incorporation of changes enables continual performance measurement and management. Maintaining bidirectional traceability of the changes provides evidence that the changes to the baselines are controlled.

The integrity of the PMB is maintained through the change management process by ensuring that changes to product requirements are incorporated into the PMB.

Performance-Based Earned Value, by Paul J. Solomon and Ralph R. Young
Copyright ©2007 IEEE Computer Society.

CAUSES OF CHANGE TO PRODUCT REQUIREMENTS

The customer or the supplier may initiate the process of changing the product requirements. When the customer requests a new system capability and that capability is not part of the features baseline, the impact of the change must be assessed before including the new feature in the baseline. If the project team has done a good job of defining the baseline to begin with, the assumption must be that any change to the baseline must affect the resources, the schedule, or the features set [1].

When the customer initiates a change to the product requirements that would cause a change to the resources or schedule, a change in the contract price is usually negotiated. Sometimes, the customer may authorize the supplier to proceed with the revised requirements before the negotiation is completed or even started. When authorization is received, the supplier changes the product plan.

Some recommendations to change the product requirements may be initiated by the supplier and offered to the customer. For example, a trade study analysis may disclose alternative solutions to requirements or design problems that may offer increased functional or performance requirements for various quality factors that are important to overall customer satisfaction. A set of quality factors is provided below [2].

QUALITY FACTORS

1. Producibility
2. Testability and integrated diagnostics
3. Distributability (including packaging and handling, transportability, and installability)
4. Usability
5. Supportability
6. Trainability
7. Disposability
8. Reliability
9. Maintainability
10. Electromagnetic compatibility
11. Electrostatic discharge
12. Health hazards
13. Environmental impact
14. System security
15. Infrastructure support
16. Any other engineering specialty bearing on the determination of functional and performance requirements for the system

Any of these quality factors may have become a product requirement if the customer decided that it was mandatory for the product to meet verified customer needs. The trade study results may have concluded that the defined Measures of Effectiveness (MOE) of one or more of these requirements may not be achieved within the cost and schedule constraints. Another possibility is that a significant improvement in some of these qualities, such as reliability or maintainability, is possible with additional investment by the customer.

After reviewing the supplier's trade study recommendations, the customer may decide to authorize an increase in one of the product requirements and the resultant increases in resources or schedule. Another possibility is that the customer authorizes a change to one product requirement and concurrently reduces another. Thus, one change in requirements offsets the other in terms of resources or schedule. In either of these situations, the supplier must identify changes that need to be made to the project plans, work packages, planning packages, and work products

Two examples follow. Example 10.1 shows a change to two product requirements of Project X that are offset in terms of resources and schedule but will require changes to the planning and work products. Example 10.2 shows how an increase in one of the product requirements causes an increase in the cost, schedule, and work packages.

Example 10.1: Trade-Off of Product Requirements, Project X

After Project X was authorized and partially developed, the customer became aware that the maximum weight must be reduced from 40 lb. to 35 lb. The customer had determined that operators of the backpack would be women as well as men. The original requirement was too heavy for women. Unfortunately, the customer was not able to provide additional funds to Project X. Instead, it chose to reduce another requirement.

The supplier's Technical Performance Measure (TPM) achievement already demonstrated that the end product would weigh 38 lb So, the team had to find three more pounds of weight reduction.

Unfortunately, Project X was well into detailed design. The customer had prepared an estimate of the change to the project plans that would be required to implement the revised weight requirement. The first activities would be additional trade studies to find a design solution to the 35 lb. requirement. The supplier estimated that the revised requirement would have several impacts on Project X's cost and schedule, as shown below:

1. **Cost increase: $150,000-$200,000 (depending on results of trade study)**
2. **Schedule increase: 1-4 months (depending on results of trade study)**
3. **Activities revised:**
   a. **New trade study**
   b. **Redesign of components in design solution: Candidates are battery and radio transmitter components**

The customer and supplier discussed the estimate. As a result, the customer authorized an additional $10,000 for the new trade study and stopped further work on the design and procurement of the battery and radio transmitter components. The customer also authorized an additional $140,000 for additional redesign activities. Both parties agreed that an additional $50,000 might be authorized, depending on the results of the trade study.

The supplier revised its master schedule, work packages, and planning packages, as follows:

1. **Master schedule and work packages:**
   a. **Added trade study ($10,000)**
   b. **Stopped work on design of two components.**
2. **Planning package: Added planning package to finish design ($140,000)**

Example 10.2: House Project Revised Product Requirement

Appendix A, *Fundamentals of Earned Value Management*, includes a case study. The project in the case study is building a house. The discussion, "Revise the PMB," states: If upgraded cabinets were added to the house subsequent to the start of work, then the additional costs and related schedule extensions would be a reason to change the baseline. Of course, that would also be an increase to the product scope and the total budget for the house.

In this example, the future owner of the house decided to upgrade the kitchen cabinets. The original cabinets were standard sizes and could be purchased "off the shelf" from inventory that was available anytime. The new cabinets would be special ordered and custom made by a supplier. Unfortunately for the owner, he decided too late in the building cycle. So he will be stuck with the additional cost of the cabinets plus the added costs of the schedule impacts. Table 10.1 shows the work packages that will be changed, the impact of the change on project schedule and cost objectives, and the reason for the impact.

TABLE 10.1 House Project—Product Requirement Change Impacts

WBS	Activity	Schedule	Cost	Reason for Impact
1.6.2	Doors and Cabinets	X	X	Custom-made cabinets to be special ordered and delivered later.
1.6.2.1 (new)	Purchase cabinets	X	X	Tom is given additional task of purchasing custom cabinets.
1.7.2.2	Painting labor	X	X	The painter will return for a small amount of rework after the cabinets have been installed.

SUMMARY

We have demonstrated several business scenarios that would cause a change to product requirements and provided examples of changes that need to be made to the project plans, work packages, planning packages, and work products resulting from those changes.

REFERENCES

[1] Leffingwell, Dean and Don Widrig. *Managing Software Requirements, A Unified Approach.* Reading, MA: Addison-Wesley, 2000, pp. 210–211.

[2] U.S. Air Force Space and Missile Systems Center (SMC). *SMC Systems Engineering Primer and Handbook.* Los Angeles Air Force Base, CA: SMC, 2004, p. 71.

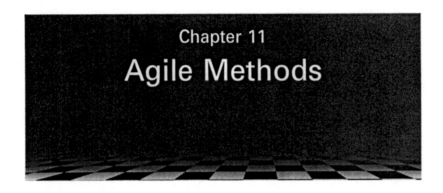

Chapter 11
Agile Methods

INTRODUCTION

Earned Value Management (EVM) requires a high degree of planning and a commitment to maintain control of the planning baselines (cost, schedule, and product quality baselines). Yet, although it is a highly plan-driven approach toward project management, it may be used with agile methods of software and systems development. Agile methods are sometimes selected when the project plan needs to change quickly in response to emerging or changing requirements or when it is not cost beneficial to comply with all the guidelines of the Earned Value Management System (EVMS) standard.

<table>
<tr><td>**GUIDELINE 4.1**</td></tr>
<tr><td>Tailor the application of PBEV to the elements of the work breakdown structure according to the risk.</td></tr>
</table>

This guidance is aimed toward those who must comply with the EVMS guidelines and those that need not comply. It enables the Project Manager (PM) to tailor the EVM processes employed according to the risks.

<table>
<tr><td>**GUIDELINE 4.2**</td></tr>
<tr><td>Tailor the application of PBEV to the phases of the system development life cycle according to the risk.</td></tr>
</table>

BUSINESS ENVIRONMENT

Many companies utilize EVM in compliance with the EVMS guidelines to satisfy a government contractual requirement. Yet they fail to seek

---

opportunities to tailor their processes to reduce the EVM implementation costs.

A growing number of companies use EVM for effective project monitoring and control even when there is no contractual requirement to comply with the EVMS guidelines. These companies need to use EVM in a cost-effective manner and to be able to change their plans quickly while still maintaining control of their cost, schedule, and quality baselines.

AGILE METHODS

Traditional EVM, used in full compliance with the EVMS guidelines, is a plan-driven approach that is not consistent with the objectives and needs of agile software development and agile methods of project management. "Agile" is the term that is used by the AgileAlliance, software professionals dedicated to promoting concepts of agile software development. PMs have begun to use agile development methods to streamline the acquisition process. Agile methods are now being applied to total systems development, even on large-scale defense projects.

For example, Mr. Blaise Durante, the U.S. Air Force Deputy Assistant Secretary for Acquisition Integration, stated that implementing Agile Acquisition requires:

1. **The use of innovative thought**
2. **Flexibility**
3. **Focusing on outcomes versus non-value-added processes and reviews**
4. **Empowering program managers to use the system versus being hampered by oversight management**

and going back to the basics of program management [1].

Alistair Cockburn advises that being agile is a declaration of prioritizing for project maneuverability with respect to shifting requirements, shifting technology, and a shifting understanding of the situation. Other priorities that might override agility include predictability, cost, schedule, process-accreditation, or use of specific tools. Referring to a concept that was stated by Boehm and Port, when there is risk associated with taking a slow deliberate approach to planning, then agile techniques are more appropriate. When there is risk associated with skipping planning or making mistakes with the plan, then a plan-driven approach is more appropriate [2].

Cockburn also discusses an agile approach to using earned value with burn charts where the requirements change frequently. He also recommends using measuring how much running functionality has been designed, programmed, and integrated. His approaches are discussed in Chapter 13 in the section on functional requirements.

Because of its scalability and its focus on requirements, PBEV can be used with agile development methods. However, as with traditional EVM, its benefits for project management increase with the project duration, cost, and team size.

The following sections provide guidance for applying PBEV in an agile manner that meets a company's information needs and objectives.

GUIDANCE FOR TAILORING CONTRACT PERFORMANCE REPORTS

The following guidance may be applied even when there are customer requirements to use a compliant EVMS.

When there is a U.S. Department of Defense requirement that the supplier use an EVMS that is compliant with the EVMS guidelines, there is also a requirement that the supplier submit a contract performance report (CPR). A Data Item Description (DID) (Contract Performance Report, DI-MGMT-81466) specifies the format and content of the CPR. However, the DID also states that the CPR is subject to tailoring per guidance in the DoD Earned Value Management Implementation Guide (EVMIG) [3].

The EVMIG includes guidance for tailoring the content of the CPR according to the risk and according to the contractor's processes. We recommend that that customer and the supplier seek opportunities to reduce project costs by tailoring the CPR requirements. The EVMIG guidance is illustrated in Table 11.1.

TABLE 11.1 EVMIG Tailoring Guide

The tailored CPR should reflect how the contractor is using EVM as a tool to manage contract performance.
All parts of the data item can be tailored as necessary based on risk analysis performed prior to contract award.
Complexity factors can usually be attributed to technical risk, schedule risk, or cost risk.
This analysis can pinpoint specific WBS elements with the highest risk that can be highlighted for more detailed reporting.

TAILORING IMPLEMENTATION OF EVM

For some projects, there may be no need for information regarding integrated schedule, technical, and *cost* performance for the full product scope or work scope of the project. It may be sufficient to utilize EVM only when cost performance information is needed because of cost-related risks or uncertainty. Otherwise, the PM may be able to control and monitor project performance with schedule and product measures.

Tailor by WBS Element

For example, the project plan may include elements of the work breakdown structure (WBS) with requirements that can be met by the purchase of commercially available hardware components that are used "off the shelf." Another possibility is that an element of the WBS may have requirements that can be satisfied by reusing a previous design and making low-risk modifications to that design.

For WBS elements that have low risk, the PM has several alternatives. Some of the alternatives follow.

> 1. **Include only the higher risk WBS elements in the Performance Measurement Baseline (PMB). In this case, the cost performance report (or contract performance report as it is called in recent U.S. federal acquisition regulations) will not equal the total project budget.**
> 2. **Include all the WBS elements in the PMB but use the Level of Effort (LOE) earned value technique to manage costs for the low-risk WBS elements. If there is a contractual requirement to comply with the EVMS guidelines, the customer and the supplier may agree that it is "impracticable" to measure these low-risk efforts (as discussed in Chapter 8); then the customer may consider tailoring the contract to allow the specified WBS elements to be measured as LOE.**

Tailor by Project Phase

In many projects, it may be impracticable to use EVM during the requirements development phase. This may occur when the customer requirements are not well defined or when trade studies are necessary to achieve a balance between the customer's cost, schedule, and technical objectives. When these conditions of uncertainty exist, the supplier may choose to defer the use of EVM. EVM may be initiated after the initial product quality requirements are known. Then the PBEV guidelines may be used to ensure management's focus on meeting the product quality requirements.

Extreme Tailoring of EVM

An extreme degree of tailoring EVM was observed during the Software Engineering Process Group (SEPG) Conference in Asia (India,

2001). Paul Solomon delivered tutorials on EVM at conference locales in Bangalore and New Delhi. He also attended tutorials and sessions to gather knowledge of the best practices in software development.

Mr. T. Balaji of CG-Smith Software in India presented a tutorial on quantitative software management. At the time, CG-Smith project managers did not use EVM, as discussed in this book, but they did use world-class methods of software development and measurement. However, when asked which measures of project performance executive level management reviewed, Mr. Balaji replied that "Magnitude to Date" is most often used. When the class understood how Magnitude to Date was derived, we realized that it is the same as the most important EVM performance index, the cost performance index (CPI) [4].

Executives may quickly compare all projects, both completed and active, by using the project level CPI. The executive review of CPI is an extreme example of tailoring EVM, The CPI is discussed in Appendix A.

SUMMARY

EVM normally requires a high degree of planning and a commitment to maintain control over the project baselines. However, when the stakeholders agree to tailor the application of EVM according to the risk, then the project may benefit from the use of agile methods of project management. The agile methods may include initiating the application of EVMS and PBEV guidelines after the requirements have been developed or applying the guidelines to only the high-risk elements of the WBS.

REFERENCES

[1] Durante, Blaise. "Agile Acquisition–Acquisition Streamlining—No Substitute for Solid Program Planning." *Agile Acquisition, the Air Force Acquisition Newsletter.* August–September 2004.

[2] Cockburn, Alistair. "Learning from Agile Software Development—Part One." *CrossTalk: The Journal of Defense Software Engineering,* October 2002.

[3] U.S. Department of Defense (DoD). *DoD Earned Value Management Implementation Guide (EVMIG).* April, 2005, Section 2-4.e.

[4] Balaji, T. *Quantitative Software Project Management—A Simplified Approach.* Tutorial, The Software Engineering Process Group (SEPG) Conference in Asia 2001, February 2001.

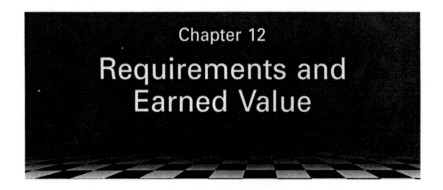

Chapter 12

Requirements and Earned Value

INTRODUCTION

Requirements management, requirements traceability, and the requirements traceability matrix (RTM) were discussed in Chapters 3 and 4. It is necessary to track the status of each requirement as it moves through life cycle activities. Measures that reflect the status of the requirements are essential to monitoring project status and serve as a scorecard to indicate that requirements are being implemented on schedule.

In this chapter, we expand the discussion of requirements management and traceability. We demonstrate how to plan and measure the progress of those activities with the RTM and use it as the source of base measures of Earned Value (EV). Finally, we discuss the importance and value of comparing the schedule variances of the requirements management and tracing activities with the variances of other project activities.

REQUIREMENTS STATUS

In Chapter 5, we listed Baxter's [1] suggested set of requirements statuses:

1. **Defined**
2. **Approved**
3. **Allocated**
4. **Designed**

Performance-Based Earned Value, by Paul J. Solomon and Ralph R. Young
Copyright ©2007 IEEE Computer Society.

5. Implemented
6. Tested
7. Verified

EARLY VALIDATION

We recommend adding three other requirements management activities to this list. The first is early validation of the requirement. We define validation as a process for confirming that the requirements are implemented in the delivered system. We need to ensure that the requirement is a real requirement (a requirement necessary to meet the real customer and user needs), that the requirement meets the criteria of a good requirement, and that the rationale (why the requirement is needed) for having the requirement in order to meet the minimum customer and user needs has been assessed. Requirements validation is critical to successful system product development and implementation. In other words, requirements are validated when it is certain that the defined set of requirements describes the input requirements and objectives and the resulting system products satisfy the requirements and objectives [2].

WAYS TO ACCOMPLISH VALIDATION

Leaving validation until the end of the project severely increases the risk of failure. Validation activities performed early in the project can reduce that risk. In Chapter 3, we noted that requirements clarifications, drivers, additions, and hidden expectations are important aspects of requirements validation. We noted there several techniques to perform early requirements validation.

We recommend that early requirements validation be completed before requirements approval. This process will reduce the possibility of the wrong product being designed and implemented. Typical early requirements validation activities include:

1. Analyze each requirement to ensure that it is unambiguous, testable, and verifiable.
2. Ensure that the set of defined acquirer requirements agrees with acquirer needs and expectations.
3. Analyze and compare identified and collected acquirer requirements to the set of defined acquirer requirements to determine downward traceability.

4. **Analyze and compare the set of defined acquirer requirements to the identified and collected acquirer requirements to determine upward traceability.**
5. **Record validation results in the information database.**

The Systems and Software Productivity Consortium (SSPC) has provided the following discussion of ways to accomplish early validation [3].

1. **Inspection**
   Focused on meeting particular customer constraints.
   Example: an inspection of a machine to see that it will fit in the desired space or an inspection of code modules to ensure their compliance with maintenance demands.

2. **Demonstration**
   Having the customer or a representative use the product to ensure it meets some minimum constraints (i.e., usability). Also can be used to perform some acceptance tests where the product is running in the intended environment versus some test or development lab.
   Example: having pilots fly an aircraft before the customer signs off on the project.

3. **Analysis**
   Using some form of analysis to validate that the product will perform as needed when demonstrating it is too costly, unsafe, or generally impractical.
   Example: using interpolation of performance load based on the worst case that is feasible to generate, to validate a need that is more stringent than this worst case. If it can be shown that there is no scaling problem, this would be sufficient to validate the performance need.

4. **Prior data**
   When a component being used has been already validated for a previous project that had similar or stricter constraints.
   Example: using a well-known encryption component to meet security needs when the component has been already validated for tougher security requirements.

SELECT A VERIFICATION METHOD FOR EACH REQUIREMENT

A second additional recommended requirements management activity is the selection of the verification method. Verification is a process for ensuring that the design solution satisfies the requirements. This should also occur before approval of the requirements to ensure that the approved verification method is included in the verification document or detailed test procedure.

TRACE THE REQUIREMENT TO THE VERIFICATION DOCUMENT

The third recommended requirements management activity is tracing the requirement to the verification document. Traceability of the requirement to the detailed test procedure ensures that necessary tests of the requirements will be included in the test procedure.

REVISED/RECOMMENDED REQUIREMENTS STATUSES

To recap, a recommended set of requirements management statuses is:

1. **Defined**
2. **Validated**
3. **Verification method determined**
4. **Approved**
5. **Allocated**
6. **Traced to verification document (test procedure)**
7. **Designed**
8. **Implemented**
9. **Tested**
10. **Verified**

DISCRETE MEASUREMENT OF REQUIREMENTS MANAGEMENT AND TRACING

When constructing a project plan, PMs often fail to establish milestones and discrete, objective measures of progress for those activities that deal with requirements development, management, and tracing. They use several rationales for concluding that these activities should be Level of Effort (LOE). However, if the PM has decided to apply EV to requirements development because of the assessed risk, than discrete EV techniques should and can be implemented.

Let's call the people that are responsible for documenting the requirements management and tracing activities requirements engineers. Requirements engineers say that the major work products of requirements management and tracing activities are the database, the RTM, and associated documents. For example, the associated documents may contain the requirements, the test procedures, and evidence of verifying the requirements.

They regard the RTM as a tool. They propose that populating the RTM with data is a support activity to the work products of engineering development (designs, test articles, test results, etc.). They also argue that the actual completion of many of activities listed above, as well as the associated documents, is the responsibility of other engineers, not the requirements management engineers. They then point to those who are actually doing the designing or testing or making related decisions. Consequently, the requirements engineers conclude that, if the allocated requirements have not been implemented into the design on schedule, or the test procedure does not yet include all necessary test cases, or the verification of requirements is behind schedule, it's not their fault. Therefore, they propose, their activities should be measured as LOE.

We recommend that, regardless of accountability, the progress of requirements, as they progress through the engineering life cycle, should be scheduled and measured against a plan. Of course, discrete earned value techniques should be used for management control. Even though the budget for the requirements engineers may be relatively small, as compared with the budgets for all other engineers, *the earned value taken in control accounts or work packages for requirements management activities can be the most important indicator of project schedule performance.* The schedule status of the set of requirements reveals more about the health of the project than any other schedule performance indicator in the Performance Measurement Baseline (PMB).

For example, if we are behind schedule in evolving the real requirements, gaining approval of the requirements by the joint (customer and developer) team, allocating the requirements to components of the system, meeting requirements in the system design, accomplishing testing of requirements, or validating the requirements, subsequent activities should not start.

USE THE RTM TO DEVELOP THE PLAN

Develop an RTM planning and status report that is organized according to the project's information needs. The requirements may be organized according to the Work Breakdown Structure (WBS), the functional architecture, the design architecture, or the key documents that contain the requirements and will be approved by the customer. For each row of the RTM, show the total number of requirements.

After the planned number of requirements has been established for each component in the RTM, develop a time-phased schedule for the planned completion of each requirements management activity. For example, specify the planned completion of the following activities for each requirement:

1. **Define**
2. **Validate**
3. **Determine verification method**
4. **Allocate**
5. **Trace to verification document**
6. **Verify**

If less measurement granularity is sufficient, than specify the planned completion of each requirement activity for the set of requirements at each component level. Summarize the planned completion data by reporting period. This will later be used to compute the time-phased BCWS.

HOW TO MEASURE PROGRESS

The measure of progress is objectively determined based on the number of completed requirements activities. It is compared with the number of activities that were planned to be completed at that time. This will enable the RTM to provide more than requirements traceability and status. It will be the source of schedule progress measures for EV.

HOW TO DETERMINE EV

When a component has many requirements, each requirement may receive an equal distribution of the total budget or may receive a weighted allocation, depending on its relative, estimated effort or business value. In other words, some requirements may be more difficult to address and therefore worth more than others for the purpose of EV.

RTM EXAMPLE

The following example includes a series of tables that demonstrate how to plan, status, and analyze schedule variances of requirements management activities. In this example, the requirements are organized according to the design architecture. For Project X, the architecture is comprised of five components:

1. **Enclosure**
2. **Radio transmitter**
3. **Battery**
4. **Control**
5. **Software**

In this example, each component goes through six typical requirements management activities. Four activities discussed previously are excluded from the example in order to minimize its complexity (Approved, Designed, Implemented, and Tested).
The typical activities include:

1. **Define the requirement.**
2. **Validate the requirement.**
3. **Determine the verification method.**
4. **Allocate the requirement.**
5. **Document the verification procedure.**
6. **Verify that the requirement has been met.**

The RTM should be used to record the status of each requirement as it progresses through this cycle. A time-phased schedule for the planned completion of these activities is the basis for the PMB. A measure of the status of the system or subsystem requirements in the RTM should be a base measure of earned value.

In the example, a system includes five components, 16 total requirements, and six systems engineering activities. The budget allocation is shown in Table 12.1.

An example of the schedule and the BCWS for the requirements management effort for one of the components, the Enclosure, is shown in Table 12.2. The time-phased BCWS is determined by allocating the budget for each activity to the month in which it is scheduled.

Table 12.3 shows the number of Enclosure requirements management activities that were completed, the EV performance, and the schedule variance.

As of the end of May, the schedule variance (SV) is −84. The activities that are behind schedule are shown in Table 12.4.

TABLE 12.1 Requirements Management Budget Allocation

SE Budget	No. Reqs.	SE Budget	Define	Valid.	Verif. Meth.	Alloc.	Verif. Doc.	Verify
Budget %			15%	15%	15%	20%	15%	20%
Component								
Enclosure	3	240	36	36	36	48	36	48
Transmitter	1	80	12	12	12	16	12	16
Battery	2	160	24	24	24	32	24	32
Control	1	80	12	12	12	16	12	16
Software	9	720	108	108	108	144	108	144
Total	16	1280	192	192	192	256	192	256

Table 12.2 Requirements Management Schedule and BCWS

		Jan.	Feb.	Mar.	Apr.	May	Jun.	Jul.	Total
Enclosure									
Schedule									
Defined		3							
Validated			2	1					
Verif. Method				1	2				
Allocated						3			
Traced to Verif.							3		
Verified								3	
BCWS current		Budget/Activity							
Defined	12	36							36
Validated	12		24	12					36
Verif. Method	12			12	24				36
Allocated	16					48			48
Traced to Verif.	12						36		36
Verified	16							48	48
Total		36	24	24	24	48	36	48	240
BCWS cumulative		36	60	84	108	156	192	240	

TABLE 12.3 Requirements Management EV Performance

		Jan.	Feb.	Mar.	Apr.	May
Enclosure						
Completed	Budget/Activity					
Defined	12		3			
Validated	12				1	1
Verif. Method	12				1	
EV cumulative		0	36	36	60	72
BCWS cumulative		36	60	84	108	156
Schedule Variance		−36	−24	−48	−48	−84

TABLE 12.4 Requirements Management Schedule Variance

Activity	Quantity	SV
Validation	1	−12
Verif. Method	2	−24
Allocated	4	−48
Total SV		−84

TOTAL REQUIREMENTS MANAGEMENT EV

Although Tables 12.2 through 12.4 illustrate just the Enclosure, the source of earned value would be the statused RTM that shows all five components and sixteen requirements. The RTM can easily be used to record the completed activities and the resultant earned value.

REASONABLENESS CHECK

When the schedule variance of the requirements management activities is compared with that of the remainder of the project, or when similar subsets are compared, we would expect that they would show a similar story. It would be hard to imagine a scenario in which the requirements management activities are significantly behind schedule and other engineering activities are not significantly behind.

Therefore, the earned value of the requirements management organization can be the leading performance indicator for the remainder of the project. We recommend that the project manager compare the relative progress of the requirements management organization with that of other engineering activities as a reasonableness or sanity check.

If the requirements management organization's work package is behind schedule, then the related development activities of other engineering organizations should also be behind schedule. If the related activities do not show similar progress, review and revise the base measures of their respective work packages to ensure that they contain consistent milestones and completion criteria with regard to the product requirements.

SUMMARY

If the requirements management and traceability activities are behind schedule, it is an early warning that the rest of the project is or will be in trouble. We recommend that a project manager look at the schedule variance of these activities early in any reviews.

The requirements management and traceability activities should be discretely planned and measured. If these activities are realistically planned, they provide a valid basis for Performance–Based Earned Value and insight into progress of the total project.

REFERENCES

[1] Baxter, Peter. "Focusing Measurement on Managers' Informational Needs." *CrossTalk: The Journal of Defense Software Engineering*, July 2002, pp. 22–25.

[2] Solomon, Paul. "Using Earned Value to Track Requirements Progress." *Proceedings of the International Symposium of the International Council on Systems Engineering (INCOSE)*, July 2006.

[3] Systems and Software Productivity Consortium. Verification and Validation Website, Topic: *Validation*. http://www.software.org/PUB/VNV/. 2006.

Using PBEV to Manage Software-Intensive Development

INTRODUCTION

In this chapter, we apply the principles and guidelines of Performance-Based Earned Value (PBEV) to software development. We provide examples of measures and completion criteria that should be used for effective management of software-intensive projects.

CHARACTERISTICS OF SOFTWARE PROJECT MANAGEMENT

The physical architecture contains both hardware and software components. Each component has its set of allocated functions. In general, the development of software components has some distinguishing characteristics as compared with hardware:

1. **Software components generally have relatively more functions, product requirements, and derived requirements than hardware components.**

2. **There is usually more incremental development until the end functionality is achieved.**

3. **Software components have a high number of subcomponents such as software modules.**

4. **The evolving product's capability to satisfy the end product requirements may be tested and measured more frequently.**

5. **More rework cycles go along with the developmental increments and frequent tests.**

6. **There is normally a higher rate and amount of change to customer requirements and derived requirements.**

PBEV provides guidance for selecting measures of performance and success criteria that address the characteristics of software development.

FUNCTIONALITY AND REQUIREMENTS

When selecting a measure on which to base earned value, the best results are achieved when the measure is directly related to indicating that the desired functionality has been implemented.

The product requirements are an excellent measure for use in determining earned value measures because they are directly related to evaluating progress in implementing the functionality required by the system. Other software measures, even though they provide other critical project information, are further removed from the implementation of the requirements and thus reduce earned value accuracy.

Requirements are applicable to all phases of the system and software development, which further increases their utility as a means of determining earned value. Additionally, the functionality that the customer wants in a new system will not be attained until the requirements are met.

The most comprehensive guide for using EVM for software development was published by the U.S. Naval Air Systems Command (NAVAIR). The guide, *Using Software Metrics & Measurements for Earned Value Toolkit* [1], was partially based on PBEV concepts. Most of the following guidance was extracted from the NAVAIR Toolkit. We acknowledge NAVAIR and the Toolkit's authors, Rick Holcombe and Phyllis Sanders, for this significant contribution to the industry and to this book.

FUNCTIONAL REQUIREMENTS

Functional requirements are requirements that specifically identify a capability that must be implemented in the software, such as:

1. **Display on the tactical plot operator-specified latitudes and longitudes.**
2. **Color all hostile targets on the tactical plot red.**
3. **Store the location, speed, altitude, and course of all tracks and targets with an accuracy of one meter.**

Each of the functional requirements is decomposed to a set of lower-level, derived requirements. The set of higher- and lower-level requirements facilitate software design. The coded software implements the software design. Also, during the initial coding phase, Source Lines of Code (SLOC) are often utilized as a sizing measure, as a cost-estimating relationship to determine budgets, and as the basis of percent complete for earned value. However, there is usually a significant error in estimating SLOC. Consequently, any progress measure based on SLOC, including a derived measure such as earned value, is highly volatile. The percent complete changes whenever the estimated SLOC changes. We recommend that the determination of percent complete should be based on the number of requirements that have been mapped or allocated to the coded software, not to the amount of SLOC.

Alistair Cockburn also advocates the use of requirements instead of SLOC as a tool for agile software development. He states that in programming the obvious unit is the line of code. These are convenient and give appropriate detail. The problem is that you won't know the actual number of lines of code needed until the very end. His suggested approach is to choose a unit of measure that won't expand. If you use a good nonexpanding measure, such as use cases, then you can use the burn-down chart, which some people find more useful [2].

Cockburn states that agile project teams measure progress not according to how many requirements have been gathered but by how much running functionality has been designed, programmed, and implemented (features that run). Cockburn also recommends that other units of accomplishment, besides features that run, be used to measure progress. These include use cases, individual steps in use cases, user interface widgets (frames, pull-down lists, buttons), interface calls used by applications, and user documentation. A database might have entities and attributes, a Web site might have articles and images, and a medical database may have medical codes as a unit of accomplishment [3].

Additional guidance on agile project management was provided in Chapter 11.

GROUPING AND TRACEABILITY OF REQUIREMENTS

Many developers do not break down cost and schedule for individual requirements for each phase. Attempting to estimate individually for every requirement adds an additional tracking and estimation burden on the developer, which may not be justified by resulting increases in EVM accuracy. It is also often impractical or impossible to estimate for individual requirements in isolation. An accurate estimate may only be possible when the requirements are considered in logical groupings, modules, Computer Software Components (CSC), or Computer Software Configuration Items (CSCIs).

If the number of requirements is sufficiently large and sufficiently detailed, the developer may choose to assume that the amount of effort required for all requirements to be implemented is equal. This simplifies and reduces the effort required to determine the budgeted cost for work scheduled (EV) for each software requirement. This assumption increases in validity as the requirements are decomposed to low levels of software requirements. These low-level software requirements are roughly equivalent to testable requirements, which is one proposed method of determining software size (see [4]). Wilson states that a testable requirement is one that is precisely and unambiguously defined, and one for which someone must be able to write a test case that would validate whether or not the requirement has or has not been implemented correctly. The number of testable requirements may be very different from the number of test cases. There are a number of reasons for this:

1. **A testable requirement may require more than one test case to validate it.**
2. **Some test cases may be designed to validate more than one testable requirement.**
3. **Testable requirements appear to have the granularity and flexibility to make earned value a practical tool for software developers.**

To utilize requirements as the basis for taking earned value, the developer must have a requirements traceability system that provides the capability to track requirements from the level of the system requirements through software requirements, builds, CSCIs, design, code, and unit test and to test procedures for all test phases.

RECOMMENDED BASE MEASURES BY PHASE

Software Requirements Analysis Phase

Software requirements analysis includes the decomposition of systems requirements into more detailed software requirements. Software requirements must be detailed enough so that the software design can be unambiguously generated from them and so that test procedures can be developed to verify them. During the software requirements analysis phase, earned value would be allocated based on how many of the systems requirements are allocated to software. If peer reviews of the requirements were performed, the successful completion of the requirements peer review, along with the correction of any identified problems, could be established as the point at which all earned value for the requirement(s) would be allocated. Using something other than successful completion of peer review to determine when the requirements analysis is complete will increase subjectivity and reduce earned value accuracy.

> EV Base Measure: Number of system requirements to be decomposed into detailed software requirements. Budget per requirement may be allocated equally to each requirement or on a weighted basis.

Code and Unit Test Phase

During Code and Unit Test (C&UT), source code is generated from the software design. Developers then conduct low-level unit testing to verify that the design has been correctly implemented. During the C&UT phase, earned value would be allocated based on the number of software requirements for which the C&UT had been completed. If peer reviews are utilized in this phase, completion of a peer review and allocation of the EV for that requirement could occur when the peer review and any noted defects had been corrected. When defects are prioritized, EV for that requirement could occur when the high-priority defects had been corrected, as specified by the organization's quality requirements and the success criteria for completing the work product.

> EV Base Measure: Number of software requirements for which CU&T has been completed and noted defects have been corrected.

Test Phase

There are a variety of test phases following C&UT to verify that the system and software requirements have been correctly implemented. Formal test procedures are executed. IEEE/EIA 12207 identifies the following test phases: software integration testing, software qualification testing, systems integration testing, and system qualification testing. During the software and systems test phases, earned value would be allocated based on how many of the systems or software requirements had been successfully tested. Successful testing for a requirement means that all associated test procedures have been executed to completion and no defects preventing the execution of the requirement have been generated. For software integration testing, software requirements will be most appropriate for taking earned value. For systems testing, the systems requirements may be more appropriate. The appropriate type of requirement for taking earned value is dependent on the type of requirements used as the basis for developing test procedures for the test phase in question.

As part of the preparation for a test phase, a test plan and test procedures must have been developed and peer reviewed. As part of the peer review, the test procedures must be checked to ensure that the procedures test all requirements and that each procedure identifies the requirements it tests. This information is essential to determining which requirements have been successfully tested and for which earned value can be allocated.

Successful completion of a test procedure is not necessarily the same as no defects occurring during the test. However, all high-priority defects should be corrected. In all cases, there should be predefined success criteria for the build or work package. Examples follow.

Example 13.1—Software Test Phase. Success criteria for taking earned value for a requirement within a software build and work package are shown in Table 13.1.

Software Rework

Software rework is the correction of defects. These defects may be in the requirements, design and other documents, or the code itself. A defective requirement will cause defective design and defective code; a defective design will cause defective code. Obviously, the sooner a defect is detected and corrected the less the cost because it will not snowball into later development phases. Cutting corners on quality processes in early development phases results in more defects that are not detected until much later in the development, with resulting significant increases in development costs.

Rework must be included in the schedule for any software development project. Additionally, if such rework phases are not planned for, it can cause severe problems to the earned value system when an attempt is made to determine how to implement it on the spur of a moment. Any project plan that does not provide time for rework is impractical and not realistic. The developer must take into consideration that some percentage of the requirements will not pass testing. The

TABLE 13.1 Success Criteria for Implementing a Software Requirement

1. All priority 1 and 2 defects must be corrected in order to take EV for a requirement.
2. No more than *n* lower priority defects will be open in order to take EV for a requirement (where *n* is specified by the organization's quality requirements and the success criteria for completing the work product).

rework must include time not only to correct the flaw in requirements, design, and/or code that caused the problem, but also to retest the corrected software. In a multirelease/build development, this may mean that some or all of the failed requirements will be rolled into the next build/release. All of this must be taken into account in the project plan.

Rework should be planned and tracked in separate work packages from the initial development of requirements, design, and code. In planning incremental builds, all builds must include budget and schedule for rework of requirements, design, and code to correct defects that were found in the current and previous builds. To ensure adequate budget and period of performance, the planning assumptions for rework should include the planned rate or number of defects expected and the budgeted resources to fix the defects. Failure to establish a baseline plan for rework and to objectively measure rework progress has caused many projects to get out of control.

Example 13.2—Software Rework.

Project Requirement: 1000 software requirements in Build A.

Assumption: None of the software requirements is on the critical path.

Program Plan: Based on the developer's experience, 10% of these requirements will fail testing, 5% will be rework of requirements that must remain in Build A, and 5% will be deferred to Build B. The program would thus plan the rework phase for Build A to include resources and schedule to allow the rework of defects impacting 50 requirements. At the end of the rework phase in Build A, 95% or 950 of the 1000 software requirements would be correctly implemented and the 50 incorrectly implemented requirements are planned to be transferred to Build B.

Often, there is a decision to close Build A even though less than 95% of the software requirements have been correctly implemented. For example, assume that a decision is made to close Build A although only 850 requirements have been met. In this case, 150 requirements will be deferred to Build B, as follows:

    1. 50 requirements that were planned to be transferred

    2. 100 requirements that are behind schedule

A recommended set of work packages (WP) for this example is shown in Table 13.2.

In the following section, we will demonstrate how to take earned value if a decision is made to complete Build A even though less than 95% of the requirements had been implemented.

TABLE 13.2 Planned Software Rework

WP #	SOW	Completion Criteria
1	C&UT 1000 requirements planned for Build A of which 950 requirements must be correctly implemented in Build A. The budget includes estimated resources for rework of code that is related to 50 of the requirements.	950 requirements must be correctly implemented in Build A.
2	C&UT 800 requirements planned for Build B of which 760 requirements must be correctly implemented in Build B plus 50 requirements that are expected to be deferred from Build B.	1. All deferred requirements from Build A have been correctly implemented in Build B. 2. 760 requirements that were baselined for Build B must be correctly implemented in Build B.

Obviously at some point all the defects must be corrected, or at least most of them. All software contains some defects when released. Additional time may be included in the final release to clean up defects, or one or more releases may be planned at the end of the development for defect correction. From an earned value point of view, the most important aspect of rework is the correct implementation of software requirements; however, an estimate of the time and resources required to perform rework will probably be based on estimates of the number of defects from historical data on previous projects or actual data from earlier rework phases in the current development. Although defect estimates may be used for estimation purposes, they are not effective for use in determining EV because they are not always directly related to requirements. In some cases several defects may need to be corrected in order to correct the implementation of a single software requirement; in other cases correcting a single defect will correct the implementation of multiple software requirements.

To use requirements as the basis for determining EV during rework, an effective requirements tracking system must be in place, which traces individual defects to the requirements they affect and identifies which defects should be corrected based on priority and contractual quality requirements. It is equally important to document the requirements baseline of each build and the budget value of meeting each requirement. Then, if more requirements are deferred from one build to another than were planned, less than 100% of the Budget at Completion (BAC) will be earned. Additional guidance and examples for rework are provided in Appendices B and G.

DEFERRED FUNCTIONALITY: DEVIATION FROM PLAN

When functionality is deferred, requirements intended for implementation as part of a specific build are delayed until a later build. If systems or software requirements intended to be implemented in Build A, do not have their design completed during the design phase; they cannot be coded and subsequently tested in Build A (or else there will be severe quality problems), they must be deferred for completion to a later build. Requirements that don't have their code completed in Build A cannot be tested in Build A. They must be deferred for completion to a later build. Deferring functional requirements has the following major impacts:

1. **If all the requirements planned for a phase are not completed, then the earned value for these deferred requirements cannot be earned as part of the build.**

2. **The phase and/or build the requirement is deferred to will require additional time and resources to complete its planned requirements and the deferred requirements. The earned value associated with these deferred requirements, that was not earned in the phase or build in which it was baselined, will instead be earned in the phase and/or build to which it was deferred.**

3. **Although requirements may be deferred to a subsequent build, the earned value must continue to show a behind-schedule condition. The deferred effort should not be replanned beyond the current month.**

Example 13.3—Deferred Functionality. To illustrate how deferred functionality should be quantified at the work package level, assume that a CSC is being developed. The development plan is to develop multiple builds with incremental functionality. The functional requirements are allocated to each build. The requirements traceability matrix documents the requirements baseline for each build. Each build has a separate work package for implementation of code. The completion criteria for each work package include:

1. **All baseline requirements have been coded, unit tested, and integrated into the build.**
2. **The build has passed peer review.**
3. **Documentation for the build has been completed.**

4. The build has been recorded as complete in the configuration management process.
5. The build is released for higher-level integration and test.

In this example, assume that there are two builds. The allocated requirements (Req) and BAC are shown in Table 13.3.1.

The baseline requirements plan is shown in Table 13.3.2.

Assume that Build A is behind schedule at the end of April, with only 90 requirements being met (coded, unit tested, and integrated). At this point, earned value would be 450 hours. The schedule variance (SV) is −50 hours. The April performance to plan and earned value is shown in Table 13.3.3.

TABLE 13.3.1 Allocated Requirements and BAC

Build	Allocated Req	Budget/Req	BAC
A	100	5	500
B	60	5	300

TABLE 13.3.2 Baseline Requirements Plan

	Jan	Feb	Mar	Apr	May	Jun	Jul	Total
Build A								
Planned Req met	25	25	25	25				100
Budget/Req: 5 hours								
BCWS current (cur)	125	125	125	125				500
BCWS cumulative (cum)	125	250	375	500				500
Build B								
Planned Req Met					20	20	20	60
BCWS cur					100	100	100	300

Table 13.3.3 Performance to Plan and Earned Value

	Jan	Feb	Mar	Apr	Total
Build A					
Planned Req Met cur	25	25	25	25	100
Actual Req Met cur	20	20	25	25	90
BCWS cur	125	125	125	125	500
EV cur	100	100	125	125	450
BCWS cum	125	250	375	500	500
EV cum	100	200	325	450	450
Schedule variance cum:					
Req Met	−5	−10	−10	−10	−10
SV	−25	−50	−50	−50	−50

There is a decision to release Build A short of its targeted functionality and baselined requirements. There will be no additional work on Build A subsequent to its release. The requirements that have not been met are deferred into Build B.

There are two options for recording and reporting earned value.

1. **Option 1: Keep the Build A work package open until all 100 baselined requirements have been met.**
2. **Option 2: Close the Build A work package and transfer the deferred requirements and budget to the Build B work package.**

Normally, project managers choose Option 2. Because all subsequent management attention and schedule visibility is on Build B, it is easier to show integration of earned value and schedule performance when the statement of work and budget that has been deferred is incorporated into the current, open build.

To implement Option 2, close the Build A work package and replan the remaining work. In this case, transfer the deferred requirements and the residual budget of 50 hours to the Build B work package. Place the budget in the first month of the Build B work package to preserve the schedule variance. If no planned builds remain, establish them through the normal internal replan process by closing the last work package and opening a new one for the next build with the unused budget [5]. Tables 13.3.4 and 13.3.5 illustrate the sequence of planning and performance.

TABLE 13.3.4 Replan of Deferred Functionality

	Apr	May	Jun	Jul	Total
Close Build A work package					
Schedule variance (cum.): Req Not Met	−10				−10
BCWS remaining	−50				−50
Build B					
Before Replan Planned Req Met		20	20	20	60
BCWS cur		100	100	100	300
Plus transfer from Build A: Req Not Met		10			
BCWS remaining		50			
After replan:					
Planned Req Met		30	20	20	70
BCWS cur		150	100	100	350

TABLE 13.3.5 Performance to Plan and Earned Value

	May	Jun	Jul	Total
Build B After Replan:				
Planned Req Met	30	20	20	70
BCWS cur	150	100	100	350
Actual Req Met cur	20			20
EV cur	100			100
Schedule variance cum:				
Req Met	−10			
SV	−50			

Although Build A includes fewer requirements than planned, the team decided to turn it over to integration testing and to transfer the unmet requirements and their allocated budget to Build B. The replan of Builds A and B are shown in Table 13.3.4. Please note that the requirements and budget that were behind schedule are transferred into the first month of the Build B work package, May. Although this statement of work had been planned for April, the constraints of the automated database prevent it from being planned before the first month of the receiving work package.

At the end of May, the work is still behind schedule. Only 10 requirements were met. The schedule variance that was inherited by the Build B work package has not been reduced, as shown in Table 13.3.5.

An effective EV system must account for deferred functionality if it is to accurately reflect project status and progress. To do this, the system or software requirements that are baselined to be implemented in each software development artifact or phase must be considered in determining EV. No matter what software measures are used as base measures of EV, requirements must also be used to determine actual program status.

TECHNICAL PERFORMANCE MEASUREMENT

Software development projects often have key technical performance requirements. Two key technical performance requirements are capacity and response time.

Capacity and Response Time Requirements Issues

Capacity and response time requirements define functionality that impacts how a large percentage of other software requirements (if not all of them) are implemented. Failure to meet these requirements can have a significant negative impact on meeting the system's cost and schedule objectives and can require significant redesign of the system hardware and/or software. For EVM to be effective, it must be able to reflect the negative cost and schedule impact on the program if such problems arise.

Capacity. Capacity requirements specify the maximum amount of available processing resources that can be used by the software application being developed. These processing resources include computer processing unit (CPU) capacity, random access memory (RAM), both dynamic and static memory, hard drives and other non-RAM static memory, interface or bus throughput, and other computer resources. Usually, for all of these resources, a maximum percentage of the total capacity of the resource is identified that the software can utilize, usually 50% for new developments or major upgrades. For example:

1. **No more than 50% of the total CPU capacity will be utilized by the system's software.**
2. **No more than 50% of the RAM is utilized by the system's software.**
3. **No more than 50% of the available interface/bus throughput is used by the system's software.**

The same applies to RAM, interfaces/buses, and other computer resources.

Response Time. Response time requirements mandate some type of response requirement on the system, usually related to reacting within a specified period of time to some input or event. For example:

1. **Within 0.25 seconds of receiving operator input the system will provide operator feedback that the input has been received.**
2. **The system will be able to process 8 Hz navigation data with no loss of data.**

CAPACITY OR PERFORMANCE REQUIREMENTS

A failure of the system to meet a capacity or performance requirement will also affect the implementation of functional requirements. Examples 13.4 and 13.5 illustrate this situation.

Example 13.4—Capacity or Performance Requirements.

1. **There are 80 functional requirements in a work package that are either completely or partially implemented in software that executes on Central Processing Unit (CPU) "A."**

2. **There is a technical performance requirement that no more than 50% of the processing capacity of CPU "A" can be utilized by the system's software.** Note that this is a Technical Performance Measure (TPM).

3. **The base measures for earned value have been determined as follows:**
   a. **Complete implementation of a functional requirement:** 1% of work package budget at completion (BAC).
   b. **TPM requirement projected to be achieved:** 20% of BAC.

4. **The performance to data follows:**
   a. **Of the requirements, 64 have been met.**
   b. **The software running on CPU "A" is using 80% of the processing capacity.**

5. **The earned value follows:**
   a. **64 completed requirements × 1% = 64%**
   b. **TPM requirement met:** 0%
   c. **Total EV % complete:** 64%

This indicates that, although 64 functional requirements have been met on the CPU, their implementation has resulted in the CPU utilization requirement for CPU "A" being exceeded by 30%. If the TPM requirement had been met, total EV would increase to 84%.

Example 13.5—Performance Requirement.

1. **There is a performance requirement that the system respond within 0.25 seconds to operator inputs.**
2. **There are 100 functional requirements related to operator inputs that are not meeting this performance requirement.**

This indicates that the requirements that relate to operator inputs are at least partially incorrect because their implementation does not meet the performance requirement for a response to operator input within 0.25 seconds.

COTS CONSIDERATIONS

Guidance is available from the SEI for using earned value to manage the development of commercial off-the-shelf (COTS)-based systems [6]. The paper illustrates how activities involving COTS products coincide with other defined system's development stages and activities. The paper includes a software WBS with COTS-based system activities that may be used to develop a performance measurement plan and to select activities and milestones for earned value.

SUMMARY

This chapter has addressed the topic of using PBEV to manage software-intensive development. Some characteristics of software project management were presented. A discussion of how PBEV evolved was provided, noting the seminal contributions made by one of the authors of this book. It was recommended that a requirements-based PBEV approach is the most effective and that requirements traceability is essential. The impact of capacity or performance requirements was illustrated. Several base measures were provided for various development phases. Rework and its impact on PBEV were discussed. Deferred functionality requires replanning for a later build. Two key technical performance measures used in software development were discussed, capacity and response time. Guidance is available concerning the use of earned value to manage the development of COTS-based systems.

REFERENCES

[1] U.S. Naval Air Systems Command (NAVAIR). *Using Software Metrics & Measurements for Earned Value Toolkit.* Lexington, MD: Department of the Navy, 2004. See https://acc.dau.mil/CommunityBrowser.aspx?id=1959/.

[2] Cockburn, Alistair. *Crystal Clear.* Boston, MA: Addison-Wesley, 2004, pp. 99–102.

[3] Cockburn, Alistair. "A Governance Model for Incremental, Concurrent, or Agile Projects." *CrossTalk: The Journal of Defense Software Engineering.* February 2006, pp. 13–17.

[4] Wilson, Peter. "Sizing Software Using Testable Requirements." Available at www.testablerequirements.com.

[5] Solomon, Paul. "Practical Software Measurement, Performance-Based Earned Value." *CrossTalk: The Journal of Defenses Software Engineering.* September 2001, pp. 28–29 (see www.stsc.hill.af.mil/crosstalk/2001/09/index.html).

[6] Staley, M., Oberndorf, P., and Sledge, C. *Using EVMS with COTS-Based Systems.* SEI Technical Report CMU/SEI-2002-TR-022, June 2002.

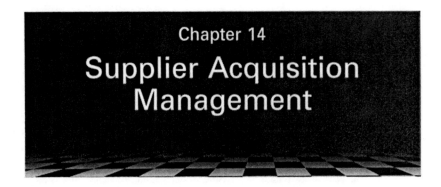

Chapter 14

Supplier Acquisition Management

INTRODUCTION

It is easy to ask a supplier to use an Earned Value Management (EVM) system that meets the guidelines of the Earned Value Management System (EVMS) Standard. It is more difficult to ensure that the supplier is using EVM effectively and that the reported performance is valid and reliable.

This chapter provides guidance to help the customer manage the supplier's behavior. Guidance is provided to motivate a supplier to integrate systems engineering processes with EVM. Additional guidance is provided for assessing whether the supplier has specified the right measures of progress and for monitoring its technical, schedule, and cost performance and its processes.

Guidance is also provided for acquisition management when the supplier is not required to use EVMS. The chapter concludes with useful guidance from the Capability Maturity Model Integration (CMMI).

CONTRACTUAL CONSIDERATIONS

The customer's contracting agent must clearly communicate requirements and expectations regarding the processes to be used by the supplier as well as all technical and management deliverables. For U. S. Department of Defense (DoD) contracts, both the contract work breakdown structure (CWBS) and the Integrated Master Plan (IMP) may be used to define the specific criteria to be satisfied for completion of program events [1]. The DoD Systems Engineering Plan (SEP)

Performance-Based Earned Value, by Paul J. Solomon and Ralph R. Young
Copyright ©2007 IEEE Computer Society.

Preparation Guide provides guidance that the SEP address the following:

1. **Contracting considerations for systems engineering**
2. **The approach and strategy for implementing event-driven technical reviews and how the review process demonstrates completion of required accomplishments by satisfying criteria in an event-driven schedule**
3. **What technical efforts are included in the EVMS measurement baseline (PMB) and how earned value is mapped to the technical reviews**
4. **How each technical baseline is developed, managed, and used to control system requirements, design, integration, verification, and validation**
5. **Specific products that constitute the technical baseline**

The DoD Integrated Master Plan (IMP) and Integrated Master Schedule (IMS) Preparation and Use Guide states that the IMP and IMS should demonstrate contractual commitment to the elements of major technical reviews and their entry and exit criteria as specified in the SEP and should serve as the foundation for effective technical execution and EVM.

Other federal agencies and commercial customers are encouraged to:

1. **Provide requirements and incentives for the supplier to establish and achieve milestones that indicate meeting the specified requirements and quality**
2. **Use Integrated Baseline Reviews to verify that the appropriate milestones and measures have been established**

INDUSTRY STANDARDS

As discussed in Chapter 1, for many contracts, the suppliers must use an EVMS that complies with the EVMS guidelines in ANSI/EIA Standard 748. The customer may also mandate that the supplier use selected systems engineering processes, work products, and definitions that are specified in one or both of the systems engineering standards that are recommended in this book. If the systems engineering standards are not mandated, then the customer should provide financial incentives to motivate the supplier to comply.

For example, the customer may require compliance with the Technical Performance Measurement (TPM) sections of the systems engineering standards in the solicitation. These sections are described in Chapter 6.

If the supplier commits to comply with both the EVMS guidelines and the specified components of the systems engineering standards, the customer will have greater confidence that the supplier's processes are able to support contract objectives.

It is essential and critical for the customer to gain insight into how well the supplier is performing against the plan and adhering to the pertinent standards. The customer may consider providing financial incentives for the supplier to meet the success criteria that are described in Chapter 5 and to achieve the planned values for technical performance that are described in Chapter 6. Of course, those technical objectives must be achieved in concert with the integrated schedule and cost objectives.

CONTRACTUAL TECHNICAL AND MANAGEMENT DELIVERABLES

The customer can obtain contractual insight by requiring key technical and management deliverables. A sample of those deliverables follows:

1. Systems Engineering Plan (SEP) with
   a. Internal and external products identified ("Product Breakdown Structure")
   b. Supporting Work Breakdown Structure (WBS)
   c. Success criteria for major technical reviews
   d. Technical Performance Measures (TPM) planned values and measurement milestones
   e. Requirements Plan specifying the requirements development, requirements management, and requirements traceability approach
   f. Trade study approach
   g. Master schedule that identifies all systems engineering products and is linked to the identified success criteria
2. Validated requirements baseline
3. Functional architecture
4. Product metrics reports
5. EVM variance analysis reports that cross-reference schedule and product metric variances

INTEGRATED BASELINE REVIEW

If the specified systems engineering approach is included in the contract, the customer should utilize the Integrated Baseline Reviews (IBR) to verify that the SEP includes all required plans, planned values, and process descriptions. For DoD contracts, the IBR should also be used to verify that the plans and success criteria in the SEP are integrated with the master schedule and are consistent with the base measures of earned value. For other U.S. federal contracts, the IBR should be used to verify that the plan includes measures of progress toward milestones in terms of capability of the investment to meet specified requirements and quality (OMB Circular No. A-11, Part 7, Section 300.5) [2].

According to the Federal Acquisition Regulation (FAR) [3], the IBR is meant to verify the technical content and the realism of the related performance budgets, resources, and schedules. It should provide a mutual understanding of the inherent risks in offerors'/contractors' performance plans and the underlying management control systems, and it should formulate a plan to handle identified risks. The IBR is a joint assessment by the offeror or contractor and the Government of the:

1. **Ability of the project's technical plan to achieve the objectives of the scope of work**
2. **Adequacy of the time allocated for performing the defined tasks to successfully achieve the project schedule objectives**
3. **Ability of the Performance Measurement Baseline (PMB) to successfully execute the project and attain cost objectives, recognizing the relationship between budget resources, funding, schedule, and scope of work**
4. **Availability of personnel, facilities, and equipment when required, to perform the defined tasks needed to execute the program successfully**
5. **Degree to which the management process provides effective and integrated technical/schedule/cost planning and baseline control**

The objective of the IBR is for the Government and the Contractor to jointly assess the technical areas, such as the Contractor's planning, to ensure complete coverage of the contract requirements, logical scheduling of the work activities, adequate resources, methodologies for earned value (budgeted cost for work performed (BCWP)), and identification of inherent risks.

More information about these topics is in Appendix D, FAR Clauses.

MONITOR SUPPLIER'S ADHERENCE WITH PERIODIC REVIEWS

Following the IBR, the customer is advised to conduct periodic reviews to ensure that suppliers are following their plans, procedures, and standards (including those for systems engineering and EVM). The customer should also perform independent assessment of the supplier's progress and verify that the correct base measures are specified and used for earned value. The PM should address TPM achievement and reporting during technical reviews.

PBEV Guidelines 2.2 and 2.4 address technical reviews. For DoD contracts, the customer should apply these guidelines when reviewing the SEP with the supplier. Use the IBR to reach agreement on the entry and exit criteria for all major technical reviews with regard to the technical baselines. The technical baselines are important work products that should be included in the IMS and work packages. The technical reviews described in the Defense Acquisition Guide (DAG) with their respective baselines and their IEEE 1220–1998 equivalents are shown in Table 14.1.

Finally, the PM should verify that the supplier has met the success criteria of event-driven technical reviews, as described in Chapter 5 and Appendix I.

UTILIZE AND ANALYZE SUPPLIER'S PERFORMANCE REPORTS

The following are key contract management responsibilities:

1. **Review the supplier's earned value reports, master schedule, and technical reports to determine whether they are consistent.**

2. **Evaluate supplier metrics (product, schedule, earned value) by understanding and questioning the information, including variance analyses.** If the information appears inconsistent or insufficient variance analysis and corrective action plans are provided, conduct reviews to obtain insight into metrics and to better understand the causes and impacts of the variances.

TABLE 14.1 DoD Technical Reviews and Baselines

Technical Review	Technical Baseline	DAG	IEEE 1220–1998
System Functional Review	System Functional Baseline	4.3.3.4.3	Validated Requirements Baseline
Preliminary Design Review	System Allocated Baseline	4.3.3.4.4	Verified Physical Architecture
Critical Design Review	System Product Baseline	4.3.3.4.5	Verified Physical Architecture
Production Readiness Review	System Product Baseline	4.3.3.9.3	Verified Physical Architecture

When evaluating the supplier metrics, particular attention should be given to the earned value that is based on the progress of the requirements as they progress through the engineering life cycle. As discussed in Chapter 12, *the earned value taken in control accounts or work packages for requirements management activities can be the most important indicator of project schedule performance* in the Performance Measurement Baseline. The recap of typical requirements management activities follows:

1. **Defined**
2. **Validated**
3. **Verification method determined**
4. **Approved**
5. **Allocated**
6. **Traced to verification document**
7. **Designed**
8. **Implemented**
9. **Tested**
10. **Verified**

Finally, perform independent assessment of the Estimate at Completion (EAC). Perform this assessment at the total contract level and at lower Work Breakdown Structure levels. Compare your assessment with that of the supplier and discuss significant differences with the supplier. Discuss the supplier's assumptions and understand the supplier's rationale for any significant improvement in cost or schedule performance compared with recent trends. Fully understand the supplier's quantified risk assessment as summarized in the Management Reserve EAC.

CMMI ACQUISITION MODULE

The following guidance was extracted from the CMMI Acquisition Module (CMMI-AM), Version 1.1 [4] published by the Software Engineering Institute. Special permission to reproduce "CMMI® Acquisition Module (CMMI-AM) Version 1.1," © 2005 by Carnegie Mellon University, is granted by the Software Engineering Institute.

> The CMMI Acquisition Module (CMMI-AM) is a stand-alone guide that describes best practices for use in the acquisition of products. . . . The Acquisition Module is a condensed form of CMMI designed to enable individual process improvement efforts within government program offices.

> The Office of the Under Secretary of Defense, Acquisition Technology & Logistics [OUSD (AT&L)] and the Office of the Assistant Secretary of Defense, Network Integration & Information [OASD (NII)] have continued to evolve systems engineering activities, to include integra-

tion of software acquisition best practices into their framework. They have agreed that the CMMI Acquisition Module will supplement the Capability Maturity Model Integration adoption on the part of Industry.

Project Monitoring and Control

Project Monitoring and Control involves establishing the planned internal activities and schedule for completion and then monitoring the status of these activities and work product completions through measurement and analysis (metrics). Included in those internal items monitored should be work product completion, . . . product performance objectives and thresholds, . . . and other activities and products included in project planning. . . . Project risk identification and mitigation should also be monitored for status.

Solicitation and Contract Monitoring

The Solicitation and Contract Monitoring process area . . . encourages creation of a contract that allows the acquirer to execute its monitoring and control of supplier activities using other process areas, such as Project Monitoring and Control. This encouragement may include levying a contractual requirement on the supplier to create a project plan that will successfully execute the contract, to define and execute the processes needed to achieve success, and to commit to execute their plan as it evolves during contract execution.

Requirements Management

The purpose of Requirements Management is to manage the requirements of the project's products and product components and to identify inconsistencies between those requirements and the project's plans and work products.

1. Requirements are managed and inconsistencies with project plans and work products are identified.
1.1 Develop an understanding with the requirements providers on the meaning of the requirements.
   The acquirer should define authorized requirements providers and an approved path by which requirements are provided to the supplier.
1.2 Obtain commitment to the requirements from the project participants.
   Commitment to the requirements by the project participants includes having coordinated and approved documents that define requirements.
1.3 Manage changes to the requirements as they evolve during the project.
   Each change to a controlled requirement should be assessed for impact to the project performance, cost, and schedule baselines and

to project risk. The existing cost, schedule, and performance baselines should be changed, as required, to accommodate the requirements change.

1.4 Maintain bidirectional traceability among the requirements and the project plans and work products.

Bidirectional traceability ensures that all higher level requirements are accounted for by the totality of the lower level requirements. It also ensures that lower level requirements are tied to a parent requirement to prevent orphan requirements at the lower levels. Bidirectional traceability also supports requirements change impact analysis when either high or lower level requirements change.

1.5 Identify inconsistencies between the project plans and work products and the requirements.

SUMMARY

This chapter emphasizes the critical role of the customer's contracting agent in ensuring that suppliers utilize EVM techniques effectively. Experience has shown that this is both difficult and often not done. Your failure to pay adequate attention to these needs could jeopardize your ability to execute the contract successfully! You are encouraged to follow good systems engineering practices, perform effective Integrated Baseline Reviews and other technical reviews, and utilize available guidance from the CMMI.

REFERENCES

[1] U.S. Department of Defense (DoD). *Work Bruakdown Structures for Defense Materiel Items.* MIL-HDBK-881A, 30 July 2005. See http://dcarc. pae.osd.mil/88/handbook/index.html.

[2] Executive Office of the President. OMB Circular No. A-11, Part 7, Section 300.5, *Planning, Budgeting, Acquisition and Management of Capital Assets,* July 2004 (see www.whitehouse.gov/omb/circulars/a11/cpgtoc.html).

[3] U.S. Federal Acquisition Regulation. See www.acqnet.gov/far/.

[4] Software Engineering Institute (SEI). *CMMI Acquisition Module (CMMI-AM).* Version 1.1. Technical Report CMU/SEI-2005-TR-011. Pittsburgh, PA: SEI, 2005. See www.sei.cmu.edu/publications/documents/05.reports/05tr011.html.

Chapter 15

Moving Forward

INTRODUCTION

This chapter provides guidance and techniques for leading and implementing process improvement. It is intended to help those organizations that decide to implement some or all of the Performance-Based Earned Value (PBEV) guidelines. The guidance is based on our experience in using the Capability Maturity Model® (CMM) Integration (CMMI®) as a framework for process improvement. However, this guidance may be applied to any process improvement framework.

Examples are provided of policies and procedures that were implemented within a sector of the Northrop Grumman Corporation to integrate systems engineering and risk management with EVM. Finally, we describe how components of PBEV were deployed, implemented, and institutionalized on a real project.

WHY IMPLEMENT PROCESS IMPROVEMENT?

Government and industry experience has shown that undertaking an organizational process improvement program results in important and tangible benefits including improved quality of work products, better use of resources, reduced rework and costs, and improved customer satisfaction. Experience shows that improving processes—sets of

SM CMM Integration and SEI are service marks of Carnegie Mellon University.
® Capability Maturity Model, Capability Maturity Modeling, CMM, and CMMI are registered in the U.S. Patent and Trademark Office by Carnegie Mellon University.

activities, methods, and practices used to accomplish tasks—has a significant positive impact. When coupled with empowerment of the work force through a total quality management approach, process improvement helps focus the organization on its key objectives and sets the stage for its transformation to higher levels of performance.

Over many years, government and industry have evolved through a series of Capability Maturity Models (CMM) from the well-known Software CMM to the CMMI. The purpose of the CMMI is to provide guidance to improve an organization's processes and its ability to manage the development, acquisition, and maintenance of products and services. The CMMI provides a framework based on best systems and software engineering practices. It facilitates identification of improvement areas based on an assessment, prioritization, development of a plan, providing leadership of the process improvement efforts, implementation of improvement activities guided by action plans, and measurement of the results.

SETTING THE STAGE FOR SUCCESS

Our experience over the past eighteen years in utilizing the CMM and the CMMI within Northrop Grumman and also in assisting and mentoring more than 90 external organizations is that there is a set of success factors that, when evolved collaboratively, set the stage for fostering an effective process improvement program. These include:

1. **Engage the organization**
2. **Ensure senior management sponsorship—don't start without this critical component!**
3. **Provide management commitment at all levels**
4. **Utilize experienced facilitators**
5. **Establish a value of continuous improvement**
6. **Provide process improvement tools and techniques**
7. **Perform a baseline assessment ("If you don't know where you are, a map won't help!")**
8. **Track progress**
9. **Encourage participation**

HOW TO IMPLEMENT A PROCESS IMPROVEMENT PROGRAM

Initial steps that a project or organization should take are:

1. **Establish the business reasons for undertaking process improvement.**

2. **Perform a baseline assessment to determine process improvement needs and priorities.**

3. **Set objectives for process improvement.** Base your approach on proven techniques to provide value, for example, utilizing peer reviews, establishing a defect prevention program, investing in the requirements process, making meetings more effective and efficient, basing decision-making on facts, and performing "PDCA" at the end of meetings and on reaching milestones.

4. **Assign resources to prioritized objectives.** Write an "Action Plan" for each improvement activity and assign the lead to a particular person.

5. **Establish an "Engineering Process Group" (EPG) to guide the improvement effort.** The members of the EPG provide leadership and determine actions that best address "points of pain."

6. **Take advantage of formal training on the selected process model.**

7. **Consider utilizing an experienced process facilitator to mentor your project or organization.**

8. **Establish an electronic process asset library that facilitates reuse of artifacts.** It's always easier to initiate needed work when one has an example of a work product with which to start. This also leverages the experience of others and provides the opportunity to take advantage of lessons learned from previous efforts.

9. **Provide orientation sessions to familiarize the project or organization with the planned process improvement initiative.** Seek suggestions and incorporate them into the planned approach. Gain buy-in of those involved.

10. **Perform formal training on how to perform peer reviews, how to perform defect prevention, how to perform requirements development and management, and other areas deemed critical for the process improvement initiative.**

11. **Execute process improvement, using periodic status reports to management that demonstrate the value of the process improvement initiative.**

Focused guidance for improving Earned Value Management (EVM) is available in a Software Engineering Institute technical paper [1]. It includes tables that map CMMI specific practices to EVMS Guidelines and describes how to map an organization's procedures to the targeted specific practices or guidelines. We recommend that this approach be applied with regard to the systems engineering standards or the PBEV guidelines.

POLICIES FOR INTEGRATING SYSTEMS ENGINEERING AND RISK MANAGEMENT

Although there are no policies to incorporate PBEV, many organizations set policies to achieve higher CMMI levels, to utilize the systems engineering standards in their processes, and to integrate risk management with EVM. Some examples of policies and procedures from the Northrop Grumman Corporation Integrated Systems Sector (NGIS) follow.

EXAMPLE 15.1: INTEGRATE ORGANIZATION PROCESSES WITH SYSTEMS ENGINEERING STANDARDS

Excerpt from NGIS Procedure: Systems Engineering

Sector processes shall align with international and national standards including, in part, ISO 15288, "Systems Engineering—System Life Cycle Processes," ISO 9000 quality assurance standards, IEEE 1220-1998, "Standard for Application and Management of the Systems Engineering Process," and shall enable each program to establish an integrated program process architecture.

All product life cycle tasks and work products shall be planned, budgeted, and included in the program's Integrated Master Schedule and shall be linked to key program events in the Integrated Master Plan.

EXAMPLE 15.2: INTEGRATE RISK MANAGEMENT WITH EARNED VALUE MANAGEMENT

Excerpt from NGIS Procedure: Manage Risk

Estimate at Complete (EAC) reviews should provide comprehensive risk assessments that quantify opportunities and risks in a Summary Risk Analysis. Specific risks will have reserve dollars identified against them. Reserves must be decreased when the risks for which they were held are resolved. Supporting detail for all significant items must be provided to enable the reviewer to determine the reasonableness of the chosen probabilities.

Risk mitigation must be integrated into the team plans such as the Integrated Master Plan, Integrated Master Schedule, control account plans, and work packages. It is imperative that the program's management utilizes this approach as the single (or most significant) method for identifying and tracking risks across the program.

IMPLEMENTATION OF PBEV

PBEV began with a series of software process improvements at NGIS. They were driven by the need to improve measurement of software development. The first improvements were based on Practical Software and Systems Measurement (PSM, 2003). Examples of performance-based measures for earned value from PSM include functional requirements status, component status, test status, and increment content-function. A complete discussion of the lessons learned, the improvement process, and examples of the types of measures that were discarded and implemented during the process improvements may be found in *CrossTalk* [2]. For example, the measurement of defects was retained as an indicator of quality and a predictor of final cost and schedule. However, various measures of achieved requirements were used for schedule progress and earned value instead of the removal of defects.

The application of PBEV guidelines to systems engineering began with a set of process improvements to:

1. **Define success criteria for technical maturity**
2. **Define criteria to differentiate between the initial development of engineering designs and rework of those designs**
3. **Define criteria for discrete measurement of rework that are based on meeting requirements**
4. **Base earned value on the above criteria**

The application of PBEV improved management's use of earned value management. The reported earned value is now a true measure of technical progress. More importantly, PBEV provides an earlier warning of deviations from the project plan and enables quick corrective actions. PBEV also provides a valid basis for estimating the cost and schedule of the remaining work.

SUMMARY

This chapter has provided guidance and techniques for leading and implementing a process improvement initiative. The rationale for undertaking a process improvement program was discussed. A set of success factors based on eighteen years of experience in using a process framework was provided. Suggestions were provided concerning how to implement a process improvement program. Policies concerning systems engineering and risk management were noted. Finally, we discussed how some PBEV guidelines were implemented on a real project.

REFERENCES

[1] Solomon, Paul. "Using CMMI to Improve Earned Value Management" (CMU/SEI-2002-TN-016). Carnegie Mellon University/SEI, October 2002 (see www.sei.cmu.edu/pub/documents/02.reports/pdf/02tn016.pdf).

[2] Solomon, Paul. "Practical Software Measurement, Performance-Based Earned Value." *CrossTalk: The Journal of Defense Software Engineering.* September 2001, pp. 25–29 (see www.stsc.hill.af.mil/crosstalk/2001/09/index. html).

Appendix A

Fundamentals of Earned Value Management

INTRODUCTION

The chapters of this book are intended for the experienced practitioner of Earned Value Management (EVM). This appendix is for the first-time user of EVM. It covers the fundamentals of EVM and includes guidelines, templates, formulas, and examples.

After reading this appendix and Appendix B, Detailed Planning Guidance, you should be able to set up a project and to measure progress against a performance measurement baseline (PMB). You will understand the basic terms and be able to understand and interpret earned value data. Most importantly, you will be able to take advantage of EVM's most powerful analytical techniques. Earned value analysis provides the ability to quickly isolate a project's most significant variances, to measure the efficiency of the resources used, and to estimate a project's final costs with proven mathematical techniques.

This appendix is consistent with the standards for project management (PMBOK Guide) and the Earned Value Management Systems standard (EVMS) that were discussed in Chapter 1. For readers that want to apply EVM in a practical manner without reference to industry EVM standards, this appendix is a primer that meets that need.

The topics include:

1. **Why use EVM?**
2. **EVM Principles**
3. **Planning and Control Processes**

Performance-Based Earned Value, by Paul J. Solomon and Ralph R. Young
Copyright ©2007 IEEE Computer Society.

4. **Product Scope and Quality**
5. **Work Breakdown Structure (WBS)**
6. **Organizational Breakdown Structure (OBS)**
7. **Control Accounts and Control Account Managers (CAMs)**
8. **Work Packages and Planning Packages**
9. **Base Measures**
10. **Performance Measurement Baseline (PMB)**
11. **House Project**
12. **Controlling a Project with EVM**
13. **Technical or Quality Variances**
14. **Schedule Variances**
15. **Cost Variances**
16. **Variance Analysis**
17. **Cost Performance Index (CPI)**
18. **Restatement of Earned Value**
19. **Rework**
20. **Maintaining the Integrity of the PMB**

WHY USE EVM?

EVM is capable of providing reliable information to answer management's questions about the status of the project. EVM also includes proven analytical techniques and formulas that management may use to answer questions about the future of the project. A set of questions that Eleanor Haupt posed when training U.S. Air Force acquisition management is shown in Figure A.1.

It must be emphasized at the outset that use of EVM techniques is contingent on management desiring honest feedback. If this is not the case, all of the effort used to provide EVM is wasted. Unfortunately, EVM and the EVMS have sometimes been more misused than used effectively—a root cause of failed application of these techniques. The project staff will provide the information that management expects—if management expects the staff to report that "all is well," that is what will be reported.

EVM PRINCIPLES

EVM compares the amount of work that was planned with what was actually accomplished to determine whether project cost and schedule performance were achieved as planned. The principles of EVM include the following:

Questions to be Answered

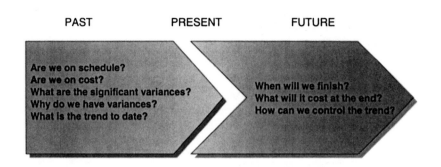

PAST   PRESENT   FUTURE

Are we on schedule?
Are we on cost?
What are the significant variances?
Why do we have variances?
What is the trend to date?

When will we finish?
What will it cost at the end?
How can we control the trend?

We analyze the past performance.........*to help us control the future*

Figure A.1 Set of Questions Answered by EVM.

1. **Plan all work scope to completion.**
2. **Decompose the program work scope into finite pieces that can be assigned to a responsible person or organization for control of technical, schedule, and cost objectives.**
3. **Integrate program work scope, schedule, and cost objectives into a performance measurement baseline against which accomplishments can be measured. Control changes to the baseline.**
4. **Use actual costs incurred and recorded in accomplishing work performed.**
5. **Objectively assess accomplishments at the work performance level.**
6. **Analyze significant variances from the plan, forecast impacts, and prepare an estimate at completion (EAC) based on performance to date and work to be performed.**

PLANNING AND CONTROL PROCESSES

EVM is used to control a project. However, the effectiveness and validity of earned value data is only as good as the project plan and the base measures of schedule progress that are specified in the planning phase of project development. In fact, if the wrong base measures are specified, than earned value data can be misleading and may fail to provide an early warning of threats to project objectives.

The intent is to construct a project plan, illustrate measures of performance, perform earned value analysis to detect deviations or variances from the plan, and take corrective actions to bring the project back under control. We will demonstrate how to develop estimates of the project's final cost and completion date in the event that no actions are taken that will result in achieving the project's cost, schedule, and technical objectives.

PRODUCT SCOPE AND QUALITY

The scope is composed of the product scope and the project scope (PMBOK Guide, Section 5.5):

1. **Product scope—the features and functions that characterize a product, service, or result**
2. **Project scope—the work that needs to be accomplished to deliver a product, service, or result with the specified features and functions.**

The product scope includes the quality baseline. The quality baseline reports the quality objectives of the project and is the basis for measuring and reporting quality performance as part of the Performance Measurement Baseline (PMB) (PMBOK Guide, Section 8.1.3.5).

WORK BREAKDOWN STRUCTURE

The planning process should include an activity to define the internal and external (deliverable) products that will be provided during the execution of the project, and then a Product Breakdown Structure (PBS). Then, the WBS can be constructed based on the PBS. The WBS is a product-oriented decomposition of project tasks depicting the breakdown of work scope for work authorization, tracking, and reporting purposes. It facilitates traceability and provides a control framework for management down to the lowest level that is needed for control, called the work package.

An excellent reference for understanding the EVMS guidelines (in Appendix C) is available on-line. It is the National Defense Industrial Association (NDIA) Program Management Systems Committee (PSMC) ANSI/EIA-748-A Standard for EVMS Intent Guide (NDIA EVMS Guide). Per this Guide, the WBS ensures that the statement of work (SOW) is entirely captured and allows for the integration of technical, schedule, and cost information.

Note that the NDIA EVMS Guide states that the WBS *allows for* the integration of technical, schedule, and cost information. The integration of technical information can only be *assured* if the WBS is traceable to the product scope requirements.

ORGANIZATIONAL BREAKDOWN STRUCTURE

The organizational breakdown structure (OBS) is the hierarchical breakdown of the organization (project) that performs the work ("performing organization"). It is used to assign responsibility for planning and managing work.

CONTROL ACCOUNTS AND CONTROL ACCOUNT MANAGERS

The intersection of the WBS and the OBS results in a management control point called the control account. A control account is managed by a control account manager (CAM). The CAM prepares, plans, and manages lower-level work assignments within the control account. These are called work packages and planning packages.

The CAM is responsible for ensuring that the control account SOW is complete and meets overall technical, budget, and schedule objectives. This is achieved by:

1. **Developing detail schedules, which are integrated horizontally and vertically with the Integrated Master Schedule (IMS) or lower-level schedules**
2. **Time-phasing of budgets**
3. **Separating discretely manageable tasks into work packages and planning packages**
4. **Selecting appropriate, objective earned value methods to measure progress**
5. **Identifying interim milestones or other base measures of progress toward completing the work package**

WORK PACKAGES AND PLANNING PACKAGES

A work package is simply a task or grouping of work. It is the point at the lowest level of the WBS at which work is planned, progress is measured, and earned value is computed.

The outcome of most work packages is a work product. A work product is an artifact that is needed for further processing in a successor work package, unless that work product is an end deliverable of the project.

BASE MEASURES

The progress of a work package is determined by using base measures. A base measure is a unit of physical work that can be planned, scheduled, and directly measured.

Example A.1: Base Measures

Examples of base measures within a work package are in Table A.1.

TABLE A.1 Examples of Base Measures

Work Product	Base Measures
Set of engineering drawings	Individual drawings completed or subtasks in the drawing process
Software module	Software code or subtasks in the coding and unit testing process. Use cases and data base entities may also be base measures.
Brick wall	Bricks laid

A planning package is a downstream effort that is budgeted and scheduled. Although it has a Statement of Work (SOW), a planning package is not detail planned and does not have an assigned earned value technique. Some of the SOW and budget from planning packages will be transferred to work packages before the heeded work begins.

Additional guidance and templates for the detailed planning of work packages are provided in Appendix B.

PERFORMANCE MEASUREMENT BASELINE

The PMB is an approved plan for the project work against which project execution is compared and deviations are measured for management control. The PMB typically integrates scope, schedule, and cost parameters of a project, but may also include technical and quality parameters (PMBOK Guide 10.3.1.5). The integration of technical and quality parameters can only be assured if the PMB includes the product scope and the quality baseline.

Management reserve (MR) is an amount of the total available budget that is withheld from the PMB to mitigate cost or schedule risks. MR is not included in the PMB, as it is not yet designated for specific work scope. It is also called a contingency reserve and is the source of budget for transfer to the PMB when risk mitigation tasks are authorized.

HOUSE PROJECT

The project to be discussed in this appendix is building a house. The developer and project manager, Peter Mann (PM), wants to build a house according to an existing architectural plan and sell it for a profit.

Cost and Schedule Objectives

He has $308,000 in cash to invest, plus his own personal time, and wants to earn a profit of $200,000 after six months of effort. He pays himself $5000 per month to be the PM. Consequently, his target price is $438,000 ($308,000 cash plus $30,000 salary for PM plus $200,000 profit).

House Quality Objectives

The house will be sold with a warranty. Consequently, the developer wants to build a house of high quality to avoid warranty expenses after the house is sold. Also, high quality should be evident to the prospective buyer and assist in a quick sale at the target price.

Some of the quality objectives of the house are:

1. **Wood shingle roof is waterproof in driving rains (up to 70 miles per hour).**
2. **Interior, painted walls look good (solid color with no streaks).**
3. **Carpeting lays flat and looks seamless.**

Example A.2: WBS for a House

The WBS for the house is shown in Table A.2.

Note that some elements of the WBS, such as the lot, are decomposed into sub-elements.

House Organizational Breakdown Structure

The PM hired three managers to manage the control account components of the project plan. They are not individually scheduled to work for the whole six months but have contracted start and stop dates based on the schedule. They each get paid $1000 per week or $25/hour.

Charley manages the lot, foundation, and roof and is scheduled to work 12 weeks. His time is not continuous but occurs when the work is being performed.

Sam manages the frame and utilities and is scheduled to work 5 weeks. His time is also not continuous because some electrical outlets, switches, and plumbing are installed after completion of interior decoration.

Tom manages the interior construction and decoration and is scheduled to work continuously. Most of Tom's time is support effort that will not be detail planned and measured. The earned value technique

TABLE A.2 WBS for a House

1.0 House
1.1 Lot (purchase and grade)
1.1.1 Purchase lot
1.1.2 Grade lot
1.1.2.1 Rent equipment
1.1.2.2 Labor
1.2 Lay foundation
1.3 Frame
1.4 Utilities (electrical and plumbing)
1.5 Roof
1.5.1 Roof shingles
1.5.2 Labor
1.6 Interior construction
1.6.1 Wallboards
1.6.1.1 CAM purchasing activity
1.6.1.2 Material
1.6.1.3 Labor
1.6.2 Doors and cabinets
1.7 Decoration (carpeting and painting)
1.7.1 Carpeting
1.7.2 Painting
1.7.2.1 Material
1.7.2.2 Labor
1.8 Program Management, including CAM Level of Effort

for support effort is called Level of Effort (LOE). Earned value is taken with the passage of time and is equal to the time-phased Budgeted Cost of Work Scheduled (BCWS). However, some of Tom's specific tasks will be planned and measured discretely, such as the ordering and receipt of materials.

The Organizational Breakdown Structure (OBS) follows:

> **Dept. P—PM**
> **Dept. C—Charley**
> **Dept. S—Sam**
> **Dept. T—Tom**

Budget and Responsibility

PM developed a project budget and allocated the budget to the WBS elements and OBS elements. The total amount available to be budgeted is $338,000. However, PM decided to distribute budget of only $308,000. He withheld $30,000 as MR. MR will only be used as a source of budget for unexpected tasks or purchases in case bad or unexpected things happen during project execution. MR is not used to provide additional budget for cost overruns.

Example A.3: Responsibility Accountability Matrix

The allocation of work responsibility and budget to the responsible organizations and their managers is called the responsibility accountability matrix (RAM). It is shown in Table A.3.

Each intersection of the WBS and OBS is the control account. It is the management control point at which the budget and a statement of work are distributed. Later, we will see how the control account becomes the control point for managing cost and schedule performance. The actual cost of work performed (AC) is always reported at the control account level. It may also be recorded and reported at the work package or lower levels. The manager of the control account is the CAM.

Schedule

PM developed a master schedule to govern the detailed planning and scheduling of his CAMs. They will develop lower-level schedule activities for inclusion on the master schedule and the work packages and planning packages to be included in the EVM data base.

The higher-level master schedule is shown below in Figure A.2.

House Control Accounts and Work Packages

Next, we will develop the project plan including a portion of the house PMB. For this purpose, and for subsequent discussion of performance and variance analysis, we will select four control accounts and selected work packages within those control accounts.

The control accounts include:

> **1.1.2 Grade the Lot**
> **1.6.1 Wallboards**
> **1.7.2 Painting**
> **1.5.1 Roof Shingles**

For selected work packages, the earned value techniques will be selected, milestones or other base measures will be selected to determine the percent complete, and the time-phased Budgeted Cost for Work Scheduled (BCWS) will be developed.

The BCWS is also called the Planned Value (PV). However, in this book, we will use the acronym BCWS. The term Planned Value will be used with regard to technical performance measurement.

Finally, during project execution, we will "take" (i.e., credit ourselves with) the value of the work that has actually been accomplished, earned value (EV), and look at a contract performance report (CPR) and the Cost Performance Index (CPI).

TABLE A.3 Responsibility Accountability Matrix for the House

WBS	OBS>Dept. P	Dept. C	Dept. S	Dept. T	PMB	MR	Total
1.0 House							
1.1 Lot							
1.1.1 Purchase lot	100,000				100,000		
1.1.2 Grade lot		500			500		
1.1.2.1 Rent equipment		1,000			1,000		
1.1.2.2 Labor		5,000			5,000		
1.2 Lay foundation			50,000		50,000		
1.3 Frame			19,900		19,900		
1.4 Utilities					30,000		
1.5 Roof							
1.5.1 Roof shingles		22,000					
1.5.2 Labor		8,000					
1.6 Interior construction							
1.6.1 Wallboards							
1.6.1.1 Purchase				150	150		
1.6.1.2 Material				2,000	2,000		
1.6.1.3 Labor				1,750	1,750		
1.6.2 Doors and cabinets				10,000	10,000		
1.7 Decoration							
1.7.1 Carpeting				6,050	6,050		
1.7.2 Painting							
1.7.2.1 Material				800	800		
1.7.2.2 Labor				8,000	8,000		
1.8 Program Management	30,000	12,000	5,000	25,850	72,850		
Total PMB	130,000	48,500	74,900	54,600	308,000		
Management Reserve						30,000	30,000
Total House					308,000	30,000	338,000

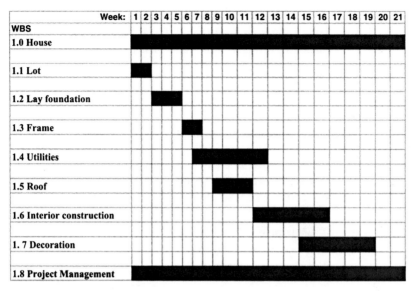

WBS	Week:	1	2	3	4	5	6	7	8	9	10	11	12	13	14	15	16	17	18	19	20	21
1.0 House																						
1.1 Lot																						
1.2 Lay foundation																						
1.3 Frame																						
1.4 Utilities																						
1.5 Roof																						
1.6 Interior construction																						
1. 7 Decoration																						
1.8 Project Management																						

Figure A.2 Master Schedule.

EV is the value of the work performed expressed in terms of the budget assigned to that work. It is also called the Budgeted Cost of Work Performed (BCWP). We will use the acronym EV in this book. It is determined by first directly measuring the progress toward completing the work package in terms of the predefined base measures. The progress is sometimes converted to the percent complete.

If "percent complete" is used, the earned value is the percent complete times the budget at completion (BAC) of the work package. If the base measures that were completed are not translated into a percent complete, then what was completed (base measures of earned value) is multiplied by the budgeted value per base measure to get the earned value. Earned value may be expressed both as a cumulative to date measure and as a measure of how much was completed in the current reporting period.

Variance analysis and corrective action or work around plans will be required when bad things happen during grading of the lot and installation of the roof shingles and when poor efficiency is realized during installation of the wallboards. Finally, the Estimate at Completion (EAC) will be developed for individual control accounts.

Grade the Lot. The control account Grade the Lot includes two work packages (WP). The SOW of WP 1 is rental of a tractor and dump truck for a period of 5 days. The rental price is $100/day so the budget at completion (BAC) is $500. The SOW of WP 2 is the labor to grade the field and haul the dirt away. Again, the planned duration is 5 days at $200/day or a BAC of $1000. The lot is 10,000 sq. ft. EV is measured and reported on a weekly basis. The EV techniques and base measures of EV follow:

Control Account—WBS 1.2: Grade the Lot: BAC: $1500

1. **WP 1—WBS 1.2.1 (rent equipment):**
   a. **BAC: $500**
   b. **EV technique: Milestone (MS) percent start/percent complete (20%/80%)**
   c. **Base measure of EV: Start and complete milestones**
   d. **Time-Phased BCWS: $100 in week 1, $400 in week 2**
2. **WP 2—WBS 1.2.2 (labor):**
   a. **BAC: $1000**
   b. **EV technique: Percent complete**
   c. **Base measure of EV: 10,000 sq. ft.**
   d. **Budget/base measure: $.10/sq. ft.**
   e. **Planned physical accomplishment: 1500 sq. ft. in week 1, 8500 sq. ft. in week 2**
   f. **Time-phased BCWS: $150 in week 1, $850 in week 2**

Example A.4: Performance Measurement Baseline. The total, time-phased PV is the PMB. The PMB of this control account is shown in Table A.4.

Wallboards. The control account Wallboards includes two work packages (WP). The SOW of WP 1 is purchase and receipt of wallboards. This is Tom's time to place the purchase order and receive the material. Although the budget in hours or dollars is a small number, if this work package is behind schedule, it is an early warning that the materials may not be on hand when needed for installation. The nominal planned value is 1 hour to prepare and submit the purchase order and 2 hours to receive and inspect the material.

TABLE A.4 Grade the Lot PMB

WBS	Week 1	Week 2	BAC
WP 1: 1.2.1			
Base measure	MS 1	MS 2	
BCWS	$100	$400	$500
WP 2: 1.2.2			
Base measure: sq. ft.	1500	8500	10,000
Budget/base measure	$10		
BCWS	$150	$850	$1,000
1.1.2 Control Account	$250	$1250	$1,500

The SOW of WP 2 is the material cost. The budgeted purchase price is $2000 for 250 wallboards.

The SOW of WP 3 is the labor to install the wallboards. The planned labor is 20 minutes per wallboard at an hourly rate of $21/hour. The BAC is $1750. The EV techniques and base measures of EV follow:

Control Account 2-WBS 1.6.1: Wallboards: BAC: $3900

1. **WP 1—WBS 1.6.1.1 (Tom purchases and receives wallboards):**
   a. **BAC: $150**
   b. **EV technique: Weighted Milestone (2 hours ($75) to order, 2 hours ($75) to receive)**
   c. **Base measure of EV: Start and completion milestones**
   d. **Time-Phased BCWS: $75 in week 12, $75 in week 13**
2. **WP 2—WBS 1.6.1.2 (Wallboards material):**
   a. **BAC: 2000**
   b. **EV technique: Milestone**
   c. **Base measure of EV: Completion milestone**
   d. **Time-Phased BCWS: $2000 in week 13**
3. **WP 3—WBS 1.6.1.3 (labor):**
   a. **EV technique: Percent complete**
   b. **Base measure of EV: 250 wallboards**
   c. **Budget/base measure: $7/wallboard**
   d. **Planned installation rate: 24 wallboards/day or 120/week**
   e. **Planned physical accomplishment: 120 in week 14, 120 in week 15, 1 in week 16**
   f. **Time-phased BCWS: $840 in week 14, $840 in week 15, $70 in week 16**

WBS	Week 12	Week 13	Week 14	Week 15	Week 16	BAC
WP 1: 1.6.1.1						
Base measure	MS 1	MS 2				
BCWS	$75	$75				$150
WP 2: 1.6.1.2						
Base measure		MS 3				
BCWS		$2,000				$2,000
WP 3: 1.6.1.3						
Base measure: wallboards			120	120	10	250
Budget/base measure			$7			
BCWS			$840	$840	$70	$1,750
1.6.1 Control Account	$75	$2,075	$840	$840	$70	$3,900

Painting. The control account Painting includes two work packages. The SOW of WP 1 is receipt of paint. The budgeted purchase price is $800 for 40 gallons. The SOW of WP 2 is the labor to paint the walls and ceilings. The planned labor is $2/sq. ft. The BAC is $8000. The CAM did not plan any rework. The EV techniques and base measures of EV follow:

Control Account 3—WBS 1.7.2: Painting: BAC: $8800

1. **WP 1 (Receive paint material):**
   a. **BAC: 800**
   b. **EV technique: Milestone**
   c. **Base measure of EV: Milestone, Receive paint ($800)**
   d. **Time-Phased BCWS: $800 in week 15**
2. **WP 2 (labor):**
   a. **BAC: $8000**
   b. **EV technique: Percent complete**
   c. **Base measure of EV: $2/sq. ft.**
   d. **Time-phased BCWS: $3000 in week 15, $3000 in week 16, $2000 in week 17**

Roof Shingles. The control account Roof Shingles includes two work packages. The SOW of WP 1 is receipt of the shingles. The earned value technique is similar to the other materials and will not be repeated here.

The SOW of WP 2 is the labor to install the shingles. The planned labor is $1/shingle. The BAC is $8000. However, there will be two specified types of measures of progress and earned value. The first measure is typical. It is based on the number of shingles installed. The second measure is based on the quality of the roof. The PM has defined a Technical Performance Measure (TPM), a schedule for taking measurements, and planned values to be achieved. The TPM will indicate whether the roof will meet its quality objective. The quality objective is for the roof to remain waterproof in a driving rain with sustained winds up to 70 miles per hour.

Control Account 4: Roof Shingles

1. **WP 2 (labor to install shingles)—Alternative 1(Ignores quality):**
   a. **BAC: $8000**
   b. **EV technique: Percent complete**
   c. **Base measure of EV: $2/sq. ft.**
   d. **Time-phased BCWS: $3000 in week 9, $3000 in week 10, and $2000 in week 11**
2. **WP 2 (labor)—Alternative 2 (Evaluate quality with TPMs)**

A better way to measure the progress of WP 2 is to consider the quality of the evolving product when assessing EV by using a TPM. In the project plan, a milestone is established to conduct a test of the roof's waterproofness. The test will be conducted after one complete section of the roof is completed at the end of week 9. A high-pressure hose will be used on the roof. If no water penetrates the shingles, the test is a success.

If the test is successful, the EV that was taken for installing shingles will remain. However, if the test fails, then $500 will be subtracted from the EV taken. In other words, the earned value after failure is $2500 ($3000 − $500). Because the quality objective was not achieved, the project is behind schedule. There will be rework to remove shingles and to reinstall them properly. The shingles had previously been individually tested for waterproofness and passed the test.

Additional guidance for integrating TPMs with EVM is provided in Appendix H.

Planning Summary

For the purpose of this educational project, the planning process is now complete. PM has established a SOW, a WBS, an OBS, and a master schedule. After considering his profit objective, PM established a MR and distributed the remaining available budget to his CAMs. The CAMs established work and planning packages and developed the time-phased BCWS. The time-phased BCWS, at any control level, is the PMB. The sum of all control account PMBs is the project PMB.

Also, this plan includes a schedule for measuring the quality or technical performance of the roof against a planned value for the TPM. The TPM plan is integrated with EVM. Finally, PM did not establish any work packages for rework. This will turn out to be an oversight.

Execution

The project has begun, and work is being performed. Work packages have been started, completed, or are still open. Earned value performance reports are prepared as part of program execution and are distributed to the CAMs and to PM.

Control Performance Reports

Earned value control performance reports (CPR) may be tabular or graphic. A commonly used graphic report looks like a set of S curves. The S curves show cumulative earned value, planned value, and actual costs.

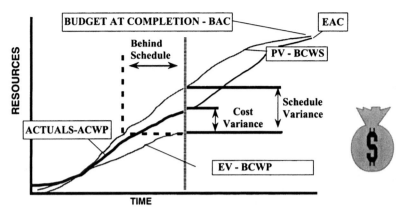

Figure A.3 S Curve.

TABLE A.5.1 Lot CPR

WBS	BCWS	EV	AC	SV	CV	CPI	BAC	EAC
1.1 Lot								
1.1.1 Purchase lot	100,000	100,000	100,000	0	0	1.00	100,000	100,000
1.1.2 Grade lot								
1.1.2.1 Rent equipment	500	400	400	−100	0	1.00	500	500
1.1.2.2 Labor	1,000	800	805	−200	−5	0.99	1,000	1,000
Total 1.1.2	1,500	1,200	1,205	−300	−5	1.00	1,500	1,500
Total 1.1	101,500	101,200	101,205	−300	−5	1.00	101,500	101,500

TABLE A.5.2 Wallboards Labor CPR

WBS	BCWS	EV	AC	SV	CV	CPI	BAC	EAC
1.6.1.3 Labor	840	403.2	504	−436.8	−336	0.80	1750	1750

The difference between two is the variance. A conceptual S curve report is shown in Figure A.3.

Example A.5: CPRs. The CPRs in Tables A.5.1 and A.5.2, have been distributed during the course of the project. The reports indicate the cumulative status of project elements at different points in time.

The summary, control account level data show both negative, cumulative schedule variances (SV) and negative, cumulative cost variances (CV). How are the variances computed and what is their significance?

The formulas are:

$$CV = EV - AC$$

$$SV = EV - BCWS$$

The data for Grade the Lot show:

$$CV = 101{,}200 - 101{,}205 = -5$$

$$SV = 101{,}200 - 101{,}500 = -300$$

In both cases, a performance parameter is compared with earned value (EV). Also, in both cases, negative is bad. When the actual costs of the work accomplished exceed the planned costs of the work accomplished, there is a cost overrun (bad). When the planned value exceeds the earned value, that activity is behind schedule (bad).

As with any control system, the variance or deviation may be significant or insignificant. For cost variances, we recommend management by exception. Establish variance thresholds so that variances that exceed the thresholds may be examined and analyzed. The threshold may be in absolute values ($300), and/or in percentage terms (5%), and/or as an index or ratio. The reports may have an exception indicator, such as color-coding, or may be sorted so that those items that exceed variance thresholds stand out.

CONTROLLING A PROJECT WITH EVM

The control process utilizes EVM metrics. These metrics include the SV and CV mentioned above and the following primary metrics:

1. **Cost Performance Index (CPI)**
2. **Schedule Performance Index (SPI)**
3. **Estimate at Completion (EAC)**

There are also some secondary or derived metrics:

1. **Budgeted Cost of Work Remaining (BCWR)**
2. **Estimate to Complete (ETC)**
3. **To Complete Performance Index (TCPI)**
4. **Variance at Completion (VAC)**

We use these metrics during variance analysis, corrective action or workaround planning, and determining most likely cost at completion, the EAC.

TECHNICAL OR QUALITY VARIANCES

A project's objectives to meet customer requirements can be translated into technical maturity or quality objectives. The PMBOK Guide calls it the quality baseline. These objectives should be defined and quantified in a technical plan and incorporated into the success criteria for milestones on the master schedule. If a project is not meeting its scheduled technical or quality objectives, then the respective milestones will not be completed on schedule. Likewise, those work packages that support the schedule milestone will also be behind schedule (as indicated by a negative schedule variance).

The core principles and guidelines of PBEV are intended to overcome traditional EVM's lack of guidance to integrate technical objectives with the PMB. Consequently, there is relatively little discussion of technical or quality variances in this appendix. Chapter 7 includes examples of technical variances.

SCHEDULE VARIANCES

For schedule variances, we recommend that the SV be converted from the budgeted currency (hours or dollars) to a time-based measure. In other words, discuss the number of periods of time that the work is behind schedule (days, weeks, or months). We should also relate the EV metric, SV, to the difference between the progress bar and time now as shown on the master schedule. During variance analysis, the SV should be discussed in terms of how many days, weeks, or months we are behind schedule. A simple way to do this is to repeatedly subtract the most recent, periodic BCWS values from the SV and to tally how many periods were utilized. For example, the SV for grading the lot is –$300. The BCWS is $1500 in the most recent week. Therefore, the task is 1/5 of a week behind schedule.

The other schedule metric is the SPI. The SPI is simply EV/BCWS. A decimal index indicates the degree to which the project element is ahead of or behind schedule. A value of less than 1.0 is bad because it indicates a behind-schedule condition. We don't find the SPI to be a very useful or effective metric. Conversion of the SV to the number of periods behind schedule provides the most meaningful information for schedule control.

COST VARIANCES

If properly planned and measured, EVM can integrate a project's cost, schedule, and technical performance. We have discussed how the technical performance should be integrated with schedule performance through the wise use of milestones and success criteria. However, we do not believe that analysis of a project's schedule metrics is sufficient to predict a project's completion date.

On the other hand, we are convinced that analysis of EVM metrics can provide insight into the efficiency with which resources are being used, can quickly detect deviations from planned cost performance, and can assist in estimating the project's final costs.

Next, we will use EVM metrics to examine the variances of the House Project and illustrate the power of EVM.

VARIANCE ANALYSIS

Effective and thorough variance analysis should incorporate the following elements:

       1. **Determine the root cause of the variance.**
       2. **Determine the impacts on cost and schedule objectives.**
       3. **Develop a corrective action or workaround plan.**
       4. **Monitor corrective action or workaround plan.**

Now, we will analyze some of the variances of the house project to see if we can bring the project under control.

Variance Analysis—Grade the Lot

The biggest variance is the SV, –$300. That's equivalent to 1 day behind schedule. The root cause was easy to determine. At the end of the fourth day of grading, a huge boulder was discovered submerged beneath the soil. All work stopped, and the grading laborers were temporarily dismissed. The corrective action plan is to call a contractor to bring heavy equipment and remove the boulder. The contractor will cost $600. The total delay to the project will be 2 days. Fortunately, the rental equipment can be returned and rented anew so there is no cost impact to that work package.

There is an additional cost impact. Both the PM and one of the CAMS, Tom, are planned as LOE. The project will take 2 days longer to complete. PM's and Tom's daily rates are $250 and $200, respectively. So the EAC will increase by $900 because the SOW of the LOE effort will be extended 2 days. The CPR above does not yet show the result of increasing the EAC.

The discovery of the boulder could not have been anticipated. PM decided to distribute additional budget of $1500 from MR to provide budget and schedule for the additional SOW.

Variance Analysis—Wallboards

The wallboards have significant schedule and cost variances. Of course, 2 days of schedule variance were caused by the boulder problem.

However, the total SV of 3 days has another cause. The wallboard installers are slower than planned. Also, because they are slower, the cost of installing a wallboard is higher than planned. So their performance inefficiency, relative to plan, causes both cost and schedule variances. The quantitative variance analysis follows.

First, the EV for installation is $403.2. It is based on the physical accomplishment, 57.6 wallboards installed times the planned value per wallboard, $7. The SV is −$436.8. One of the causes of the SV is the 2-day boulder delay (48 wallboards × $7) = −$336. The more important cause is the low efficiency of the workers. They are completing an average of 2.4 wallboards per hour instead of the planned rate of 3 wallboards per hour. They are operating at 80% of the budgeted efficiency. So after starting 2 days late and working for 3 days, only 57.6 wallboards have been installed. The plan was to have 120 wallboards installed by the end of that week. The SV during those 3 days is $100.8 (14.4 wallboards × $7). Based on the planned BCWS per day of $168, this is equivalent to a delay of .6 days. So the project is behind schedule by 2.6 days.

There is also a growing cost problem. The actual labor costs are $504. The EV is $403.2, so the CV is −$100.8. The labor rate is exactly as planned, $168/day. However, only 19.2 wallboards were completed per day instead of 24. Conversely, the cost of installing one wallboard is $8.75 instead of $7.

COST PERFORMANCE INDEX

EVM has a very powerful metric of resource efficiency, the Cost Performance Index (CPI). The formula is simple. CPI = EV/AC. It is the ratio of what we accomplished at the planned cost for that accomplishment divided by the actual costs. If the CPI is less than 1, it's bad. It indicates that it costs more to produce a unit of earned value than was planned.

Using the Wallboards data, CPI = $403.2/$504 = 0.8. This, of course, is the same as the 80% of budgeted efficiency that was discussed previously. Not surprisingly, if we divide what it should cost to install one wallboard by the actual cost, $8.75, the ratio is also 0.8.

So we have some inefficient labor. Now what's the impact on the project? Actually, there are two impacts, both bad.

Cost Impact—Wallboards

First, unless corrective action is taken, there will be a cost overrun at completion. This is sometimes called the Variance at Completion or VAC.

If the rest of the wallboards are also installed at a CPI of .8, the cost of the remaining work will be $1683.5 (192.4 wallboards × $8.75). Another way to estimate the remaining costs is to divide the Budgeted Cost of Work Remaining (BCWR) by the expected future performance efficiency. The BCWR is the BAC less the EV ($1750 − $403.2 = $1346.8). Let us assume that the expected future efficiency is no better than the past. If so, the BCWR divided by the expected future efficiency is $1346.8/.8 = $1683.5. There are two EVM terms and acronyms for the phrases used above. The expected future efficiency is the To Complete Performance Index (TCPI). The estimate of the remaining costs is the Estimate to Complete (ETC).

$$EAC = AC + ETC.$$

Using these formulas, the EAC for the wallboard labor = $504 + $1683.5 = $2187.5. This will cause a cost overrun or VAC (BAC − EAC) of −$437.5.

Warning. Be cautious when using a TCPI to derive the ETC. Although we have discussed the merits of using the TCPI, it is, after all, only a mathematical technique. The real ETC should be determined by identifying all of the remaining tasks and the resources needed to complete those tasks.

Normally, the CPI is used to develop a TCPI. It is recommended that the CPI first be adjusted to eliminate any nonrecurring variances. Also, determine whether the CPI should be based on cumulative performance since the beginning of the effort or whether more recent cost performance is more representative of the future. Often a CPI based on the last three or six months provides the best indicator of future performance.

There are a few other caveats. First, the CPI at a summary level of the WBS is less valid than at the lower levels. For example, the CPI for the Wallboard control account is composed of three work package components: Tom's labor, purchase of the material, and installation labor. Yet all of the CV is related to the installation labor. Consequently, a more accurate ETC will be obtained by determining the TCPI at the level of the installation labor instead of the control account level.

Finally, using a mathematical technique based on past performance does not take into account corrective action plans and other management actions to bring the project back under control.

Schedule Impact—Wallboards

There will also be a significant schedule impact because of the unfavorable CPI. Worse yet, the late finish may cause additional cost overruns to other activities unless successful corrective actions are taken.

First, based on the TCPI of .8, the remaining work will take slightly over 10 days to complete (192.4 wallboards/19.2 wallboards per day). The plan was to complete the remaining 192.4 wallboards in a little over 8 days. So the project will have a late finish of 4.4 days, as follows:

SV to date: 2.4 days

Future SV: 2.0 days

There will be an additional cost impact for PM's and Tom's time (remember, they were LOE) of $450/day, or $1980.

Corrective Action Plan

Fortunately, PM has a corrective action plan. He developed a process improvement that will increase the future cost and schedule performance efficiency. Instead of fastening the wallboards to the studs with a hammer and nails, PM rented a few nail guns, trained the workers to use the new tools, and was able to bring the project back under control, except for the 2-day delay caused by the boulder. Later, we will demonstrate how to do an internal replan to incorporate the process improvement.

Variance Analysis—Painting

The performance report for Painting reveals only one significant cost variance. There is an underrun of $200 for purchase of the paint. However, there is a significant problem.

The earned value for the painting labor is $1800. It is based on completing 900 sq. ft. at $2/sq. ft. There is even a small cost underrun of $20. The CPI is 1.01. The SV is apparently zero. The data showed that the job is 22.5% complete.

However, when PM inspected a few of the painted rooms, it was apparent that the paint did not have a smooth, opaque appearance. There were streaks and an apparent uneven application of the paint. Tom, the painting CAM, determined that he had bought the wrong paint. He thought that he had purchased a one-coat paint at a bargain price. In fact, he purchased paint that required two coats on new plasterboard.

After apologizing to the PM, Tom came up with a corrective action plan. It required taking negative earned value to show the true percent complete and a replan of the remaining work. Tom proposed that the some of the remaining paint be used to apply a second coat to the 900 sq. ft. that was already painted. New paint, the kind that requires only one coat, would be purchased for the remaining 3100 sq. ft.

The ETC was computed as follows:

1. **Purchase one-coat paint to cover 3100 sq. ft.: 31 gallons @ $30 per gallon = $930.**
2. **Labor to apply one coat to 4000 sq. ft. based on TCPI of 1.01: $7920**

Tom has agreed not to be paid for the additional time to complete his SOW because of his error.

RESTATEMENT OF EARNED VALUE

After the paint quality error was discovered, PM restated EV, as follows.

WP 1: Receive paint
Because there was only enough paint on hand to cover 19.5% of the area to be painted (including the second coat), negative EV was taken to report EV at 19.5% complete instead of 100% complete. The remaining 81.5% of EV will be taken when the new paint is received.

WP 2: Because all 4000 sq. ft. remain to be painted, including the rework of 1900 sq. ft., EV of the paint labor work package is restated to zero. The restatement is important for three reasons:

1. EV reflects the true percent complete and a more realistic indicator of the amount of work remaining. Anything higher would be misleading.
2. The PMB is reset so that EV can be used to track progress.
3. The CPI and CV reflect reality.

If rework had been anticipated during the planning process, it should have been planned as a separate work package, as will be discussed next.

REWORK

Rework is a normal activity that should be estimated and planned during engineering development. Often, even when three-dimensional models are used for parts design, the fabricated parts do not fit together properly or fail to fit in the available space. Rework of the drawings is required.

Software functionality or requirements are rarely met during early reviews or testing. Even if a requirement was achieved earlier, subsequent integration testing often discloses a defect related to that requirement. Again, rework is required.

The budget for rework should be established during the planning process. It should be based on historical data and revised to consider improvements in processes and tools, differences in labor skills, and other factors.

Normally, rework should not be budgeted and scheduled in the same work package as the original effort. Establishing a separate work package for rework enables improved planning, control, and analysis.

First, the project will have clear visibility of the baseline finish date of the initial development of requirements, design, or other activities. Normally, the completion of these activities and their respective work products is a constraint to another activity. If rework is combined with the initial development, it is more difficult to establish the baseline schedule constraints and the baseline start dates of dependent activities.

Second, if the initial development is behind schedule, a forecasted slip to the completion of the work package will be shown as ETC beyond the baseline completion date. Consequently, the management control system provides useful information to the impacted, constrained activities. If rework is combined with the initial development, then only a slip to the completion of all rework will be visible as extended ETC. The manager of the downstream activity will have to rely on meetings or personal communication to learn of any slip to the initial development.

Third, the analysis of cost variances is easier to perform if rework is planned in a separate work package. This is especially true after rework has begun. It is easier to analyze the variances, discuss the root causes, and address the impacts if rework is based on separate and distinct performance data and is not commingled with the initial development.

Fourth, if rework is planned separately, it may preclude the need to report a reduction in cumulative earned value or negative earned value in the current period. Earned value should be decremented when new information discloses that activities or work products that were previously assessed as complete no longer meet the success or completion criteria. However, if rework is expected and planned, then the realization of the rework may not indicate a behind-schedule condition and a correction to earned value.

Additional discussion of rework, with examples of alternate planning techniques, is provided in Appendices B and G.

MAINTAINING THE INTEGRITY OF THE PMB

One of the most important principles of EVM is to maintain the integrity of the PMB. This requires both strong discipline and internal controls to preclude changing the PMB when bad or unexpected things happen.

Schedule Integrity

We have heard CAMs or higher-level managers explain or complain that the plan or baseline is "too dynamic" and should be changed to reflect reality. They would like to "move the baseline schedule to the right" instead of reporting a behind-schedule condition and a future slip to a milestone completion date. Their opinion seems justified if the behind-schedule condition is "not their fault" because their predecessor activity is behind schedule. They have not received the work product that is needed to begin their work package.

In this situation, we believe that the PM should strictly control the ability to rebaseline the same work to the right. If the project, or an activity within the project, is behind schedule, than the expected recovery plan, including the resource needs, should be shown as revised, re-time-phased ETC, not re-time-phased BCWS.

The same principle holds true when the behind-schedule work is transferred to another organization, to a supplier as a result of a make vs. buy decision, or to the internal organization from a supplier. Although the ETC for the corrective action plan should show the expected workflow, the cumulative BCWS should not be changed. Otherwise, the negative schedule variance will disappear and the performance data will not show the real progress. However, it is permitted to replan future BCWS to reflect a recovery plan as long as the activity will be completed by its need date.

Budget Integrity

The principle of maintaining the integrity of the PMB also applies to the budget. It is normally not justifiable to issue additional budget to cover a current or future cost overrun. Again, managers believe that, if the work is transferred to another organization, or to a supplier because of a make vs. buy decision, then the receiving CAM or organization should receive budget that is sufficient to cover the total estimated cost. They believe that the receiving CAM should not be penalized or constrained by the original baseline and past performance. We recommend that the budget baseline be maintained, even if the work is being transferred as part of a corrective action plan. Otherwise, cost overruns will appear to have been mitigated.

Revise the PMB for Work Scope Revisions

So when is it appropriate to change the baseline? When there is clearly a change to the authorized work scope. For example, if upgraded cabinets were added to the house subsequent to the start of work, then the additional costs and related schedule extensions would be reason to change the baseline. Of course, that would also be an increase to the product scope and the total budget for the house.

Another situation that could justify changing the PMB is a real change to the work scope even though there is no change to the product scope. The boulder problem is a good example. The activity and cost of removing the boulder were clearly out of scope to the CAM's authorized SOW. PM decided to budget all costs that were caused by the boulder so that the affected CAM would not have to report a cost overrun.

Revise the PMB When It Is No Longer Pertinent

Sometimes during project execution, the variances become too big and the baseline for the remaining work becomes obsolete and unachievable. Under those conditions, the key stakeholders may agree to develop a new baseline for the remaining work and to track performance against the new baseline. After the new baseline has been implemented, EVM will again become a useful tool for management control.

SUMMARY

In this appendix, we discussed the fundamental characteristics of EVM, developed a PMB for a typical project, prepared a Contract Performance Report, and performed variance analysis.

In Appendix B, we will provide guidance for developing work packages.

REFERENCES

Other guidance for using earned value management is provided below.

[1] Fleming, Quentin W. and Joel M. Koppelman. *Earned Value Project Management*, 3rd ed. Upper Darby, PA: Project Management Institute, 2005.

[2] Humphreys, Gary C. *Project Management Using Earned Value*. Orange, CA: Humphreys & Associates, Inc., 2002.

[3] Project Management Institute. *Practice Standard for Earned Value Management*. Upper Darby, PA: Project Management Institute, 2005.

Detailed Planning Guidance

INTRODUCTION

Appendix A introduced the fundamentals of earned value management. It provided enough information to help you understand the planning and performance measurement of a typical project. This appendix supplements Appendix A with additional guidance and templates for establishing work packages. The following topics are discussed:

1. **Detailed Planning of the Project**
2. **Detailed Planning of a Work Package**
3. **Work Products**
4. **Completion Criteria**
5. **Earned Value Methods**
6. **Technical Performance Matrix Worksheet Templates**
7. **Replan for Change in Number of Base Measures**
8. **Rework**
9. **Minimize Number of Work Packages**

DETAILED PLANNING OF THE PROJECT

Work packages are an outcome of developing the detailed plan for a project.

The detailed planning activities follow:

1. **Develop an Integrated Master Schedule (IMS) to include all tasks that require visibility by the Program Manager and other team members and that have interdependencies with other tasks.**

Performance-Based Earned Value, by Paul J. Solomon and Ralph R. Young
Copyright ©2007 IEEE Computer Society.

2. Analyze the critical path to assess risk and ensure successful program execution.
3. Decompose the project work scope into manageable pieces of work called work packages and planning packages.
4. Allocate budget (resources) to each work and planning package.
5. Develop time-phasing of budgets for each work and planning package according to the expected workflow.
6. Do a check for realism in resource loading. Do not be too optimistic regarding the availability of resources.

DETAILED PLANNING OF A WORK PACKAGE

1. Each work package is distinguishable from other work packages by a unique statement of work.
2. Planned start and completion dates are consistent with the IMS activity that it supports.
3. Size and duration are consistent with the nature of the task.
4. A work package is planned to its logical conclusion.
5. Define and quantify the qualities and completion criteria of the work product that is the outcome of the work package. Completion criteria may be stated in terms of product or process quality, functional requirements, and/or other technical performance requirements.
6. Plan rework separately from the basic work effort for better control and analysis.
7. Budgets are normally expressed in labor hours or material dollars, but may be in terms of any resource that is suitable to the PM and the organization's processes.
8. Establish the base measures of earned value by determining the interim work products for which physical accomplishment can be directly measured.
9. The time phased budget of a discrete work package is determined by multiplying its base measures by the budget that was allocated to those measures.
10. Choose an appropriate earned value method for each work package and document the selection.
11. Establish and document objective measures for interim performance measurement.

Additional guidance for detail planning a work package is provided below.

WORK PRODUCTS

Examples of work products were provided in Chapters 4 and 5. Additional examples are provided in Appendix E, Enabling Work Products.

COMPLETION CRITERIA

Sometimes customer approval, quality assurance approval, successful qualification test, or some other form of acceptance by another party is a criterion for completing a work package. If such a criterion exists, retain a reasonable amount of budget for the completion activity and for possible rework, corrective action, and retest.

Examples of completed work products and work packages:

1. **All drawings of the configuration item completed per engineering procedures, signed off, and entered into database as complete.**
2. **Computer software module was unit-tested and peer reviewed and includes all baselined functionality and requirements.**
3. **Technical data package for design of fire detection system completed per engineering procedures and meets all baselined, allocated requirements and technical performance measures (as verified by analyses, simulations, etc.).**
4. **Courseware module complete per engineering procedures and contains all baselined, allocated requirements.**
5. **Test procedure complete and approved and includes all baselined, allocated requirements.**

EARNED VALUE METHODS

A set of generally accepted earned value methods is given in Table B. It includes guidance and examples for each method.

TECHNICAL PERFORMANCE MATRIX WORKSHEET TEMPLATES

To minimize administrative costs, combine related tasks that have small budget values into higher level, discrete work packages instead of setting up individual work packages for each task. Fewer work packages will result in fewer variances to be reviewed by management. A worksheet should be prepared to document the combining of lower level tasks. Examples of this worksheet, called a Technical Performance Matrix, follow.

Prepare a work sheet to record the time-phasing of the base measures of earned value (equivalent units, interim milestones, tasks, events, measurements, or process steps planned to be completed). This is the documented basis for time-phasing the BCWS.

Several templates for preparing Technical Performance Matrix worksheets may be used with the Objective Indicators method to document the development of time-phased BCWS and the objective assessment of % complete for EV.

TABLE B EV Methods

EV Method	Guidance	Example
Milestone (100% at completion)	1. Best to use when start and complete are in the same period. 2. This method fails to indicate if the task did not start on schedule. Consequently, the next method is preferred.	100% at complete
Percent at Start/Percent at Complete	Document percent of budget allocated to start/complete. If duration exceeds 2 periods, the following methods are preferred. They enable interim performance measurement.	25%/75%

Interim Milestones with Objective Indicators	1. Document % of budget allocated to each milestone (MS), (start, interim milestones, completion milestone).
	2. To take partial % complete toward the next milestone, document objective indicators to be used as base measures with % of budget allocated to each measure.
		MS 1 = 20%
		MS 2 = 50%
		MS 3 = 30%
		
		MS 2 has 3 subtasks:
		  Subtask 1: 10%
		  Subtask 2: 80%
		  Subtask 3: 10%

Objective Indicators (sometimes called Percent Complete)	1. If base measures have equal budget value, document number of measurands. 2. If base measures have unequal budget value, document number of measurands and budget allocated to each measurand. 3. May be used to combine many subtasks or events into one work package. Prepare Technical Performance Matrix to document budget allocation. Examples of Technical Performance Matrices follow in the next section.	1. 10 units, equal value 2. Drawing complexity: Complexity 1: 20 drawings at 40 hours each (800). Complexity 2: 40 drawings at 60 hours each (2400). Complexity 3: 10 drawings at 90 hours each (900). Total: 70 drawings with BAC = 4100. 3. Multiple tasks with unequal budget allocation.
Apportioned	Planning and progress are tied to another work package based on the ratio of their respective BACs. Both the time-phased BCWS and the earned value are apportioned with that ratio.	Inspection activity earns proportionally to the inspected activity

TABLE B *Continued*

EV Method	Guidance	Example
Level of Effort	Value is earned solely by the passage of time. There is no tangible work product at the completion of the work package. The planned value for a work period is automatically credited as earned value at the end of the period. There is never a schedule variance.	Support type activity such as project management and customer liaison.

Example B.1: Budget Allocated to Tasks

In this example, there is a series of tasks in the work package. Each task is scheduled and is allocated a percentage of the Budget at Completion (BAC). Table B.1 shows the development of the time-phased BCWS.

Example B.2: BAC Allocated to Similar Work Products and Tasks

In this example, the work package SOW is a set of similar work products (test benches and special test equipment). Each work product is the outcome of the same sequence of operations or tasks. Each work product is scheduled and is allocated a percentage of the BAC. In the Technical Performance Matrix, the budget allocation to each work product is shown in the second column. The allocation of each work product's budget to the sequential tasks is shown in the second row. Table B.2 shows the recording of physical accomplishment and the computation of earned value. A set of linked work sheets can be used to develop and document the time-phased BCWS. In the second work sheet, enter the planned completion date of each task in the cell. In a third work sheet, develop a formula to compute the BCWS for a period based on the tasks that have planned completion dates in the same period.

Example B.3: Drawings of Different Complexities

In this example, the SOW is a set of drawings. The drawings have been assigned to three categories depending on their relative complexity. Drawings with higher complexity receive a higher budget allocation. Table B.3 shows the development of the time-phased BCWS and the earned value (EV) for a set of work products with different complexity.

TABLE B.1 Time-phased BCWS

TASK/EFFORT	BAC	% OF BAC (Add to 100)	BCWS/ Task	Plan Complete	BCWS/ Month
BAC	400				
Document Shell		1	4	Jan.	
Preface		1	4	Jan.	8
Executive Summary		2	8	Feb.	
1.1: General		1	4	Feb.	
1.2: Background		1	4	Feb.	
1.3: Test Item Description		3	12	Feb.	
1.4: Overall Test Objective		1	4	Feb.	
1.5: Constraints & Limitations		1	4	Feb.	
1.6: Test Resources		2	8	Feb.	
1.7: Safety Requirements		1	4	Feb.	
1.8: Security Requirements		1	4	Feb.	
1.9: Test Project Management		1	4	Feb.	
2.x: General Test Objectives		2	8	Feb.	
2.x.x: Specific Test Objectives		4	16	Feb.	
2.x.x.x: Measures of Performance		4	16	Feb.	
2.x.x.x.1: Success Criteria		4	16	Feb.	112
2.x.x.x.2: Evaluation Criteria		4	16	Mar.	
2.x.x.x.3: Final Data Products		4	16	Mar.	
2.x.x.x.4: Data Requirements		4	16	Mar.	
2.x.x.x.5: Algorithms/Processes		5	20	Mar.	
2.x.x.x.6: Test Methodology		6	24	Mar.	
2.x.x.x.7: Expected Results		3	12	Mar.	
3.1: Pretest Briefing		1	4	Mar.	
3.2: Test Execution		1	4	Mar.	
3.3: Posttest Briefing		1	4	Mar.	
3.4: Quick-Look Data Analysis		2	8	Mar.	
4.1: Deficiency Reports		1	4	Mar.	
4.2: Preliminary Report of Results		2	8	Mar.	
4.3: Technical Report		3	12	Mar.	148
5.1: Logistics		3	12	Apr.	
References		2	8	Apr.	
App 1: Test Conditions Matrix		3	12	Apr.	
App 2: Requirements Traceability		3	12	Apr.	
App 3: Parameter List		3	12	Apr.	
App 4: Data Analysis Plan		2	8	Apr.	
App 5: Instrumentation Plan		2	8	Apr.	
App 6: Logistics Support Plan		2	8	Apr.	
App 7: List of Abbreviations, Acronyms & Symbols	2	8	Apr.		
App 8: Distribution List		2	8	Apr.	
Initial Formatting		3	12	Apr.	
Revisions		3	12	Apr.	
Final Formatting		3	12	Apr.	132
WORK PACKAGE TOTAL		100	400		400

TABLE B.2 EV for a Set of Similar Work Products

Task % of BAC	WP % of BAC	Analysis 20%	Requirements, Procure 23%	Design Support 25%	Install 15%	Integrate & Test 15%	Rework 2%	BAC 100%	Earned Value
Work Product (WP)	WP % of BAC								
1553 Patch Panel	10%	120	138	150	90			600	498
Battery Bay	5%	60	69	75	45	45	6	300	300
C&TC 3	5%	60	69	75	45			300	249
Display Bench	15%	135	207	225				900	567
Display Brassboard	10%	120	138	150	90			600	498
Computer Interface	15%	135	207	225	90			900	657
Comms. Simulator	10%	60	138					600	198
Special Display	30%	360	414	450				1800	1224
TOTAL	100%	1054	1380	1350	360	45	6	6000	4191

TABLE B.3 EV for a Set of Work Products with Different Complexity

Drawings			Mar	April	May	BAC
	Complexity	# Drawings				
	1	35	10	15	10	35
	2	25	10	7	8	25
	3	18	8	4	6	18
Total Units		78	28	26	24	78
Budget/Drawing						
40	1					
60	2					
90	3					
BCWS						
Complexity 1			400	600	400	1400
Complexity 2			600	420	480	1500
Complexity 3			720	360	540	1620
Total BCWS			1720	1380	1420	4520
EV						
Units						
Complexity 1			8	4		
Complexity 2			8	4		
Complexity 3			6	3		
Total Units—Current			22	11		
EV						
Complexity 1			320	160		
Complexity 2			480	240		
Complexity 3			540	270		
Current EV			1340	670		
Cumulative (cum.) EV			1340	2010		

REPLAN FOR CHANGE IN NUMBER OF BASE MEASURES

Sometimes the detailed planning of an open (already started) work package must be changed when there is a better understanding of the work or when the number of intermediate or enabling work products changes. When this occurs, both the base measures of earned value and the assessed earned value should be changed in a controlled manner. If the changes are made properly, the reported earned value will reflect the real percent complete and be an accurate indicator of the remaining work. The following example uses drawings. It also applies to the number of requirements or any set of tasks.

Example B.4: Replanning for Growth in Number of Drawings

Background. The original SOW was estimated to be a set of 40 drawings that define the design of an end work product. After the work was 50% complete, the complete work requirements were known. The SOW is now 50 drawings. The functionality and product quality requirements of the end work product are unchanged. There will be no additional budget because this is not a change in the product scope. This is just a better understanding of the tasks and intermediate work products that make up the design.

In April, the number of remaining drawings was changed. Some drawings were decomposed. Now there are 50 drawings. Two more drawings were completed. The revised plan and resulting performance are shown in Table B.4.2.

Note that the cumulative percent complete declined after the replan, from 50 percent in March to 44 percent in April, despite completing two more drawings. We have restated the budget value per each drawing, including completed drawings from 40 hours to 32 hours.

Some managers abhor negative earned value and prefer to hold earned value constant until the completion of future drawings causes

TABLE B.4.1 Original Plan—Growth in Number of Drawings

Drawings	Jan.	Feb.	Mar.	Apr.	May	Total
Planned number of drawings	8	8	4	10	10	40
Budget/Drawing: 40						
Planned % Complete: cumulative (cum.)	20	40	50			
BCWS—current	320	320	160	400	400	1600
BCWS—cum	320	640	800			
Completed drawings—current	8	6	6			20
% Complete—cumulative	20	35	50			50
EV—current	320	240	240			800
EV—cumulative	320	560	800			800

TABLE B.4.2 Revised Plan—Growth in Number of Drawings

Drawings: Revised (Rev.)	Jan.	Feb.	Mar.	Apr.	May	Total
Planned number of drawings	8	8	4	15	15	50
Rev. Budget/Drawing: 32						
Completed drawings—cur.	8	6	6	2		22
Completed drawings—cum.	8	14	20	22		22
Drawings % Complete				44		44
EV—cur.	320	240	240	−96		704
EV—cum.	320	560	800	704		704
EV % complete—cum.	20	35	50	44		

earned value "catch up" to the previously reported percent complete. However, management should not structure earned value information just to "look good." If earned value is valid and is properly analyzed, it discloses the variance from plan and can be used to estimate the final cost at completion. The purpose of taking negative earned value in April is to show the real status and to better understand the magnitude of the remaining work. Had we not taken negative earned value, the cumulative earned value would be misleading and we might underestimate the final cost and the completion date.

Another, agile method for replanning a work package when there is a change in the number of base measures, is proposed by Alistair Cockburn, (first mentional in Chapter 13). Cockburn is an advocate of the burn-down chart to show progress against a plan and be the basis of earned value. However, Cockburn normally encounters projects in which the scope is frequently changing. He cites a situation in which a team was given 130 story points to deliver in three iterations. After each iteration, the customer added new stories and revised the relative sizes of the remaining stories. Both increased the amount of work remaining.

Cockburn wanted to demonstrate how to illustrate actual accomplishments against a changing scope. The burn-down chart in Figure B.1, shows the scope increase and remaining work after each iteration. The chart is from Cockburn's *Crystal Clear*, a book that illuminates the fundamentals of agile development. Cockburn, *Crystal Clear: Human Powered Methodology for Small Teams*, Figure 3.35 p. 104, © 2005 Pearson Addison Wesley. All rights reserved.

The situation portrayed in Figure B.1 may be handled several ways with regard to earned value. If the change in story points is not

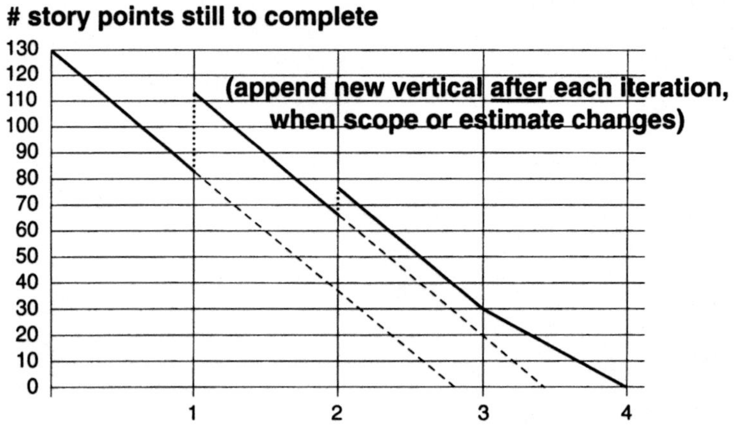

 # story points still to complete

Figure B.1 *Burn-Down* **Chart Showing Scope Increase after Each Iteration.**

considered a change in the customer's requirements (product scope), then it is analogous to Table B.4.2. With no change in the product scope, there is normally no change in the total budget of the work package.

On the other hand, if the additional story points are considered a change in product scope, the customer should be expected to pay more and additional budget should be allocated to the work package. Changes in work scope are discussed in Chapter 10.

There is another approach to handling a growth in the number of base measures when there is no additional budget. That approach is to revise the Performance Measurement Baseline of the remaining work in the work package without making the unpopular negative adjustment to earned value. Note in Figure B.1, the second iteration was an increase in the remaining work from 70 to 75 story points. An approach to replanning the work package is to take the remaining budget (total budget at completion less cumulative earned value) and to divide that by the remaining 75 story points. This would yield a lower budget to be earned for completion of each future story point than was earned for the completed story points.

There are advantages and disadvantages to this approach in terms of the value of management information. The remaining work could still be measured objectively against the revised plan and provide valid earned value for schedule performance analysis. On the other hand, the cumulative cost performance information, and a derived measure such as the cumulative Cost Performance Index (CPI), would no longer be a valid measure of past performance or provide a reliable estimate of the remaining costs. To compensate for the revised budget cost per unit, cost performance analysis and the CPI should be based on the actual costs incurred and earned value since the last iteration of the plan.

To illustrate how to revise the remaining plan while holding the past constant, we have revised the data in Table B.4.2 to show April earned value without revising the past. The 30 remaining drawings have a remaining budget of 800. Therefore, each remaining drawing has a revised budget/drawing of 26.7 (800/30), as compared with the original budget of 40. The result is shown in Table B.4.3.

Please note that the physical work (drawings) is 44 percent complete at the end of April. However, the cumulative EV is 53 percent of the total budget (853.4/1600). For effective and intuitive schedule assessment and variance analysis, the cumulative earned value and the base measures of physical or technical accomplishment should be the same percent complete, as was shown in Table B.4.2.

TABLE B.4.3 Revalue only the Remaining Drawings

Drawings: Revised (Rev.)	Jan.	Feb.	Mar.	Apr.	May	Total
Planned number of drawings	8	8	4	15	15	50
Original Budget/Drawing: 40						1600
Rev. Budget/Drawing: 26.7						
Completed drawings—cur.	8	6	6	2		22
Completed drawings—cum.	8	14	20	22		22
Drawings % complete cum.				44		44
EV—cur.	320	240	240	53.4		853.4
EV—cumulative	320	560	800	853.4		853.4
EV % complete cum.	20	35	50	53		

REWORK

As discussed in Appendix A, rework should be planned separately from the initial development of work products. A separate work package for rework enables improved planning, control, and analysis because:

1. **The initial development of the work product has a distinct, baseline completion date.**
2. **Progress can be tracked toward meeting that date.**
3. **Slips and impacts can be shown on the IMS and in the ETC.**
4. **Variance analyses for the initial development and for rework are based on separate and distinct performance data.**

Two examples if planning rework with discrete earned value techniques follow. In Example B.5, rework was not planned. Negative earned value is taken if a previously completed drawing is now incomplete and must be reworked. In Example B.6, rework is in a separate work package (Preferred Method).

Example B.5: Negative EV If Enabling Work Products Must Be Reworked

Rework was not planned separately. Negative earned value is taken if a previously completed drawing must be reworked. The planning assumptions for this example follow:

1. **50 drawings are planned during January through May.**
2. **Basis of estimate for the budget included an assumption that there would be 10% rework.**
3. **Rework is not specifically planned, scheduled, and tracked.**
4. **Budget value per drawing = 40.**
5. **Total budget = 2000.**
6. **Rework of drawings is planned to begin in April.**
7. **Negative earned value taken when a drawing must be reworked: −40.**

TABLE B.5.1 Planned Rework

Drawings	Jan.	Feb.	Mar.	Apr.	May	Total
Planned number of drawings	8	10	12	10	10	50
BCWS	320	400	480	400	400	2000

TABLE B.5.2 Rework—February Earned Value

Drawings	Jan.	Feb.	Mar.	Apr.	May	Total
Completed drawings	8	10				18
EV	320	400				720

TABLE B.5.3 Rework—March Earned Value

Drawings	Jan.	Feb.	Mar.
Completed drawings	8	10	12 − 2 = 10
EV current	320	400	400
BCWS current	320	400	480
BCWS cum.	320	720	1200
EV cum.	320	720	1120
Schedule variance	0	0	−80

With these ground rules, if a drawing received credit for completion but later requires rework, the organization would decrease EV (negative earned value) until the reworked drawing is completed. The time-phased BCWS for drawings is shown in Table B.5.1.

Assume that work was on schedule through February. February cumulative EV is 720 hours based on 18 drawings completed, as shown in Table B.5.2.

During March, the IPT discovered that two drawings need rework. One had an incorrect interface, and the other required reduced dimensions to fit into the available space. The rework will be completed in June. Twelve drawings were completed in March, as scheduled.

Earned value performance at March month end is shown in Table B.5.3.

Example B.6: Rework Is in a Separate Work Package (Preferred Method)

The same work and budget from above are now in two work packages. The initial drawings now receive 90% of the previous budget, or 36 hours each as shown in Table B.6.1.

TABLE B.6.1 Initial Development in a Separate Work Package

Initial Development of Drawings	Jan.	Feb.	Mar.	Apr.	May	Total
Planned number of drawings	8	10	12	10	10	50
BCWS	288	360	432	360	360	1800

TABLE B.6.2 Rework in a Separate Work Package

Rework of Drawings	Jan.	Feb.	Mar.	Apr.	May	Total
BCWS			60	70	70	200

The rework is anticipated to start in March and complete in May. The planning assumption, based on historical data, is that rework will require a BAC of 200 hours. There is no way to estimate the planned number of drawings to be reworked. However, the time phasing usually begins in the third month. BCWS is planned as shown in Table B.6.2.

Discrete EV for Rework

We recommend that that a discrete earned value technique, not LOE, be used for rework. It is tempting to justify the LOE technique for rework because the number of requirements, drawings, or other work products that require rework cannot be precisely planned. However, there is always a discrete date when rework must be complete. Otherwise, the incomplete work will constrain a subsequent activity.

It is preferable to measure rework discretely based on the planned technical maturity or quality of the work products. For example, at the end of May, a quality target may be defined that the number of drawings in rework is less than 5%, or 2 drawings. At the end of April, the quality target may be that the number of drawing in rework is less than 10%, or 5 drawings. If the number of drawings requiring rework exceeds those percentages, than no earned value may be taken.

The same principle or rule is applicable to the number of requirements that have been met. With this type of ground rule, rework would be discretely planned with earned value measures that indicate the number or percentage of requirements that were met. For example, the milestones during the last three months of rework follow:

1. **Last month: 100% of requirements were met.**
2. **Last month—1 month: 95% of requirements were met.**
3. **Last month—2 months: 85% of requirements were met.**

Example B.7: Rework Is in a Separate Work Package (Part LOE, Part Completion Milestone)

The initial set of drawings is developed in one work package. Each drawing is complete based on the organization's engineering process but without regard to meeting the allocated product requirements. A separate work package is established for planned rework of the drawings until the product requirements are met. The rework work package is part LOE and part completion milestone.

The same work and budget from above are now in two work packages. The initial development of drawings now receives 90% of the previous budget, or 36 hours each, as shown in Table B.7.1.

The rework is anticipated to start in March and complete in May. The planning assumption, based on historical data, is that rework will require a BAC of 200 hours. The actual number of drawings to be reworked, the time phasing of when the deficiencies will be discovered, and the time phasing of completion of rework cannot be estimated with precision. However, the time phasing usually begins in the third month. BCWS is shown in Table B.7.2.

Rework is sometimes considered LOE because the number of requirements, drawings, software modules, or other work products that will be reworked cannot be precisely planned. However, rework cannot be entirely LOE because, as a minimum, there is always a discrete date when rework must be complete without having an adverse impact on subsequent activities. So, the Budgeted Cost for Work Scheduled (BCWS) for rework must be discretely planned, no later than its need date. One approach is to plan rework in two work packages, one LOE and the other discrete, as shown in Table B.7.3.

If rework has not been completed in May, than no earned value can be taken and the work package will be behind schedule. A late completion should be shown on the schedule and estimate to complete (ETC).

TABLE B.7.1 Initial Development in a Separate Work Package

Initial Development of Drawings	Jan.	Feb.	Mar.	Apr.	May	Total
Planned number of drawings	8	10	12	10	10	50
BCWS—cur.	288	360	432	360	360	1800

TABLE B.7.2 Rework Work Package

Rework of Drawings	Jan.	Feb.	Mar.	Apr.	May	Total
BCWS—cur.			60	70	70	200

TABLE B.7.3 Planned Rework in Two Work Packages (Part LOE, Part Discrete)

Rework of Drawings	Mar.	Apr.	May	Total
LOE BCWS—cur.	60	70		130
Completion Milestone BCWS			70	70

The work packages will be complete when there are no drawings to be reworked and all requirements have been met. Additional rework of the drawings may likely occur in the future if testing in a subsequent phase of the engineering life cycle discloses that the drawings no longer meet requirements. This may happen during qualification testing or system acceptance testing. However, rework in those phases is planned and budgeted separately from the rework of the engineering design phase.

Additional guidance and examples for the discrete planning of requirements-based rework are provided in Appendix G, Examples G.2 and G.3. Chapter 13 includes a section on software rework.

MINIMIZE NUMBER OF WORK PACKAGES

For cost-effective (Lean) PBEV, try to minimize the number of work packages. The number of discrete work packages should be limited to only those that are an effective measure of progress toward meeting the project's technical, schedule, or cost objectives. (Additional guidance is provided in Chapter 5).

Determine whether tasks, although measurable, should be Level of Effort (LOE) because they are recurring events such as meetings, reports, reviews, or updates, which normally aren't a measure of technical progress. This will result in a leaner, more cost-effective PMB. (Additional guidance is provided in Chapter 8).

A checklist that may be used to determine whether a work package is truly needed, whether it may be combined with other tasks into a larger discrete, work package, or whether it should be discrete vs. LOE, is provided in Table B.8.

TABLE B.8 Tests for Lean Work Package Planning

Conditions to Determine the Need for a Discrete Work Package (WP) per PBEV Guidelines	Examples of SOW or Work Product	Should normally be discrete. Yes (Y) No (N)	May be combined with other related tasks into one WP. Yes (Y) No (N)	Rationale for PBEV Guidance
The outcome of a WP is a technical work product that constrains the start or completion of another technical WP.	A set of requirements, designs, or test procedures that is needed, as a set, for a downstream task. A trade study that is needed to make a decision.	Y	N	If the completed work product constrains the start or completion of a subsequent, technical WP, analyze significant schedule variances to determine the impact on downstream activities. If this work product were combined with others into one WP, its linkage with a successor activity would be difficult to document.
The outcome of a WP is a set of technical work products. An individual work product that is a component of the end work product may be the input to a subsequent WP before completion of the set but is not, in itself, a constraint. The same is true for a task or subtask that is performed to produce the work product.	An individual requirement, design, or test procedure within the WP that is an input to a downstream task but is, in itself, not a constraint. A set of tasks that result in an individual requirement, design, or test procedure.	Y	Y	If an individual work product is not a constraint to a downstream task, there is no need to monitor its progress at the WP level. It may be combined with other similar work products in a WP. Only the work package completion must be linked with a successor activity. A Technical Performance Matrix should be used to plan and monitor the progress of the individual work product and the tasks and subtasks that are performed to produce the work product. This matrix is the source of planning and performance information for the WP.

TABLE B.8 *Continued*

Conditions to Determine the Need for a Discrete Work Package (WP) per PBEV Guidelines	Examples of SOW or Work Product	Should normally be discrete. Yes (Y) No (N)	May be combined with other related tasks into one WP. Yes (Y) No (N)	Rationale for PBEV Guidance
The outcome of a WP is a scheduled process improvement that is required to meet a project cost or schedule objective.	A process improvement that must be implemented to achieve planned cost performance efficiencies or schedule performance rates. The process improvement may include improved labor processes and/or the implementation of productivity improvement tools.	Y	N	If a corrective action plan for a cost or schedule variance states that a process improvement will be implemented to improve future cost efficiency and/or schedule performance, the corrective action plan should include the implementation date of the new process. Although the tasks that lead to the process improvement do not indicate progress toward meeting the project's technical objectives, failure to implement the corrective action plan on time will adversely affect planned cost and/or schedule objectives. Consequently, the corrective action plan is important to the PM. The plan to implement that process should be budgeted, scheduled, and measured with discrete earned value.

TABLE B.8 *Continued*

	N	Y
The outcome of a WP is a recurring work product that does not constrain the start or completion of another, recurring WP (other than the next recurring WP). Both the completion of the work product and the tasks that are performed to produce the work product are planned, scheduled, and measurable.	A recurring status report, database update, or documentation of a recurring meeting.	A recurring work product, although scheduled, rarely constrains another task (other than the next recurring task to produce the next period's work product). Consequently, there is no significant schedule impact to downstream tasks. Schedule variances normally are corrected in the near future, either by completing the work product or by management's decision that the work product for that period is no longer needed or that it will be combined with that of the following period. EVM is not cost justified for control because deviations from the plan have no significant impact on downstream tasks and on the completion of the end system product. Consequently, the measurement of performance is impracticable.
The outcome of a WP is a nonrecurring work product that does not constrain the start or completion of another, nonrecurring WP.	Documentation to report that a technical review was performed or that a technical meeting was completed Examples include preliminary	The occurrence of a technical review or meeting provides no information regarding the technical maturity of the evolving product. Normally, the purpose of the meeting is to assess technical maturity, to approve the technical work products such as requirements, designs, test plans, test

TABLE B.8 *Continued*

Conditions to Determine the Need for a Discrete Work Package (WP) per PBEV Guidelines	Examples of SOW or Work Product	Should normally be discrete. Yes (Y) No (N)	May be combined with other related tasks into one WP. Yes (Y) No (N)	Rationale for PBEV Guidance
Both the completion of the work product and the tasks that are performed to produce the work product are planned, scheduled, and measurable.	design reviews, detailed or critical design reviews, and technical interchange meetings.			results, or trade study recommendations. Some reviews or meetings are held to review variances from the plans and corrective actions. In any case, the important outcomes of these meetings and reviews, with regard to measuring technical progress, are the approvals of the completed work products or the agreements that they meet the product quality requirements. Although a review or meeting may be completed on schedule, the outcomes of the meeting may be that work products are not approved or that the planned technical maturity has not been achieved. These are the important measurements for earned value. Conversely, the schedule status of the review or meeting itself is less relevant and need not be discretely measured for PBEV. In this case, the discrete measurement of performance is impractical. LOE is recommended.
Work scope is of a general or supportive nature for which measurement of performance is impossible or impractical.	Program management, administrative support, and database administration.	N	Y	Multiple LOE tasks within a control account may be combined into one work package. Supporting detail regarding the development of the time phased budget at the task level should be maintained.

Appendix C

American National Standards Institute (ANSI)/Electronics Industries Alliance (EIA) Standard-748, Earned Value Management Systems (EVMS) Guidelines

The Guidelines in this Appendix are excerpts from "Earned Value Management Systems" (ANSI/EIA 748A), Copyright ©1998, reaffirmed 2002, Government Electronics and Information Technology Association, a Sector of the Electronic Industries Alliance. All Rights Reserved. Reprinted with Permission.

Additional information for interpretation and implementation of EVMS is provided in the Reference section of this appendix.

GUIDELINES BY MAJOR CATEGORY

Organization

> **Guideline 1. Define the authorized work elements for the program. A work breakdown structure (WBS), tailored for effective internal management control, is commonly used in this process.**

> **Guideline 2. Identify the program organizational structure including the major subcontractors responsible for accomplishing the authorized work, and define the organizational elements in which work will be planned and controlled.**

Performance-Based Earned Value, by Paul J. Solomon and Ralph R. Young
Copyright ©2007 IEEE Computer Society.

Guideline 3. Provide for the integration of the company's planning, scheduling, budgeting, work authorization and cost accumulation processes with each other, and, as appropriate, the program WBS and the program organizational structure.

Guideline 4. Identify the company organization or function responsible for controlling overhead (indirect costs).

Guideline 5. Provide for integration of the program WBS and the program organizational structure in a manner that permits cost and schedule performance measurement by elements of either or both structures as needed.

Guideline 6. Schedule the authorized work in a manner that describes the sequence of work and identifies significant task interdependencies required to meet the requirements of the program.

Planning, Scheduling, and Budgeting

Guideline 7. Identify physical products, milestones, technical performance goals or other indicators that will be used to measure progress.

Guideline 8. Establish and maintain a time-phased budget baseline, at the control account level, against which program performance can be measured. Budget for far-term efforts may be held in higher-level accounts until a planning package appropriate time for allocation at the control account level. Initial budgets established for performance measurement will be based on either internal management goals or the external customer negotiated target cost including estimates for authorized but undefinitized work. On government contracts, if an over-target baseline is used for performance measurement reporting purposes, prior notification must be provided to the customer.

Guideline 9. Establish budgets for authorized work with identification of significant cost elements (labor, material, etc.) as needed for internal management and for control of subcontractors.

Guideline 10. To the extent it is practical to identify the authorized work in discrete work packages, establish budgets for this work in terms of dollars, hours or other measurable units. Where the entire control account is not subdivided into work packages, identify the far-term effort in larger planning packages for budget and scheduling purposes.

Guideline 11. Provide that the sum of all work package budgets plus planning package budgets within a control account equals the control account budget.

Guideline 12. Identify and control level of effort activity by time-phased budgets established for this purpose. Only that effort which is unmeasurable or for which measurement is impractical may be classified as level of effort.

Guideline 13. Establish overhead budgets for each significant organizational component of the company for expenses that will become indirect costs. Reflect in the program budgets, at the appropriate level, the amounts in overhead pools that are planned to be allocated to the program as indirect costs.

Guideline 14. Identify management reserves (MR) and undistributed budget (UB).

Guideline 15. Provide that the program target cost goal is reconciled with the sum of all internal program budgets and MRs.

Accounting Considerations

Guideline 16. Record direct costs in a manner consistent with the budgets in a formal system controlled by the general books of account.

Guideline 17. Summarize direct costs from control accounts into the WBS without allocation of a single control account to two or more WBS elements.

Guideline 18. Summarize direct costs from the control accounts into the contractor's organizational elements without allocation of a single control account to two or more organizational elements.

Guideline 19. Record all indirect costs which will be allocated to the contract.

Guideline 20. Identify unit costs, equivalent units cost, or lot costs when needed.

Guideline 21. For EVMS, the material accounting system will provide for:

(1) Accurate cost accumulation and assignment of costs to control account in a manner consistent with the budgets using recognized, acceptable, costing techniques.

(2) Cost performance measurement at the point in time most suitable for the category of material involved, but no earlier than the time of progress payments or actual receipt of material.

(3) Full accountability of all material purchased for the program including the residual inventory.

Analysis and Management Reports

Guideline 22. At least on a monthly basis, generate the following information at the control account and other levels as necessary for management control using actual cost data from, or reconcilable with, the accounting system:

(1) Comparison of the amount of planned budget and the amount of budget earned for work accomplished. This comparison provides the schedule variance (SV).

(2) Comparison of the amount of the budget earned with the actual (applied where appropriate) direct costs for the same work. This comparison provides the CV.

Guideline 23. Identify, at least monthly, the significant differences between both planned and actual schedule performance and planned and actual cost performance, and provide the reasons for the variances in the detail needed by program management.

Guideline 24. Identify budgeted and applied (or actual) indirect costs at the level and frequency needed by management for effective control, along with the reasons for any significant variances.

Guideline 25. Summarize the data elements and associated variances through the program organization and/or WBS to support management needs and any customer reporting specified in the contract.

Guideline 26. Implement managerial actions taken as the result of earned value information.

Guideline 27. Develop revised estimates of cost at completion (EAC) based on performance to date, commitment values for material, and estimates of future conditions. Compare this information with the Performance Measurement Baseline (PMB) to identify variances at completion important to company management and any applicable customer reporting requirements including statements of funding requirements.

Revisions and Data Maintenance

Guideline 28. Incorporate authorized changes in a timely manner, recording the effects of such changes in budgets and schedules. In the directed effort prior to negotiation of a change, base such revisions on the amount estimated and budgeted to the program organizations.

Guideline 29. Reconcile current budgets to prior budgets in terms of changes to the authorized work and internal replanning in the detail needed by management for effective control.

Guideline 30. Control retroactive changes to records pertaining to work performed that would change previously reported amounts for actual costs, earned value, or budgets. Adjustments should be made only for correction of errors, routine accounting adjustments, effects of customer or management directed changes, or to improve the baseline integrity and accuracy of performance measurement data.

Guideline 31. Prevent revisions to the program budget except for authorized changes.

Guideline 32. Document changes to the PMB.

REFERENCES

U.S. Department of Defense (DoD) Earned Value Management Implementation Guide. April 7, 2005. See https://acc.dau.mil/CommunityBrowser.aspx?id=19557. This document provides guidance to be used during the implementation and surveillance of Earned Value Management Systems (EVMS) established in compliance with DoD Guidelines.

National Defense Industrial Association (NDIA) Program Management Systems Committee (PMSC) *ANSI/EIA-748-A Standard for Earned Value*

Management Systems Application Guide, Working Release for User Comment. Arlington, VA, 2005. This guide defines a standard approach to applying Earned Value Management (EVM) that ensures a common understanding of expectations and encourages efficiencies through the use of uniform guidance for all parties implementing ANSI/EIA 748, Earned Value Management Systems (EIA-748).

NDIA PMSC ANSI/EIA-748 Standard for Earned Value Managment Systems Intent Guide. January 2005. This guide was created by the National Defense Industrial Association—Program Management System Committee to promote a clearer understanding of the ANSI/EIA-748A. For each of the 32 earned value management guidelines this Guide provides: the value to management, an intent statement, typical attributes, and examples of objective evidence. Excerpts from the *NDIA PMSC ANSI/EIA-748-A Intent Guide* are included in Appendix C-1.

Excepts from NDIA PMSC ANSI/EIA-748-A Standard for Earned Value Management Systems Intent Guïde

National Defense Industrial Association
2111 Wilson Blvd., Suite 400
Arlington, VA 22201
(703) 522-1820
Fax: (703) 522-1885
www.ndia.org

Guideline 1. Define the authorized work elements for the program. A work breakdown structure (WBS), tailored for effective internal management control, is commonly used in this process.

Intent Guideline 1
A WBS is a direct representation of the work scope in the project, documenting the hierarchy and description of the tasks to be

---

Performance-Based Earned Value, by Paul J. Solomon and Ralph R. Young
Copyright ©2007 IEEE Computer Society.

performed and relationship to the product deliverables. The WBS breaks down all authorized work scope into appropriate elements for planning, budgeting, scheduling, cost accounting, work authorization, measuring progress, and management control. The WBS must be extended to the level necessary for management action and control based on the complexity of the work. Each item in the WBS is assigned a unique identifier. These identifiers can provide a structure for a hierarchical summation of costs and resources. A WBS dictionary defines the work scope for each element in the WBS.

Typical Attributes:

- Only one WBS is used per project and it contains all project work including revisions for authorized changes and modifications.
- WBS contains all contract line items and end items.
- WBS identifies all WBS elements specified for external reporting.
- WBS is extended at a minimum to the control account level.
- WBS elements include a complete definition of work scope requirements.
- WBS will evolve as the project requirements change.

Guideline 6. Schedule the authorized work in a manner that describes the sequence of work and identifies significant task interdependencies required to meet the requirements of the program.

Intent Guideline 6

The scheduling process documents and the resulting project schedule provides a logical sequence of work leading to a milestone, event, and/or decision point, to ensure that the schedule supports the project objectives. There is a clear definition of what constitutes commencement and completion of a task. The schedule describes the sequence of discrete authorized work and their significant task interdependencies. Government development programs typically schedule the discrete authorized work through the use of a network. Production programs typically schedule using an MRP or ERP tool employing a line of balance schedule that supports the project objectives.

The master schedule must agree with the project objectives, include all key events, and reflect a logical sequence of events. It is essential for monitoring progress, analyzing variances, and tracking corrective actions to ensure that all team members are working to the same project schedule.

Schedules add a timeline to the project plan to accomplish the technical scope, allow managers to evaluate actual progress against the established baseline, and to forecast completion dates for remaining work. No specific scheduling software is required, but there must be horizontal and vertical integration through the framework of the WBS and OBS.

Typical Attributes:
An integrated network scheduling system has the following characteristics:

- The schedule reflects all the time phased discrete work to be accomplished that is traceable to the WBS and the statement of work.
- Critical target dates, project milestones, contractual events, accomplishment criteria, and project decision points are identified and are being used to plan, status, and monitor progress of the work.
- The schedule describes the sequence of work through use of the significant interdependencies that are indicative of the actual way the work is accomplished and link key detail tasks with summary activities and milestones.
- Task durations and estimates are meaningful and are relatively short (short duration tasks are preferred and should be reflective of the ability to manage).
- Longer tasks need objective interim measures to enable accurate performance assessments.
- Resource estimates from the budget plan are reasonable and are available to support the schedule.
- The baseline schedule is the basis for measuring performance.
- The schedule provides current status and forecasts of completion dates for all discrete authorized work.
- The schedule network relationships can support the development of a critical path for development projects.

Guideline 7. Identify physical products, milestones, technical performance goals or other indicators that will be used to measure progress.

Intent Guideline 7
Identify objective interim measures within tasks to enable accurate performance assessment each month. The master schedule includes key program and contractual requirements. It enables the team to predict when milestones, events, and program decision points can be expected to occur. In a development environment, lower tier schedules must contain specific task start and finish dates that are based on physical accomplishment and are clearly integrated with program time constraints. These tasks will align with the objective interim measures within long work packages to enable accurate performance assessment. A sufficient number of interim measures will be defined after the detailed schedule is established to ensure performance is measured as accurately as possible. Interim measures will be based

on the completion criteria developed for each increment of work to provide a basis for objectivity, limiting the subjectivity of work accomplished. Accurate schedule status depends on the selection of objective measures of progress to indicate work completion. These measures are necessary to substantiate technical achievement against the schedule plan and justify progression to the next task. A key feature of an interdependent schedule is that it establishes and maintains the relationship between technical achievement and progress statusing.

Typical Attributes:
- Objective completion criteria are determined in advance and used to measure progress to determine achievement of milestones or other indicators.
- Interim milestones and lower tier tasks serve as indicators of progress against which progress is monitored by the control account manager.

Guideline 8. Establish and maintain a time-phased budget baseline, at the control account level, against which program performance can be measured. Budget for far-term efforts may be held in higher-level accounts until a planning package appropriate time for allocation at the control account level. Initial budgets established for performance measurement will be based on either internal management goals or the external customer negotiated target cost including estimates for authorized but undefinitized work. On government contracts, if an over-target baseline is used for performance measurement reporting purposes, prior notification must be provided to the customer.

Intent Guideline 8
The assignment of budgets to scheduled segments of work produces a plan against which actual performance can be compared. This is called the performance measurement baseline (PMB) [. . . .] The PMB is a vehicle for comparison of work accomplished with work scheduled, and actual cost with value of work performed.

Typical Attributes:
- PMB reflects the work scope, time phased consistent with the integrated schedule.
- PMB reflects the budget value for the work scope in control accounts and higher level summary planning accounts.

Guideline 10. To the extent it is practical to identify the authorized work in discrete work packages, establish budgets for this work in terms

of dollars, hours or other measurable units. Where the entire control account is not subdivided into work packages, identify the far-term effort in larger planning packages for budget and scheduling purposes.

Intent Guideline 10
Effort contained within a control account is distributed into either work packages or planning packages. Work packages are single tasks assigned to a performing organization for completion, and should be natural subdivisions of control account effort resulting in a definable end product or event. Work package descriptions must clearly distinguish one work package effort from another. A key feature from the standpoint of evaluating accomplishment is the desirability of having work packages that incorporate frequent, objective indicators of progress. When work packages are relatively short, little or no assessment of work-in-progress is required. As work package length increases, work-in-process measurement becomes more subjective, unless objective techniques, such as discrete milestones with preassigned budget values or completion percentages, subdivide them.

Each work package will have the following characteristics:

- It represents units of work at the level where work is performed.
- It is clearly distinguishable from all other work packages.
- It is assigned to a single organizational element, or in an integrated product team environment, there could be a single integrated product team responsible with multiple functional disciplines performing the scope of work.
- It has scheduled start and completion dates and, as applicable, interim milestones, all of which are representative of physical accomplishment.
- It has a budget or assigned value expressed in terms of dollars, labor hours, or measurable units.
- Its duration is limited to a relatively short span of time. Longer tasks need objective interim measures to enable accurate performance assessments, or it is level of effort (LOE).
- It is integrated with detailed engineering, manufacturing, or other schedules.

Work for a given control account that cannot be planned in detail at the outset, will be divided into larger segments and placed into planning packages within the control account. Planning packages are aggregates of future tasks and budgets, beyond the detail plan, that will be divided into work packages at the earliest practical point in time. Time phased budgets assigned to planning packages must be supported by a specified scope of work and this relationship must be maintained when detailed planning of the effort occurs.

Typical Attributes:

- Control account plans (CAPs) represent the work assigned to one responsible organizational element on one program WBS element. This is the lowest level in the structure at which the comparison of actual costs to planned budgets and earned value are required. It is also the cost collection point that identifies the cost elements and factors contributing to cost and/or schedule variances.
- Work packages represent detailed jobs, or material items. They are units of work at levels where work is performed and are clearly distinguishable from all other work packages. They are assigned to a single organizational element; have scheduled start and completion dates and, as applicable, interim milestones; have a budget or assigned value expressed in terms of dollars, labor hours, or other measurable units; duration is limited to a relatively short span of time, or it is subdivided by discrete value milestones to facilitate the objective measurement techniques of work performed, or it is LOE; and is integrated with detailed engineering, manufacturing, or other schedules.
- A planning package is the logical aggregation of work within a control account, normally the far-term effort, that can be identified and budgeted in early baseline planning, but can not yet be defined into discrete, apportioned, or level of effort work packages. Planning package plans must reflect the manner in which the work is to be performed.

Guideline 12. Identify and control level of effort activity by time-phased budgets established for this purpose. Only that effort which is unmeasurable or for which measurement is impractical may be classified as level of effort.

Intent Guideline 12

Each task on the project needs to be assessed using the best method to budget and measure its progress toward completion. Level of effort is defined as having no measurable output or product at the work package level. Level of effort must be limited to those activities that are unable to be measured discretely to avoid distorting project performance data. Level of effort work packages should be separately identified from discrete effort work packages and apportioned effort work packages. Budgets for level of effort activity must have a sound basis of estimate and be time phased to properly reflect when work will be accomplished.

Typical Attributes

Level of effort work packages contain tasks of a general or supportive nature which do not produce definite end products, must be separately evaluated from discrete work packages within the control account, and contain time-phased budgets for planning and control.

- The amount of LOE activity will vary among performing organizations, but it must be held to the lowest practical level.
- Level of effort budgets should be separately substantiated and planned as direct labor, material/subcontract, or other direct costs. Level of effort should be budgeted on a time-phased basis for control and reporting purposes.
- When level of effort and discrete work packages are mixed within the same control account, the control account manager must ensure visibility into the earned value technique for measuring performance of the discrete effort.
- The earned value for level of effort work packages equals the time-phased budget.

Guideline 14. Identify management reserves (MR) and undistributed budget (UB).

Intent Guideline 14

Identify and control management reserve (MR) and undistributed budget. Management reserve is budget for work scope that will arise during the course of the project, but cannot be identified in advance. Because management reserve is budget that is not as yet tied to work, it does not form part of the performance measurement baseline. The management reserve budget should be commensurate with the level of risks identified by the project and/or withheld for management control purposes.

Guideline 27. Develop revised estimates of cost at completion (EAC) based on performance to date, commitment values for material, and estimates of future conditions. Compare this information with the Performance Measurement Baseline (PMB) to identify variances at completion important to company management and any applicable customer reporting requirements including statements of funding requirements.

Intent Guideline 27

On a monthly basis, the control account manager should review the status of the expended effort and the achievability of the forecast and significant changes briefed to program management. A comprehensive EAC is accomplished on a periodic basis using all available information to arrive at the best possible estimate at completion. This is done by:

    a. Evaluating performance to date efficiency achieved by performing organizations for completed work and comparing it to remaining budgets;

b. Assessing commitment values for material to complete the remaining work;

c. Estimating future conditions to derive the most accurate estimate at completion.

Comparisons of this estimate to budgets for the associated effort must be made frequently enough for management to ensure project performance and resource availability will not be adversely impacted. Prudent maintenance of the control account level EAC by the control account manager ensures that the EAC reflects a valid projection of project costs.

Typical Attributes:

- Timely and comprehensive assessments of the effort required for completing all work packages and planning packages in the control account plan.
- Control account manager updates the EAC to reflect changes in budget and/or integrated master schedule when there is material significance.
- Time-phased ETC based on an analysis of remaining tasks in the integrated master schedule and projected resource plan.
- Control account manager should generate the EAC at the work package and planning package level and then sort and summarize by WBS and OBS to the control account level.
- Contract performance report totals for the EAC should reconcile with the corresponding time-phased resource plan.
- EACs should consider all emerging risks and opportunities within the project's risk register (or other similar database) which will impact the integrated master schedule and resource plan for the remainder of the work.
- EAC results are communicated to the customer in internal reports and in funding documents.

[Federal Register: July 5, 2006 (Volume 71, Number 128)]
[Rules and Regulations]

DEPARTMENT OF DEFENSE

GENERAL SERVICES ADMINISTRATION

NATIONAL AERONAUTICS AND SPACE ADMINISTRATION

48 CFR Parts 2, 7, 34, and 52

ACTION: Final rule.

SUMMARY: The Civilian Agency Acquisition Council and the Defense Acquisition Regulations Council (Councils) have agreed on a final rule amending the Federal Acquisition Regulation (FAR) to implement earned value management system (EVMS) policy. FAR coverage is necessary to help standardize the use of EVMS across the Government. The final rule specifically impacts contracting officers, program managers, and offerors/contractors required to manage contracts by utilizing earned value management systems for major acquisitions.

DATES: Effective Date: July 5, 2006.

PART 2—DEFINITIONS OF WORDS AND TERMS

2. Amend section 2.101 in paragraph (b) by adding, in alphabetical order, the definition "Earned value management system" to read as follows:

2.101 Definitions.

(b) Earned value management system means a project management tool that effectively integrates the project scope of work with cost, schedule and performance elements for optimum project planning and control. The qualities and operating characteristics of an earned value management system are described in American National Standards Institute/ Electronics Industries Alliance (ANSI/EIA) Standard-748, *Earned Value Management Systems* (see OMB Circular A-11, Part 7).

PART 7—ACQUISITION PLANS

3. Amend section 7.105 by revising paragraph (b)(3) and amending paragraph (b)(10) by adding two sentences to read as follows:

7.105 Contents of written acquisition plans.

(b) (3) Source-selection procedures. Discuss the source-selection procedures for the acquisition, including the timing for submission and evaluation of proposals, and the relationship of evaluation factors to the attainment of the acquisition objectives (see Subpart 15.3). When an EVMS is required (see FAR 34.202(a)) and a pre-award IBR is contemplated, the acquisition plan must discuss—

　　(i)　How the pre-award IBR will be considered in the source selection decision;

　　(ii)　How it will be conducted in the source selection process (see FAR 15.306); and

　　(iii)　Whether offerors will be directly compensated for the costs of participating in a pre-award IBR.

(10) If an Earned Value Management System is to be used, discuss the methodology the Government will employ to analyze and use the earned value data to assess and monitor contract performance. In addition, discuss how the offeror's/contractor's EVMS will be verified for compliance with the American National Standards Institute/ Electronics Industries Alliance (ANSI/EIA) Standard-748, Earned Value Management Systems, and the timing and conduct of integrated baseline reviews (whether prior to or post award). (See 34.202.)

PART 34—MAJOR SYSTEM ACQUISITION

4. Revise section 34.000 to read as follows:

34.000 Scope of part.

This part describes acquisition policies and procedures for use in acquiring major systems consistent with OMB Circular No. A-109; and the use of an Earned Value Management System in acquisitions designated as major acquisitions consistent with OMB Circular A-11, Part 7.

5. Amend section 34.005-2 by adding paragraph (b)(6) to read as follows:

34.005-2 Mission-oriented solicitation.

(b) (6) Require the use of an Earned Value Management System that complies with the guidelines of ANSI/EIA Standard-748 (current version at time of solicitation). See 34.201 for earned value management systems and reporting requirements.

6. Add subpart 34.2 to read as follows:

Subpart 34.2—Earned Value Management System

Sec.
34.201 Policy.
34.202 Integrated Baseline Reviews.
34.203 Solicitation provisions and contract clause.

34.201 Policy.

(a) An Earned Value Management System (EVMS) is required for major acquisitions for development, in accordance with OMB Circular A-11. The Government may also require an EVMS for other acquisitions, in accordance with agency procedures.

[[Page 38246]]

(b) If the offeror proposes to use a system that has not been determined to be in compliance with the American National Standards Institute/Electronics Industries Alliance (ANSI/EIA) Standard-748, Earned Value Management Systems, the offeror shall submit a comprehensive plan for compliance with these EVMS standards. Offerors shall not be eliminated from consideration for contract award because they do not have an EVMS that complies with these standards.

(c) As a minimum, contracting officers shall require contractors to submit EVMS monthly reports for those contracts for which an EVMS applies.

(d) EVMS requirements will be applied to subcontractors using the same rules as applied to the prime contractor.

(e) When an offeror is required to provide an EVMS plan as part of its proposal, the contracting officer will determine the adequacy of the proposed EVMS plan prior to contract award.

34.202 Integrated Baseline Reviews.

(a) When an EVMS is required, the Government will conduct an Integrated Baseline Review (IBR).

(b) The purpose of the IBR is to verify the technical content and the realism of the related performance budgets, resources, and schedules. It should provide a mutual understanding of the inherent risks in offerors'/contractors' performance plans and the underlying management control systems, and it should formulate a plan to handle these risks.

(c) The IBR is a joint assessment by the offeror or contractor, and the Government, of the—

    (1) Ability of the project's technical plan to achieve the objectives of the scope of work;

    (2) Adequacy of the time allocated for performing the defined tasks to successfully achieve the project schedule objectives;

    (3) Ability of the Performance Measurement Baseline (PMB) to successfully execute the project and attain cost objectives, recognizing the relationship between budget resources, funding, schedule, and scope of work;

    (4) Availability of personnel, facilities, and equipment when required, to perform the defined tasks needed to execute the program successfully; and

    (5) The degree to which the management process provides effective and integrated technical/schedule/cost planning and baseline control.

(d) The timing and conduct of the IBR shall be in accordance with agency procedures. If a pre-award IBR will be conducted, the solicitation must include the procedures for conducting the IBR and address whether offerors will be reimbursed for the associated costs. If permitted, reimbursement of offerors' pre-award IBR costs is governed by the provisions of FAR Part 31.

34.203 Solicitation provisions and contract clause.

(a) The contracting officer shall insert a provision that is substantially the same as the provision at FAR 52.234-2, Notice of Earned

Value Management System—Pre-Award IBR, in solicitations for contracts that require the contractor to use an Earned Value Management System (EVMS) and for which the Government requires an Integrated Baseline Review (IBR) prior to award.

(b) The contracting officer shall insert a provision that is substantially the same as the provision at 52.234-3, Notice of Earned Value Management System—Post Award IBR, in solicitations for contracts that require the contractor to use an Earned Value Management System (EVMS) and for which the Government requires an Integrated Baseline Review (IBR) after contract award.

(c) The contracting officer shall insert a clause that is substantially the same as the clause at FAR 52.234-4, Earned Value Management System, in solicitations and contracts that require a contractor to use an EVMS.

PART 52—SOLICITATION PROVISIONS AND CONTRACT CLAUSES

7. Add sections 52.234-2, 52.234-3, and 52.234-4 to read as follows:

52.234-2 Notice of Earned Value Management System—Pre-Award IBR.

As prescribed in 34.203(a) use the following provision:

NOTICE OF EARNED VALUE MANAGEMENT SYSTEM— PRE-AWARD IBR (JUl 2006)

(a) The offeror shall provide documentation that the Cognizant Federal Agency has determined that the proposed earned value management system (EVMS) complies with the EVMS guidelines in ANSI/EIA Standard-748 (current version at time of solicitation).

(b) If the offeror proposes to use a system that has not been determined to be in compliance with the requirements of paragraph (a) of this provision, the offeror shall submit a comprehensive plan for compliance with the EVMS guidelines.

(1) The plan shall—
    (i) Describe the EVMS the offeror intends to use in performance of the contracts;
    (ii) Distinguish between the offeror's existing management system and modifications proposed to meet the guidelines;
    (iii) Describe the management system and its application in terms of the EVMS guidelines;
    (iv) Describe the proposed procedure for administration of the guidelines, as applied to subcontractors; and

   (v) Provide documentation describing the process and results of any third-party or self-evaluation of the system's compliance with the EVMS guidelines.

  (2) The offeror shall provide information and assistance as required by the Contracting Officer to support review of the plan.

  (3) The Government will review and approve the offeror's plan for an EVMS before contract award.

  (4) The offeror's EVMS plan must provide milestones that indicate when the offeror anticipates that the EVM system will be compliant with the ANSI/EIA Standard—748 guidelines.

(c) Offerors shall identify the major subcontractors, or major subcontracted effort if major subcontractors have not been selected subject to the guidelines. The prime Contractor and the Government shall agree to subcontractors selected for application of the EVMS guidelines.

(d) The Government will conduct an Integrated Baseline Review (IBR), as designated by the agency, prior to contract award. The objective of the IBR is for the Government and the Contractor to jointly assess technical areas, such as the Contractor's planning, to ensure complete coverage of the contract requirements, logical scheduling of the work activities, adequate resources, methodologies for earned value (budgeted cost for work performed (BCWP)), and identification of inherent risks.

(End of provision)

52.234-3 Notice of Earned Value Management System—Post Award IBR.

As prescribed in 34.203(b) use the following provision:
  NOTICE OF EARNED VALUE MANAGEMENT SYSTEM - POST AWARD IBR (JUL 2006)

(a) The offeror shall provide documentation that the Cognizant Federal Agency has determined that the proposed earned value management system (EVMS) complies with the EVMS guidelines in ANSI/EIA Standard - 748 (current version at time of solicitation).

(b) If the offeror proposes to use a system that has not been determined to be in compliance with the requirements of paragraph (a) of this provision, the

[[Page 38247]]

offeror shall submit a comprehensive plan for compliance with the EVMS guidelines.

(1) The plan shall—

    (i) Describe the EVMS the offeror intends to use in performance of the contracts;

    (ii) Distinguish between the offeror's existing management system and modifications proposed to meet the guidelines;

    (iii) Describe the management system and its application in terms of the EVMS guidelines;

    (iv) Describe the proposed procedure for administration of the guidelines, as applied to subcontractors; and

    (v) Provide documentation describing the process and results of any third-party or self-evaluation of the system's compliance with the EVMS guidelines.

(2) The offeror shall provide information and assistance as required by the Contracting Officer to support review of the plan.

(3) The Government will review and approve the offeror's plan for an EVMS before contract award.

(4) The offeror's EVMS plan must provide milestones that indicate when the offeror anticipates that the EVM system will be compliant with the ANSI/EIA Standard -748 guidelines.

(c) Offerors shall identify the major subcontractors, or major subcontracted effort if major subcontractors have not been selected, planned for application of the guidelines. The prime Contractor and the Government shall agree to subcontractors selected for application of the EVMS guidelines.

(End of provision)

52.234-4 Earned Value Management System.

As prescribed in 34.203(c), insert the following clause:

EARNED VALUE MANAGEMENT SYSTEM (JUL 2006)

(a) The Contractor shall use an earned value management system (EVMS) that has been determined by the Cognizant Federal Agency (CFA) to be compliant with the guidelines in ANSI/EIA Standard—748 (current version at the time of award) to manage this contract. If the Contractor's current EVMS has not been determined compliant at the time of award, see paragraph (b) of this clause. The Contractor shall submit reports in accordance with the requirements of this contract.

(b) If, at the time of award, the Contractor's EVM System has not been determined by the CFA as complying with EVMS guidelines or the Contractor does not have an existing cost/schedule control system that is compliant with the guidelines in ANSI/EIA Standard-748 (current version at time of award), the Contractor shall—

(1) Apply the current system to the contract; and

(2) Take necessary actions to meet the milestones in the Contractor's EVMS plan approved by the Contracting Officer.

(c) The Government will conduct an Integrated Baseline Review (IBR). If a pre-award IBR has not been conducted, a post award IBR shall be conducted as early as practicable after contract award.

(d) The Contracting Officer may require an IBR at—

(1) Exercise of significant options; or

(2) Incorporation of major modifications.

(e) Unless a waiver is granted by the CFA, Contractor proposed EVMS changes require approval of the CFA prior to implementation. The CFA will advise the Contractor of the acceptability of such changes within 30 calendar days after receipt of the notice of proposed changes from the Contractor. If the advance approval requirements are waived by the CFA, the Contractor shall disclose EVMS changes to the CFA at least 14 calendar days prior to the effective date of implementation.

(f) The Contractor shall provide access to all pertinent records and data requested by the Contracting Officer or a duly authorized representative as necessary to permit Government surveillance to ensure that the EVMS conforms, and continues to conform, with the performance criteria referenced in paragraph (a) of this clause.

(g) The Contractor shall require the subcontractors specified below to comply with the requirements of this clause: [Insert list of applicable subcontractor

----

(End of clause)

Appendix E

Enabling Work Products

Examples of work products were given in Chapters 4 and 5. A representative sample of typical work products, by CMMI Process Area, follows in Table E.1. When decomposing the work into discrete work packages, we recommend that the work products be similar to those shown in this book. You may also establish intermediate or enabling work products that result in work products that are similar to those shown.

EXAMPLE E.1: TYPICAL WORK PRODUCTS IN CMMI
See Table E.1.

EXAMPLE E.2: ENABLING WORK PRODUCTS FROM PROJECT X
Set of drawings that are part of the define design solution to the backpack requirements:

1. **Subset of drawings that define the framework**
2. **Subset of drawings that define the exterior skin**
3. **Subset of the exterior skin drawings that define the components that close and seal the opening of the backpack (clasps, zippers, etc.)**

None of these drawings can be individually evaluated for its ability to meet product requirements. Even the full set of drawings of the skin cannot be analyzed for its potential ability to meet the waterproof requirement. However, the drawings can be inspected or analyzed

TABLE E.1 Typical Work Products

CMMI Process Area	Typical Work Products
Requirements Development	Customer requirements Derived requirements Product requirements Product-component requirements Interface requirements Functional architectures Activity diagrams and use cases Object-oriented analyses with services identified Technical performance measures Records of analysis methods and results Results of requirements validation
Technical Solution	Product component operational concepts, scenarios, and environments Use cases Documented relationships between requirements and product components Product architectures Product-component designs Technical data packages Allocated requirements Product component descriptions Key product characteristics Required physical characteristics and constraints Interface requirements Material requirements Verification criteria used to ensure that requirements have been achieved Conditions of use (environments) and operating/usage scenarios, modes, and states for operations, support, training, and verifications throughout the life cycle Interface design specifications Interface control documents Implemented design Product support documentation (training materials, users manual, maintenance manual, online help)
Requirements Management	Requirements traceability matrix
Validation	Validation results
Verification	Exit and entry criteria for work products Verification results
Measurement and Analysis	Specifications of base and derived measures
Decision Analysis and Resolution	Results of evaluating alternate solutions

to determine whether the gap between adjacent subcomponents of the skin are within acceptable limits. Similarly, a prototype of the skin can be built and tested against the waterproof product requirement.

Regarding the framework, perhaps analysis, models, or simulation can be used to determine its ability to meet the weight and impact resistance requirements.

Appendix F

Trade Studies

Trade studies are often performed during all phases of the engineering life cycle, including systems definition, before the product requirements are known. During systems definition, they are performed to identify the recommended set of requirements and constraints in terms of risk, cost, schedule, and performance impacts. Later, trade studies lead to functional allocation of requirements and selection of the preferred design approach. Other typical areas of trade studies are:

1. **Risk reduction**
2. **Technology evaluation**
3. **Physical architecture evaluation**
4. **Cost/performance decisions**
5. **Make/buy decisions**
6. **Material decisions**
7. **Life cycle cost decisions**

A trade study is an analysis or evaluation of alternatives leading to a recommended solution. We have worked with many engineers and managers who say that trade studies are not measurable, that the LOE technique is sufficient. They base their opinion on the "dynamic" (their words) nature of many trade studies. Often, the original set of proposed alternatives is substantially changed or abandoned when new information is obtained or customer requirements change. Sometimes, the evaluation of an alternative is suddenly abandoned. They question the feasibility of applying objective earned value to such dynamic activities.

Performance-Based Earned Value, by Paul J. Solomon and Ralph R. Young
Copyright ©2007 IEEE Computer Society.

Our response to the question and our approach for objective measurement is based on two premises:

1. **The outcome of a trade study is usually a recommendation that is needed to make a decision.** The decision constrains and guides further progress. Consequently, a trade study must be measured discretely and result in a work product, the documented trade study results.

2. **An organization's engineering processes should include a process and structured approach for performing trade studies.** That process should include both interim and final work products that can be planned, scheduled, and measured.

We examined the procedures, activities, and work products of two organizations to distill an outline of the trade study process, activities, and recommended work products:

1. **U.S. Air Force Space & Missile Systems Center Systems Engineering Primer and Handbook (SMC)**
2. **Northrop Grumman Integrated Systems, Airborne Early Warning & Electronic Warfare Systems Procedure, Trade Studies (NG)**

One recommended trade study outline is based on SMC, as follows:

1. **Purpose of study**
   a. **Resolve an issue**
   b. **Perform decision analysis**
   c. **Perform analysis of alternatives**
2. **Scope of study**
   a. **State level of detail of study**
   b. **State assumptions**
   c. **Identify influencing requirements and constraints**
3. **Trade study description: Describe trade studies to be performed to make trade-offs among:**
   a. **Concepts**
   b. **User requirements**
   c. **System architectures**
   d. **Design**
   e. **Program schedule**
   f. **Functional performance requirements**
   g. **Life cycle costs**
4. **Analytical approach**
   a. **Identify candidate solutions**
   b. **Measure performance**
      i. **Develop models and measures of merit**
      ii. **Develop values for viable candidates**
   c. **Selection criteria** (normally risk, performance, cost)

5. Scoring
   a. **Determine measures of results to be compared to criteria**
   b. **Assign weights to measures of results reflecting their relative importance**
   c. **Perform sensitivity analysis**
6. **Documentation of trade results**
   a. **Select user/operational concept**
   b. **Select system architecture**
   c. **Derive requirements**
      i. **Alternative functional approaches to meet requirements**
      ii. **Alternative functional views**
      iii. **Requirements allocations**
   d. **Derive technical/design solutions**
   e. **Cost analysis results**
   f. **Risk analysis results**
   g. **Understand trade space**

A similar approach is seen in the set of typical activities and work products, from the Northrop Grumman procedure (Table F.1).

TABLE F.1 Trade Study Plan Typical Activities

Activity	Work Product
1. Generate trade study plan	Trade study plan
2. Establish objectives	Trade objectives
3. Establish evaluation criteria	Evaluation criteria
4. Define/baseline candidates	Candidate definition: Include performance characteristics and/or models, engineering drawings, schematics, flow diagrams, equations etc.
5. Establish candidate evaluation methods: Approaches include preliminary design, analysis/evaluations, prototyping, simulation, analytical modeling, lessons learned, analysis.	Evaluation methods
6. Establish interpretation guidelines	Interpretation guidelines
7. Trade study stakeholder review	Stakeholder review report
8. Evaluate candidates	Results of performing evaluation
9. Prioritize according to best fit	Trade study recommendations
10. Establish refinement criteria (if necessary): Accommodate new information	Refinement criteria and methods

TRADE STUDY PROGRESS

Measuring the progress of a trade study requires more flexibility and agility than other engineering activities. This is especially true for evaluating the candidates or alternatives. Most of the other activities in a trade study are of relatively short duration. For these activities, the percent start/percent complete method is recommended.

Most managers find it difficult to measure the actual evaluation of the candidates or alternatives. For example, assume that the trade study plan calls for the evaluation of five candidates with the elimination of three candidates after three months of evaluation activities followed by a final selection after one more month. Often, one or more of the candidates will be eliminated before all the process steps have been completed. Sometimes a new candidate is added. Can earned value be used effectively with these scenarios?

Yes. The following example will illustrate how to set up the base measures of earned value for the evaluation of candidates.

EXAMPLE F.1: EVALUATE TRADE STUDY CANDIDATES

The activity, evaluate candidates, is successfully decomposed. First, two major milestones are defined:

1. **Down select two candidates.**
2. **Select recommended alternative.**

Next, we will decompose the activity that leads to the down select of two candidates:

1. **Assess, test, analyze, and document results of each of five candidates. Some candidates may be disqualified by engineering analysis prior to testing carded**
2. **Select final two candidates.**

The scheduling of the base measures of earned value and the time-phased budget that will be allocated to the base measures of earned value are illustrated in Chapter 6, Guidelines 2.5 and 2.6. The revision of the trade study plan is discussed in Example F.2.

Recap

The base measures of earned value have been established. If the tests for all five candidates are executed to completion, earned value is taken for each candidate and for the down select.

EXAMPLE F.2: TRADE STUDY EVALUATE CANDIDATES ACTIVITY

The trade study activity, evaluate candidates, has the following budget allocation and schedule constraints:

1. **Budget for total evaluation activity: 1000 hours**
   a. **Down select two candidates: 750 hours**
   b. **Select recommended alternative: 250 hours**
2. **Period of performance: 4 months**

Next, we will decompose the activity that leads to the selection of two, final candidates, establish the base measures of Earned Value (EV), and decompose the budget to base measures. The initial decomposition of activities results in the following tasks:

1. **Test, analyze, and document results of each of five candidates.**
2. **Select final two candidates.**

The milestones that are the base measures of Earned Value are given in Table F.2.1.

The budget allocation to the milestones has been added to Table F.2.2 and the resultant time-phased Budgeted Cost of Work Scheduled (BCWS) is shown.

EXAMPLE F.3: TRADE STUDY FROM PROJECT X

This trade study is based on Figure 3.13, RTM for the Mobile (backpack) Command and Control Center for Unmanned Reconnaissance Helicopter. The specific requirements for the trade study are the requirements for the allocated enclosure requirements: ENCL002, ENCL003, and ENCL004.

1. Purpose of Study

The purpose of this study is to resolve two separate but closely related issues in the design of the enclosure component for the Mobile (back-

TABLE F.2.1 Trade Study Evaluation Milestones

Trade Study Base Measures: Evaluation Activity	Time Period
Initial evaluation of each of 5 candidates has three milestones:	
1. Test has been set up	1
2. Tests are executed to completion	2
3. Test results are analyzed and documented.	3
Document the down select from 5 candidates to 2 candidates.	3
Document selection of recommended alternative.	4

TABLE F.2.2 Trade Study Evaluation BCWS

Trade Study Base Measures: Evaluation Activity	Time Period	BCWS/ candidate (hours)	BCWS/ Period
Initial evaluation of each of 5 candidates has three milestones. Evaluations are done in parallel:			
1. Test has been set up	1	40/candidate	200
2. Tests are executed to completion	2	40/candidate	200
3. Test results are analyzed and documented.	3	40/candidate	200
Document down select from 5 candidates to 2 candidates	3	150	150
Document selection of recommended alternative	4	250	250
Total Budget at Completion (BAC)			1000

pack) Command and Control Center for Unmanned Reconnaissance Helicopter. The two sets of alternatives to be determined are:

1. **Whether to use a rigid (frame based) enclosure over which a waterproof material is fitted or a semi-rigid material that does not need an underlying frame**
2. **Assuming the rigid frame solution is selected, what material is the most suitable for the external shell?**

2. Scope of Study

This trade study is limited to the following allocated product component requirements:

ENCL002: The Mobile C2 Center shall be waterproof in continuous (up to 2 hours) driving rain with a wind speed of up to 65 miles per hour and rainfall of up to 4 inches per hour.

ENCL003: The Mobile C2 Center shall show no damage after at least 3 successive impacts with a hard abrasive surface of up to 15 lbs./sq. in.

ENCL004: The Mobile C2 Center Enclosure component shall retain full operational capability after at least 3 successive impacts with a hard abrasive surface of up to 30 lbs./sq. in.

The level of detail is expected to be sufficient to prove what type of frame is appropriate for the backpack enclosure and what type of fabric covering is most suitable.

The only assumption relevant to this trade study is:

Each combination of frame architecture and covering will be subjected to 25 wash cycles before testing.

3. Trade Study Description

The trade study will be performed by:

1. **A review of trade literature on similar products**
2. **The military's experience with similar products**
3. **Informal testing of sample products obtained from interested vendors**

4. Analytical Approach

There are two sets of alternatives in this trade study. First is the choice between a rigid frame based architecture and a semi-rigid frame. If the preferred solution is the semi-rigid frame architecture, the trade study is complete. If the choice is the rigid frame architecture, the trade study continues with an evaluation of coverings that comprise the second alternative.

The attributes for each set of alternatives will be:

1. **Enclosure weight**
2. **Durability**
3. **Water resistance**
4. **Puncture resistance**
5. **Comfort in use**

The scoring is determined by:

1. **Score each attribute for each alternative based on the attribute scoring scale described in Table F.3.1.**
2. **Multiply each attribute score by the priority-weighting factor to form a weighted attribute score.**
3. **Add the weighted attribute scores for each alternative to form a composite score for each alternative.**

Develop a matrix for recording the scores or each alternative and attribute, as shown in Table F.3.1.

5. Scoring

Priority Weighting. The customer priority-weighting factor will be based on the following scale:

Low	Medium	High
1	2	3

Attribute Scoring. Each attribute described above will be scored according to the following scale:

Not Acceptable	Somewhat Acceptable	Moderately Acceptable	Very Acceptable	Completely Acceptable
1	2	3	4	5

6. Documentation of Trade Results

Document each alternative/attribute, as shown in Table F.3.2.

TABLE F.3.1 Trade Study Scoring Matrix

Customer Requirement Attribute	Customer Priority	Rigid Frame with Covering	Semi-rigid Frame No Covering	Treated Fabric Covering	Multi-layer Membrane Covering
		Score is equal to Customer Priority times Attribute Acceptability			
Enclosure Weight	3				
Durability	3				
Water Resistance	2				
Puncture Resistance	1				
Comfort in Use	2				
Total					

TABLE F.3.2 Documentation of Trade Results

Customer Requirement Attribute	Customer Priority	Rigid Frame with Covering		Semi-rigid Frame No Covering		Treated Fabric Covering		Multi-layer Membrane Covering	
		Score is equal to Customer Priority times Attribute Acceptability							
Enclosure Weight	3	4	12	3	9	3	9	4	12
Durability	3	4	12	3	9	2	6	4	12
Water Resistance	2	5	10	5	10	3	6	5	10
Puncture Resistance	1	5	5	1	1	4	4	2	2
Comfort in Use	2	3	6	5	10	3	6	4	8
Total			45		39		31		44

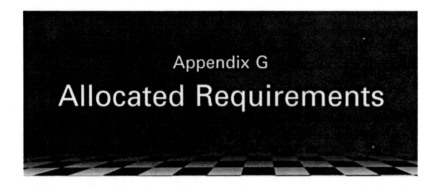

Appendix G
Allocated Requirements

ALLOCATED REQUIREMENTS

Product requirements are developed, allocated, implemented into design, and tested. Establishing a time-phased product requirement baseline against which progress can be consistently measured is the most important EVM step. It drives the budget and the schedule. The technical requirements also establish the criteria for completing tasks. Of equal importance are a disciplined requirements traceability process and a requirements traceability database.

Requirements are applicable to all phases of the system and software development, which further increases their utility as a means of determining earned value. Additionally, requirements are directly related to producing the functionality the customer wants in a new system. When selecting a measure on which to base earned value, the best results are achieved when the measure is directly related to the degree to which the desired functionality has been implemented. Requirements are an excellent measure for use in determining earned value measures because they are directly related to evaluating progress in implementing the functionality required by the system. Other measures, even though they provide other critical project information, are further removed from the implementation of the requirements and thus reduce earned value accuracy [1].

In Chapter 3, we introduced the topic of allocated requirements, requirements that were assigned to elements of the system design such as subsystems, components, and parts. In this appendix, we measure the progress of the requirements as they proceed from

Performance-Based Earned Value, by Paul J. Solomon and Ralph R. Young
Copyright ©2007 IEEE Computer Society.

development, to implementation into the design, and then to being tested successfully.

Table G is a list of examples in this appendix of techniques for basing earned value on meeting the requirements.

REQUIREMENTS DEVELOPMENT

As discussed in Chapter 3, it is critically important to invest sufficient time and effort to evolve the real requirements. Yet requirements development is the most difficult stage to estimate and to measure. During the system definition stage, and with the evolutionary acquisition approach, the real product requirements are not yet known [2]. Both the total time and the duration of requirements development are a function of how well the customer understands and communicates the initial requirements. Then the customer and the supplier keep communicating until the validated requirements baseline is completed. Often, trade studies are performed to aid in defining the real requirements, as discussed earlier. After the validated requirement baseline has been defined, these requirements and requirements that have been derived from the validated requirements baseline should be used as a basis for earned value. Example G.1 illustrates how to allocate the budget for requirements development to the product requirements and the derived functional requirements.

Example G.1: Requirements Development

This example is taken from Project X, Figure 3.13, RTM for the Mobile (backpack) Command and Control Center for Unmanned Reconnaissance Helicopter.

The product requirement: "PROD006 The Mobile C2 center shall use encryption for all transmissions" was converted from its source customer requirement along with seven other product requirements.

TABLE G Examples of Basing EV on Meeting the Requirements

Example #	Title
G.1	Requirements Development
G.2	Design EV Based on Completion of Drawings and Meeting Requirements
G.3	Negative EV When Rework is Necessary
G.4	Test Organization EV Based on Executing Tests and Meeting Requirements

The objective indicator earned value method is appropriate for developing the product requirements. Assume that each of the eight product requirements receives an equal allocation of the total work package budget. Also, assume that three functional requirements will be derived and developed from PROD006, as follows:

1. **FUNC001: The Mobile C2 center shall support up to 256-bit cipher strength encryption at a minimum.**
2. **FUNC002: The Mobile C2 center shall at a minimum use the Data Encryption Standard (DES) in accordance with FIPS Pub 46-3 (Triple DES).**
3. **FUNC003: The Mobile C2 center shall incorporate digital signatures using public key encryption technology.**

The allocation of the budget for requirements development within a work package (WP) is shown in Tables G.1.1 and G.1.2.

DESIGN PHASE

The time-phased plan for the design phase should include milestones that define the number or percentage of requirements to be met at those points. Earned value should then be based on the actual requirements that were met.

Example G.2: Design EV Based on Completion of Drawings and Meeting Requirements

Engineering analysis is also performed by other engineering science organizations to determine whether the evolving design meets allocated requirements. Methods used include prototypes, models and simulation, and other analytical techniques.

Detailed schedules are established for all work packages. Success milestones are also established for meeting individual requirements.

TABLE G.1.1 Product Requirements Development Budget Allocation

Product Req.	Req.	Budget
PROD001	Weight	100
PROD002	Waterproof	50
PROD003	Abrasion Resistance	50
PROD004	Impact Resistance	50
PROD005	Battery Charge	150
PROD006	Encryption	200
PROD007	Control Channels	200
PROD008	Select Sensors	200
Total WP		1000

TABLE G.1.2 Functional Requirements Development Budget Allocation

PROD006	Encryption	
Functional Req.	Req.	Budget
FUNC001	256 bit	60
FUNC002	DES standard	60
FUNC003	10 kHz separation	80
Total WP		200

When the PBEV guidelines are applied, the progress of the initial design work package is measured both by the initial completion of the enabling work products and by meeting the requirements. Closure of the work packages is determined by success in meeting the requirements.

This Appendix also provides examples of alternative methods for measuring the progress of rework and of testing. Rework of a drawing is performed when, after its initial completion, subsequent engineering, build, or test activities disclose that it no longer meets the requirements.

Assume that a set of 50 drawings has a budget at completion (BAC) of 2000 hours and that each drawing is weighted equally in terms of effort. Each drawing receives a budget allocation of 40 hours.

The output of a work package is the design of a component of a subsystem, a set of wire harnesses. There are two requirements that are allocated to the wire harnesses. maximum weight and maximum diameter. The requirements are:

1. **Maximum weight: 200 lb.**
2. **Maximum diameter: 1 in.**

The progress and earned value of the work package is measured both by the completion of the enabling work products (drawings) and by meeting the requirements. The schedule for completing the drawings and for meeting the requirements is shown in Table G.2.1.

TABLE G.2.1 Schedule for Drawings and Requirements

Schedule Plan	Jan.	Feb.	Mar.	Apr.	May	Total
Drawings	8	10	12	10	10	50
Requirements met:						
Weight				1		1
Diameter				1		1

TABLE G.2.2 Net EV Based on Component Requirements

Design (drawings)	Jan.	Feb.	Mar.	Apr.	May	Total
Planned drawings	8	10	12	10	10	50
BCWS—cur.	320	400	480	400	400	2000
BCWS—cum.	320	720	1200	1600	2000	2000
Actual drawings completed	9	10	10	12		
EV (drawings)—cur.	360	400	400	480		
EV (drawings)—cum.	360	760	1160	1640		
Negative EV (reqs)—cum.				−100		
Net EV (drawings and reqs)				1540		
Schedule Variance	40	40	−40	−60		

The budget is allocated as follows:

1. **The work package for a component has a budget at completion of 2000 hours. Each drawing has a budget value of 40 hours.**
2. **EV is dependent on the engineering analyses that are performed to determine that the design meets the requirements. EV is decremented (negative EV) if a requirement was not met on schedule. EV is restored when the requirement is finally met. The total possible negative earned value is 300 hours, as follows: component weight requirement (req.) not met: −100, diameter req. not met: −200.**

The schedule status at April month end follows:

1. **Cumulative (cum.) drawings completed: 41**
2. **Diameter req. met**
3. **Component weight req. not met**

Table G.2.2 shows the time-phased Budgeted Cost for Work Scheduled (BCWS), how EV increases for completing the drawings and is reduced if the design fails to meet requirements.

The unfavorable schedule variance analysis should state that the drawings are ahead of schedule by one (+40) but the design has not met the planned requirements (−100). There will be an unfavorable impact to both the cost and schedule objectives as the drawings are reworked until the design meets the requirements.

Example G.3: Negative EV When Rework is Necessary

If EV was previously taken for meeting the requirements and it is later determined that the requirements are no longer met, EV should be reduced to show the current, behind-schedule condition. A technique for reducing EV when enabling products, such as drawings, are returned for rework is shown in Appendix B, Example B.5. In that example, when a "completed" drawing no longer meets a requirement, the cumulative EV is reduced by the budget value of the drawing.

In this example, the negative EV that is associated with not meeting a requirement on schedule is also applied subsequent to the time when that requirement was assessed as being met.

The schedule status at May month end follows.
Cumulative (cum.) drawings completed:

1. 41 through April
2. 10 in May
3. −2 returned for rework related to diameter

The May cumulative earned value is reduced to account for both the returned drawings and the requirements not met, as shown in Table G.3.1.

TABLE G.3.1 Negative EV When Rework is Necessary

Design (drawings)	Jan.	Feb.	Mar.	Apr.	May	Total
Planned drawings	8	10	12	10	10	50
BCWS—cur.	320	400	480	400	400	2000
BCWS—cum.	320	720	1200	1600	2000	2000
Actual drawings completed	9	10	10	12	10	
Drawings returned for rework					2	
EV (drawings)—cur.	360	400	400	480	320	
EV (drawings)—cum.	360	760	1160	1640	1960	
Negative EV (reqs)—cum.				−100	−300	
Net EV (drawings and reqs)				1540	1660	
Schedule Variance	40	40	−40	−60	−340	

TABLE G.3.2 Rework Causes Negative Earned Value

Design (drawings)	Jan.	Feb.	Mar.	Apr.	May	Total
Planned drawings	8	10	12	10	10	50
BCWS—cum.	320	720	1200	1600	2000	2000
Drawings completed	9	10	10	11		
Drawings returned				–5		
Net drawings—cur.	9	10	10	6		
Net drawings—cum.	9	19	29	35		
EV—cur.	360	400	400	240		
EV—cum.	360	760	1160	1400		
EV—cum.	0	40	–40	–200		

The unfavorable schedule variance analysis should state that the drawings are now behind schedule by one (–40) after accounting for the drawings returned for rework and the design is now behind schedule for meeting both requirements (–300). There will be an unfavorable impact to both the cost and schedule objectives as the drawings are reworked until the design meets the requirements.

The planning assumptions for this example follow:

1. **50 drawings are planned during January through May.**
2. **Budget value per drawing = 40.**
3. **Rework of drawings is planned to begin in April.**
4. **Negative earned value taken when a drawing must be reworked: –40.**

During April, seven initial drawings are completed and five drawings are returned for rework. Two had an incorrect interface and three required reduced dimensions to fit into the available space. The EV as of April month end is shown in Table G.3.2.

The five returned drawings resulted in a decrement to EV of 200. If rework had not been assessed, than the work package would appear to be on schedule. Furthermore, the overstatement of real EV would fail to indicate the true cost performance and might be misleading regarding the most likely EAC and completion date.

REWORK

Discussion of rework to meet the requirements, including examples, is provided in Appendix B. Chapter 13 includes a section on software rework.

Previously, the PMB for the engineering design organization was developed. Next, the test organization's related SOW and PMB will be examined.

TESTING

Example G.4: Test Organization EV Based on Executing Tests and Meeting Requirements

Successful testing for a requirement means that all associated test procedures have executed to completion and the requirement has been met. During a testing activity, it is recommended that the test organization utilize two measures in combination, as base measures of earned value.

1. **Execution of the test plan to completion.**
2. **Requirements tested successfully.**

Some test managers believe that their EV should be based only on executing the tests. They acknowledge responsibility for having the test assets (laboratories, calibrated test equipment, processes, etc.) and the required, skilled people ready and suitable for executing the tests. Their rationale is that they are responsible for conducting the tests and that, if the test resources, including labor, are available and the tests are being executed on schedule, they are doing their job.

They argue that they should not be held accountable (statused as behind schedule) if the testing could not even start because of late engineering design or late development of the test plan. They also argue that they should not be measured as behind schedule if the test cannot be completed because the testing was aborted because of a test failure (of the product being tested). They reason that, if the test results are not successful, it is not their fault but the fault of the requirements, design, or development organizations. Consequently, they propose that they should not be penalized by showing a behind-schedule condition if subsequent tests must be performed after the rework has been completed.

In this situation, the test manager is taking the point of view of the test organization rather than that of the team as a whole. In our judgment, the interests of the project team are best served by taking EV for testing based on both executing the test steps to completion and meeting the requirements.

Therefore, we recommend that a portion of EV be performance based. Even if the test manager may not be at fault, the test SOW should only be complete when the product requirements have been met.

Execution of the Test Plan

The base measures for executing the test plan may be any measures of progress, depending on the detailed test plan and the organization's test procedures. Sometimes a time-phased burn-up or burn-down plan is used, with each measurement in the plan being a defined test activity, test points, or other measure. The portion of the total test budget that is allocated to the base measures of executing the test plan is allocated to the base measures and time-phased accordingly.

Requirements Tested Successfully

The remainder of the total test budget is allocated to test success. Success is the determinant that a requirement was met. Test success is usually determined after analysis of the test data. Consequently, success is not always determined at the time of test execution. Also, an allocated requirement may be traceable to more than one test activity or test point. However, the schedule should include milestones for successful testing of the requirements. Then, when that requirement has been met, the test activity may receive EV based on the budget that had been allocated to that event. In the period of test success, both the test activity and the engineering design activity would take EV for meeting the requirement.

Testing Planning Assumptions:

1. **The detailed test plan for execution of tests to completion is comprised of 140 sequential test steps.**
2. **There are 16 requirements to be tested until success.**

The schedule for test execution, for analysis of the results, and for successful testing of the requirements follows.

Assume that the detailed test plan for execution of tests to completion is comprised of 140 sequential test steps. There are 16 requirements to be tested. The test steps are scheduled through June. The first requirements will be met in February. The analysis of the data will be completed in July. The test plan schedule for the base measures of EV is shown in Table G.4.1.

The test organization has a total budget of 780 hours. Now we will allocate the time-phased budget to the base measures of EV. This will be allocated to execution of the test to completion, 700 hours and test

TABLE G.4.1 Text Plan

Test Organization	Jan.	Feb.	Mar.	Apr.	May	June	Jul.	Total
Test steps executed		20	30	20	30	40		140
Requirements tested successfully			3	3	4	3	3	16

TABLE G.4.2 Test Plan BCWS

Total test org. BCWS	Jan.	Feb.	Mar.	Apr.	May	Jun.	Jul.	Total
Test steps executed		100	150	100	150	200		700
Requirements tested successfully			15	15	20	15	15	80
Total BCWS		100	165	115	170	215	15	780

success, 80 hours. Each test step will earn 5 hours. Each requirement tested successfully will earn 5 hours. The time-phased BCWS is shown in Table G.4.2.

DEFERRED REQUIREMENTS

Guidance and examples to account for the deferral of requirements from one work package to another when work is behind schedule are provided in Chapter 13.

SOFTWARE DEVELOPMENT

For software development, the milestones may indicate the planned, incremental functionality as well as the number of requirements met. Additional guidance for software is provided in Chapter 13.

REFERENCES

[1] U.S. Naval Air Systems Command (NAVAIR). *Using Software Metrics & Measurements for Earned Value Toolkit.* Lexington, MD: Department of the Navy, 2004.

[2] Young, Ralph R. *Effective Requirements Practices.* Boston, MA: Addison-Wesley, 2001.

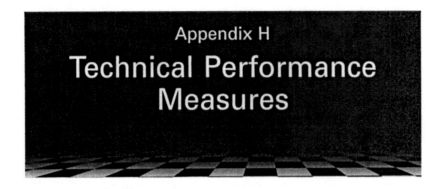

This appendix contains examples of using Technical Performance Measures (TPMs). Techniques for planning, budgeting, and taking earned value when using TPMs are discussed in Chapter 6. The examples fall into two categories of TPMs, physical qualities, such as weight, and software quality.

TPM WORK PRODUCTS: EVIDENCE OF ACHIEVING PLANNED TPM VALUES

When a TPM is used to verify that technical performance requirements have been met, the evidence of achieving the planned values becomes a pertinent work product. The evidence is normally documentation of the analysis of TPM results and conclusions reached.

CONCEPT OF BASING EV ON TPMS

The following discussion and examples illustrate techniques for basing EV on achieving, or not achieving, planned technical performance. Often, during the early stages of design such as drawing development, it may be too early to measure TPM progress. For tasks that are scheduled to complete before the first TPM milestone, EV would be based only on completing drawings per the organization's process quality procedures and standards. Eventually, enough drawings will have been completed to enable the measurement of TPM achievement. If a percentage of the work package budget had been allocated to completing

Performance-Based Earned Value, by Paul J. Solomon and Ralph R. Young the drawings and another percentage to achieving planned TPM values, then the work package would be held to less than one hundred percent complete until the TPM planned values are achieved.

The simple EV technique is to allocate part of the work package budget to achieving the TPM planned value and to take EV when the value is achieved, as illustrated in Example H.1.

A preferred technique is to take negative EV if a TPM planned value is not achieved when scheduled, as shown in Example H.2.

Commonly, thresholds or tolerance bands are used with TPMs. A technique for taking partial EV when the achieved value does not meet the objective but is within tolerance is shown in Example H.3.

The achievement of significant performance requirements may not be measurable at the lowest WBS and work package level. If the design of a component is at the work package level, completion of the design may depend on achieving planned TPM values or other quality objectives that are only measurable at a higher level of the system architecture or WBS. A technique for constraining EV for a component-level work package is to earn part of the work package budget when the performance objective is met at the higher level of the WBS, as shown in Example H.4.

TPM: PLANNED VALUE FOR PHYSICAL QUALITIES

Example H.1: Budget Is Allocated to Achieving TPM Planned Value for Weight

In this example, a percentage of the available budget is allocated to achieving planned TPM values for weight. Techniques for establishing the planned values and for taking EV based on achieving those values are demonstrated.

Planning assumptions:

1. Subcomponent requires 100 drawings.
2. Subcomponent has a weight limit of 300 lb.
3. TPM plan assumes weight can be determined by analysis beginning in the sixth month.
4. BAC: 5000 hours.
5. EV method and budget allocation:
   a. Allocate 90% of the BAC to developing the drawings = 4500 hours, 45 hours/drawing.
   b. Allocate 10% of the BAC to planned TPM achievement milestones = 500 hours.
   c. Time-phase BCWS per planned accomplishment.

6. **Take EV based on drawings:** Drawing is completed per the organization's process, including quality assurance process: 45 hours.
7. **TPM milestones and success criteria.**
   a. **Total EV for the set of drawings is taken when the TPM achieved is 300 lb.: 500 hours.**
   b. **Interim milestones are established for measuring TPMs with planned values at those milestones and associated, potential EV, as follows: 6 months: 330 lb. Potential EV = 100 hours 8 months: 315 lb. Potential, incremental EV = 300 hours.**

A Caution. One drawback of the preceding technique is that the initial completion of a drawing will receive less EV than should have been budgeted, based on its estimated cost. For example, if a drawing had a basis of estimate (BOE) for the budget of 50 hours and the drawing was completed in 50 hours, there should be no cost variance (CV), and the CPI should be 1.0. By withholding part of the potential EV, an artificial CV is created. In the above example, a cost overrun of 5 hours per drawing would be created. The CV would increase until the planned TPM value is achieved. At that time, the artificial CV would be reversed. If the percent of BOE that is withheld is small, then the artificial CV would also be small and possibly insignificant.

A recommended, alternative technique precludes an "artificial" CV, as follows.

Example H.2: Negative EV If TPM Planned Value Is Not Achieved

The preferred technique is to allocate budget to the base measure of EV consistently with its BOE instead of reducing provided budget for the TPM achievement. However, if either the scheduled TPM measurement is not taken or the value of the measurement does not achieve its planned value for that TPM, then negative EV is taken. After the EV has been decreased, the cumulative EV will indicate that the project is behind schedule because the evolving product has failed to meet its technical performance objective.

The technique to reduce cumulative EV when a requirement is not met is illustrated in Appendix G, Example G.2. In Example G.2, there are two technical performance requirements, maximum weight and maximum diameter. Negative EV is taken when TPM planned values are not achieved.

Example H.3: Partial EV If TPM Is Within Tolerance of Planned Value

Another variant of this technique is to take partial EV if the TPM achieved is within a predefined tolerance threshold of the planned value. For example, a weight target may be established with a threshold of 5%. An EV rule could be documented that, if the measured weight exceeds the planned value, but is within the threshold, then 80% of potential negative EV will be the decrement, not 100%.

EV solution:

1. TPM planned value at 8 months is 300 lb.
2. Negative budget value for not achieving TPM planned value = 300 hours.
3. Threshold is 5%. 5% TPM planned value = 15 lb.
4. At 8 months, measured weight = 310 lb.
5. Measured weight is over TPM planned value but under threshold.
6. Negative EV = 80% × 300 hours = 240 hours.
7. Negative EV = 0 hours when weight objective has been met.

Example H.4. EV When TPM Is at a Higher WBS Level

Example H.4 is a typical situation during development of a project. A TPM objective is established at the subsystem level. The TPM objective is often measurable only at the system or subsystem level. Many, if not all of the components of the system or subsystem contribute to technical performance. For a weight TPM, all components play a part. For other TPMs, such as response time, a subset of the components, including both hardware and software components, contributes to the subsystem or system objective. In Example H.4, earned value at the component level is based on both the weight of the component and the weight of the subsystem to which it belongs. The Systems Engineering Plan (SEP) or another planning document should define the technique and criteria.

A typical technique that may be defined in the SEP follows. When setting up a work package for one of several components, define completion criteria that include meeting both the component and subcomponent weight objectives. Decrease (negative) EV when the either of the objectives is not met on schedule. Then take 100% EV when the subsystem objective is finally met, even if the component's weight is still heavier than its objective.

The amount of negative EV is arbitrary and is not related to effort. It is established only to portray a behind-schedule condition when the design fails to meet technical objectives.

The assumptions of this example are:

1. **The component is one of four components that form a subsystem.**
2. **The subsystem's TPM objective is 4000 lb.**
3. **The SEP states that some components may be overweight at completion if there are offsets in other components as long as the total subsystem weight does not exceed 4000 lb.**

In this example, the total possible negative EV is 500 hours, as follows:

1. **Component weight TPM planned value not met: −100**
2. **Subsystem weight TPM planned value not met: −2200**
3. **Diameter req. not met: −200**

In this example, the EV of the work package for a component is dependent on the both the measured weight of the component and the weight of the other components within the same subsystem. If both the component and the subsystem weight planned values were not achieved at the April milestone, the net EV would be 1340 hours, as shown in Table H.1. This technique may also incorporate higher levels of the WBS.

TABLE H.4 Net EV Based on Component and Subsystem TPMs

Design (drawings)	Jan.	Feb.	Mar.	Apr.	May	Total
Planned drawings	8	10	12	10	10	50
BCWS–cur.	320	400	480	400	400	2000
BCWS—cum.	320	720	1200	1600	2000	2000
Actual drawings completed	9	10	10	12		
EV (drawings)—cur.	360	400	400	480		
EV (drawings)—cum.	360	760	1160	1640		
Negative EV (component weight) —cum.				−100		
Negative EV (subsystem weight)— cum.				−200		
Net EV (drawings and reqs including TPMs)				1340		
Schedule Variance	40	40	−40	−260		

Example H.5: Waterproofness—Project X

A nonsoftware example can be taken from Figure 3.14, Mobile C2 Center Critical MOPs and Related TPMs. In this case the design requirement is:

> ENCL002 The Mobile C2 Center shall be waterproof in continuous (up to 2 hours) driving rain with a wind speed of up to 65 miles per hour and rainfall of up to 4 inches per hour.

The TPM related to this requirement is classified as a failure rate of testing of a material that exceeds a threshold, namely:

> The moisture content according to the probe shall not increase by more than 5% during the duration of the test.

In this case the analyst decides that, because of the increased risk involved with this requirement and associated TPM, that 25% (or about $10,000) of the value of the work package to develop the enclosure will be allocated to the TPM. Once again, when the test described in Figure 3.14 is passed, EV for the TPM will be taken. If the successful test is later than originally planned EV will either be decremented or simply not taken when the TPM is planned, but, regardless, it will be taken when the test is successful.

TPM: SOFTWARE QUALITY

Quality as a Constraint to EV

An example of applying PBEV involves constraining EV based on the quality (or lack of quality) of the evolving product. The "Hammervold Constraint" places an arbitrary limit on the percent complete when quality objectives are not being met. A software engineering manager, Rich Hammervold of the Northrop Grumman Corporation, uses this technique to limit EV to 80% (or any other limit) when the defect rate is higher than planned (an indicator of quality). Even if the percent complete of the enabling work products were higher (as measured by requirements, components, use cases, or other measures), reported EV is limited to 80%. The rationale is that the higher rate of defects indicates lower quality and more rework than planned. The constraint prevents progress from being overstated or misleading.

TPM of Software Quality

The indicated quality of the software may be determined by the defect density rate. The TPM objective is that the defect density rate does not exceed 20 defects per 1000 Source Lines of Code (SLOC) at the completion of integration testing. The work product is evidence of achieving that objective.

Example H.6: TPM of Software Quality—Project X
The software that instantiates the following Project X requirements comprises a single self-contained subcomponent of the software being developed (or purchased):

> FUNC004 The Mobile C2 center shall support up to three sets of channels simultaneously.
>
> FUNC005 The Mobile C2 center shall have five channels per channel set, one set for each helicopter being controlled.
>
> FUNC006 The Mobile C2 center shall have a separation of 10 kHz (Kilo Hertz) between channels.

There is one work product in the WBS (and its respective work package) that supports the development of this subcomponent. If the nature of the software supports lower-level work packages and it makes sense to do so, the analyst may wish to create such lower-level work packages, to gain more control over the task, as necessary. For example, the software to control the frequency separation between the channels (FUNC006) may have its own work package, separate from the work package set up for the FUNC004 and FUNC005 requirements.

A portion of the total work package BAC (say 15%, equivalent to 300 labor hours or the comparable dollar amount of 300 labor hours) for these work packages is allocated to the TPM appropriate for this subcomponent. The TPM in this case is the quality of the software as measured by defects or a maximum allowable defect density rate.

Continuing with the single work package example (all three requirements), let's assume that the defect density rate for the number of defects (per 1000 SLOC) is set to 20 at the completion of integration testing. If the number of defects exceeds 20 in the time period when this TPM is scheduled (or if the count is not taken because the schedule slips), we would decrement the EV by 300 labor hours and both the current and cumulative SV will show a behind schedule condition. When corrected, the 300 labor hours will be restored to EV.

Software Quality Principle Applied to other Engineering Activities
In the preceding example, the TPM measured the quality of the work product as being inversely related to the number or rate of defects. This same principle may be applied to other engineering activities or functions. Some examples follow.

1. **The percentage of drawings returned for rework exceeds a threshold.**
2. **The failure rate of testing a material exceeds a threshold.**
3. **Other quality objectives are not being met, as determined by the organization's quality assurance process.**

If the achieved quality is less than the planned quality, per the TPM plan, than EV will be constrained or decremented, per the specified EV technique and budget allocation.

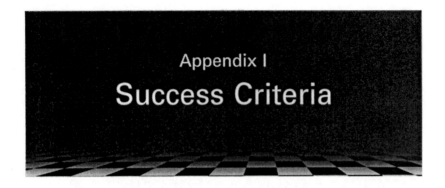

Appendix I

Success Criteria

EVENT-DRIVEN ENTRY AND EXIT CRITERIA FOR SUCCESS

Meeting entry and exit criteria for technical reviews, on schedule, is an important control for effective project management. Most interim progress measurements that are made before the technical reviews are logical precedents to the entry and exit criteria of the technical reviews. If the team is making steady, planned progress toward the next technical review, it may be confident that the project is going well. If the success criteria for the technical review are well defined, the review team will be able to review all related artifacts, documentation, and other evidence to assess whether the engineering development of the evolving product is truly on schedule.

The major stakeholders should agree in advance on the entry criteria for significant technical reviews. Then, if the performance indicators show that all the entrance criteria will not be met, the technical review may be deferred or may be refocused on those criteria that will not be met and their impacts on program objectives.

For significant technical reviews, there should be milestones in the integrated master schedule (IMS) and in work packages that depend on the entry and exit criteria. Exit criteria should clearly establish define successful execution of the project and include stakeholder agreement that the criteria were met, including all required documentation. Success criteria are discussed more thoroughly in Guideline 2.4. This appendix includes the following useful information from IEEE 1220 and examples of success criteria.

1. Guidance and success criteria from IEEE 1220 for completion of technical reviews at several phases of engineering development (Tables I.1 through I.4)
2. Excerpts from entrance and exit criteria for a Critical Design Review (CDR) (Example I.1)
3. An example from Project X of success criteria for the completion of detailed design (Example I.2)
4. Excerpts of success criteria from the Defense Acquisition Guide (DAG) [1] for major technical reviews (Example I.3)

EXAMPLE I.1: ENTRANCE AND EXIT CRITERIA FOR CRITICAL DESIGN REVIEW (CDR)

An excerpt from a CDR checklist follows.

Purpose

The CDR confirms that the detailed design is ready to proceed with coding, fabrication, assembly and integration efforts, and verifies that:

TABLE I.1 Guidance for Technical Reviews At Completion of the Preliminary Design Stage

IEEE 1220	Technical Reviews at the completion of the preliminary design stage (paraphrased)
	Subsystem reviews to ensure that (5.2.4.1) a) Subsystem definition is sufficiently mature to meet SE master schedule (SEMS) criteria; b) Component allocations and preliminary component specifications are reasonable and provide a sound subsystem concept; c) Subsystem risks have been assessed and mitigated to a level appropriate to continue development; d) Trade study data are adequate to substantiate that subsystem requirements are achievable; e) Decisions made in arriving at the subsystem configuration definition are well supported by analysis and technical data. System review (5.2.4.2) When: after completion of subsystem reviews. Purpose: to determine whether: • The total system approach to detailed design satisfies the system baseline; • Unacceptable risks are mitigated; • Issues for all subsystems, products, and life cycle processes are resolved; • Accomplishments and plans warrant continued development effort.

TABLE I.2 Guidance for Technical Reviews At Completion of the Detailed Design Stage

IEEE 1220	Technical Reviews at the completion of the detailed design stage. (paraphrased)
	Component reviews (5.3.4.1) When: At the completion of the detailed design stage. Purpose: to ensure that: a) Each detailed component definition is sufficiently mature to meet measure of effectiveness/measure of performance (MOE/MOP) criteria; b) Component specifications are reasonable and provide a sound component concept; c) Component and related life cycle process risks have been assessed and mitigated to a level appropriate to support Fabrication, Assembly, Integration, and Test (FAIT); d) Trade study data are adequate to substantiate that detailed component requirements are achievable; e) Decisions made in arriving at the detailed component definition configuration are well supported by analysis and technical data. **Subsystem reviews (5.3.4.2)** When: after completion of component reviews associated with the subsystem. Purpose: to determine whether: • The subsystem detailed design satisfies the design to baseline; • Risks are mitigated and remaining risks are acceptable; • Issues for all components, assemblies, and life cycle processes are resolved; • Accomplishments and plans warrant continuation with FAIT. **System review (5.3.4.3)** When: after completion of subsystem detailed design reviews. Purpose: to determine whether: • The detailed design of the system satisfies the system baseline; • Unacceptable risks are mitigated; • Issues for all subsystems, products, and life cycle processes are resolved; • Accomplishments and plans satisfy criteria for continuation of the technical effort • The system is ready to continue into FAIT by having resolved outstanding product or life cycle process issues.

1. The detailed design satisfies that the contractually required functionality and performance, have been achieved.
2. The detailed design addresses both the stated and derived requirements with sufficient traceability,
3. The interface control documents and draft detail specification are complete.
4. Exit criteria have been met.

TABLE I.3 Guidance for Technical Reviews At Completion of Functional Verification

IEEE 1220	Technical Reviews at the completion of functional verification (paraphrased)
	Functional verification (6.4) Purposes: • To assess the completeness of the functional architecture in satisfying the validated requirements baseline • To produce a verified functional architecture for input to synthesis. Verify architecture completeness (6.4.2.1) Verify that system functional and operational requirements included in the requirements baseline are traceable to the functional architecture. Verify functional and performance measures (6.4.2.2) Verify that all system-level functional and performance requirements of the requirements baseline are traceable to the established functional architecture. Verify satisfaction of constraints (6.4.2.3) Verify that all system-level policy, procedural, standardization, functional, and design constraints of the requirements baseline are traceable to the established functional architecture.

TABLE I.4 Guidance for Technical Reviews at Completion of Design Verification

IEEE 1220	Technical Reviews at the completion of design verification (paraphrased)
	Design verification (6.6) Ensuring that: a) The requirements of the lowest level of the design architecture, including derived requirements, are traceable to the verified functional architecture; b) The design architecture satisfies the validated requirements baseline. Verify architecture completeness (6.6.2.1) Verifies that: a) Design elements descriptions are traceable to requirements of the functional architecture (upward traceability); b) The requirements of the functional architecture are allocated and traceable to the design architecture. All internal and external design interfaces should be upward and downward traceable to their source requirement. Verify functional and performance measures (6.6.6.2) Verify that the evaluation results from activities defined by 6.6.1 (Select verification approach) satisfy the functional and performance requirements (including human performance requirements) of the validated requirements baseline. Verify satisfaction of constraints (6.6.2.3) Verify that the: a) Evaluation results from activities, as defined by 6.6.1, satisfy the constraints, including interfaces, of the functional architecture; b) Constraints of the established design architecture are traceable to the validated requirements baseline.

Scope

The CDR is conducted for each subsystem of the system to determine whether the system element designs and design requirements are complete and to determine whether the supplier is prepared to proceed with software coding, hardware fabrication, assembly and integration, and development testing.

The detailed specification requirements are discussed and evaluated to determine whether these requirements are completely allocated and traceable to subsystem requirements. Derived requirements are completely allocable to subsystem requirements.

The design is evaluated to determine whether the design correctly and completely implements all requirements, and that traceability to requirements is maintained.

Entry Criteria

1. Design data package [specifications, critical drawings, and internal interface control documents (ICD)] is complete (engineering release acceptable per the supplier's documented processes) and placed under the supplier's configuration management control.
2. All preliminary design review (PDR) action items have been closed.
3. All subsystem PDRs and CDRs have been successfully conducted and documented, and action items (supplier and subcontractor) resulting from them have been closed.
4. All developmental test data is available at CDR demonstrating that the detailed design is ready to proceed with coding, fabrication, assembly, and integration efforts.
5. The design correctly and completely implements all requirements, and traceability of design to requirements is maintained.
6. The following documents have been delivered to the customer before the CDR:
   a. Detailed specification revision
   b. Scientific and technical reports
   c. System characteristics and performance data report
   d. System electrical loads analysis report
   e. System structural analysis report
   f. System environmental impact assessment report
   g. System basic dimensional data report
   h. Stress/structural/loads/analysis documentation
   i. Dynamic modeling, analysis, and simulation results
7. Functions have been allocated to configuration items (allocated baseline established).
   a. Verify that the ICD and draft detail and product specifications are complete for each configuration item.

    b. At least 80% of each subsection critical drawings/schematics complete.

    c. Design is mature and stable—design "frozen."

Exit Criteria

1. Performance results based on latest technical performance data indicate that the system will meet all performance requirements.

2. Subsystem design is finalized and meets all allocated design and interface and all derived requirements.

3. System design:

    a. Meets all allocated design, interface and derived requirements.

    b. Traceability of design to requirements is maintained.

    c. Satisfies reliability, safety, logistics, product assurance, maintainability, and producibility requirements.

    d. Software requirements and preliminary designs are mature enough to proceed with detailed design and coding.

    e. Design data package is adequate to support development hardware.

EXAMPLE I.2: SUCCESS CRITERIA FOR COMPLETION OF DETAILED DESIGN, PROJECT X

The Project X customer and supplier agreed on the success criteria to be reached at the completion of detailed design. Some of these criteria follow.

1. Ninety percent of engineering design drawings are complete and releasable to manufacturing.

2. All stakeholders agree that ninety percent of drawings are complete and the design is producible.

3. Completion of subsystem design reviews:

    a. Enclosure

    b. Radio transmitter

    c. Battery

    d. Control

    e. Software

4. Prototype of enclosure demonstrated that the design meets the following requirements:

    a. RQMT002: Waterproof in continuous rain (per requirement ENCL002 in Chapter 3, Figure 3.13)

    b. RQMT003: Impact resistant (per requirement ENCL003 in Chapter 3, Figure 3.13)

5. Software integration testing results demonstrated that the software meets the following requirements:

    a. FUNC007: The Mobile C2 center shall allow the user to select a visible image of the terrain being surveilled.

b. FUNC008: The Mobile C2 center shall allow the user to select an infrared image of the terrain being surveilled.

c. FUNC009: The Mobile C2 center shall allow the user to select either a high-pass or a low-pass filter to enhance the visible image of the terrain being surveilled.

6. All stakeholders agree that there are no critical, Priority 1 software defects.

EXAMPLE I.3: SUCCESS CRITERIA AND TECHNICAL BASELINES FROM THE DEFENSE ACQUISITION GUIDE

The technical reviews and technical baselines shown in Table I.5 are discussed in the Defense Acquisition Guide (DAG). The iterations of the technical baseline are key systems engineering work products. Completion of these work products should be dependent on accomplishing the success criteria that are discussed below.

4.3.2.4.1. System Requirements Review

The SRR is conducted to ascertain progress in defining **system technical requirements**.

SRR Success Criteria. Typical System Requirements Review (SRR) success criteria include affirmative answers to the following exit questions:

1. Can the system requirements, as disclosed, satisfy the Capability Development Document?

2. Are the system requirements sufficiently detailed and understood to enable system functional definition and functional decomposition?

3. Is there an approved system performance specification?

4. Are adequate processes and metrics in place for the program to succeed?

5. Have Human Systems Integration requirements been reviewed and included in the overall system design?

6. Are the risks known and manageable for development?

7. Is the program schedule executable (technical and/or cost risks)?

8. Is the program properly staffed?

9. Is the program executable within the existing budget?

10. Does the updated cost estimate fit within the existing budget?

11. Is the software functionality in the system specification consistent with the software sizing estimates and the resource-loaded schedule?

TABLE I.5 DAG Technical Baselines

Technical Review	Technical Baseline
System Requirements Review	System Technical Requirements Baseline
System Functional Review	System functional baseline
Preliminary Design Review	System allocated baseline
Critical Design Review	System product baseline

4.3.3.4.3 System Functional Review

The System Functional Review (SFR) is a multidisciplined technical review to ensure that the system under review can proceed into preliminary design and that all system requirements and functional performance requirements derived from the Capability Development Document are defined and are consistent with cost (program budget), schedule (program schedule), risk, and other system constraints. Generally this review assesses the system functional requirements as captured in system specifications (functional baseline), and ensures that all required system performance is fully decomposed and defined in the functional baseline. System performance may be decomposed and traced to lower-level subsystem functionality that may define hardware and software requirements. The SFR determines whether the systems functional definition is fully decomposed to a low level, and whether the IPT is prepared to start preliminary design.

Completion of the SFR should provide:

1. An established system functional baseline
2. An updated risk assessment for the System Development and Demonstration phase
3. An updated Cost Analysis Requirements Description (CARD) (or CARD-like document) based on the system functional baseline
4. An updated program development schedule including system and software critical path drivers
5. An approved Product Support Plan with updates applicable to this phase.

The SFR determines whether the system's lower-level performance requirements are fully defined and consistent with the mature system concept, and whether lower-level systems requirements trace to top-level system performance and the Capability Development Document. A successful SFR is predicated upon the IPT's determination that the system performance requirements, lower-level performance requirements, and plans for design and develop-ment form a satisfactory basis for proceeding into preliminary design.

The program manager should tailor the review to the technical scope and risk of the system, and address the SFR in the Systems Engineering Plan. The SFR is the last review that ensures the system is credible and feasible before more technical design work commences.

Typical SFR success criteria include affirmative answers to the following exit questions:

1. Can the system functional requirements, as disclosed, satisfy the Capability Development Document?
2. Are the system functional requirements sufficiently detailed and understood to enable system design to proceed?
3. Are adequate processes and metrics in place for the program to succeed?
4. Are the risks known and manageable for development?
5. Is the program schedule executable (technical/cost risks)?
6. Is the program properly staffed?
7. Is the program with the approved functional baseline executable within the existing budget?
8. Is the updated Cost Analysis Requirements Description consistent with the approved functional baseline?
9. Does the updated cost estimate fit within the existing budget?
10. Has the system Functional Baseline been established to enable preliminary design to proceed with proper Configuration Management?
11. Is the software functionality in the approved functional baseline consistent with the updated software metrics and resource loaded schedule?

4.3.3.4.4. Preliminary Design Review

The Preliminary Design Review (PDR) is a multidisciplined technical review to ensure that the system under review can proceed into detailed design and can meet the stated performance requirements within cost (program budget), schedule (program schedule), risk, and other system constraints. Generally, this review assesses the system preliminary design as captured in performance specifications for each configuration item in the system (allocated baseline) and ensures that each function in the functional baseline has been allocated to one or more system configuration items. Configuration items may consist of hardware and software elements and include such items as airframes, avionics, weapons, crew systems, engines, trainers/training, etc. Completion of the PDR should provide:

1. An established system allocated baseline
2. An updated risk assessment for System Development and Demonstration
3. An updated Cost Analysis Requirements Description (CARD) (or CARD-like document) based on the system allocated baseline
4. An updated program schedule including system and software critical path drivers
5. An approved Product Support Plan with updates applicable to this phase.

The PDR evaluates the set of subsystem requirements to determine whether they correctly and completely implement all system requirements allocated to the subsystem. The PDR also determines whether subsystem requirements trace with the system design.

Typical PDR success criteria include affirmative answers to the following exit questions:

1. Does the status of the technical effort and design indicate operational test success (operationally suitable and effective)?
2. Can the preliminary design, as disclosed, satisfy the Capability Development Document?
3. Has the system allocated baseline been established and documented to enable detailed design to proceed with proper configuration management?
4. Are adequate processes and metrics in place for the program to succeed?
5. Have human integration design factors been reviewed and included, where needed, in the overall system design?
6. Are the risks known and manageable for development testing and operational testing?
7. Is the program schedule executable (technical/cost risks)?
8. Is the program properly staffed?
9. Is the program executable with the existing budget and with the approved system allocated baseline?
10. Does the updated cost estimate fit within the existing budget?
11. Is the preliminary design producible within the production budget?
12. Is the updated Cost Analysis Requirements Description consistent with the approved allocated baseline?
13. Is the software functionality in the approved allocated baseline consistent with the updated software metrics and resource-loaded schedule?

The program manager should conduct the PDR when all major design issues have been resolved and work can begin on detailed design.

The PDR should address and resolve major system-wide issues.

4.3.3.4.5. Critical Design Review

The Critical Design Review (CDR) is a multidisciplined technical review to ensure that the system under review can proceed into system fabrication, demonstration, and test and can meet the stated performance requirements within cost (program budget), schedule (program schedule), risk, and other system constraints. Generally this review assesses the system final design as captured in product specifications for each configuration item in the system (product baseline), and ensures that each product in the product baseline has been captured in the detailed design documentation. Product specifications for hardware enable the fabrication of configuration items and may include production drawings. Product specifications for software (e.g., Software Design Documents) enable coding of a Computer Software Configuration Item. Configuration items may consist of hardware and software elements and include items such as airframe, avionics, weapons, crew systems, engines, trainers/training, etc. Completion of the CDR should provide:

1. An established system product baseline
2. An updated risk assessment for System Development and Demonstration
3. An updated Cost Analysis Requirements Description (CARD) (or CARD-like document) based on the system product baseline
4. An updated program development schedule including fabrication, test, and software coding critical path drivers
5. An approved Product Support Plan with updates applicable to this phase.

The subsystem detailed designs are evaluated to determine whether they correctly and completely implement all system requirements allocated to the subsystem, and whether The traceability of final subsystem requirements to final system detail design is maintained.

Typical CDR success criteria include affirmative answers to the following exit questions:

1. Does the status of the technical effort and design indicate operational test success (operationally suitable and effective)?
2. Does the detailed design, as disclosed, satisfy the Capability Development Document?
3. Has the system product baseline been established and documented to enable hardware fabrication and software coding to proceed with proper configuration management?
4. Has the detailed design satisfied Human Systems Integration (HSI) requirements?
5. Are adequate processes and metrics in place for the program to succeed?

6. Are the risks known and manageable for developmental testing and operational testing?
7. Is the program schedule executable (technical/cost risks)?
8. Is the program properly staffed?
9. Is the program executable with the existing budget and the approved product baseline?
10. Is the detailed design producible within the production budget?
11. Is the updated CARD consistent with the approved product baseline?
12. Are Critical Safety Items and Critical Application Items identified?
13. Does the updated cost estimate fit within the existing budget?
14. Is the software functionality in the approved product baseline consistent with the updated software metrics and resource-loaded schedule?
15. Have key product characteristics having the most impact on system performance, assembly, cost, reliability, or safety been identified?
16. Have the critical manufacturing processes that impact the key characteristics been identified and their capability to meet design tolerances determined?
17. Have process control plans been developed for critical manufacturing processes?

The program manager should conduct the CDR when the "build-to" baseline has been achieved, allowing production and coding of software deliverables to proceed.

Glossary

	Word or Phrase	Definition
evms	Actual Cost (AC)	The costs actually incurred and recorded in accomplishing work performed.
3.2	Allocated Requirements	Requirements that have been assigned to elements of the system design (e.g. subsystems, components, or parts).
evms	Apportioned Effort	Effort that is not readily measured or divisible into discrete work packages but which is proportionately related to the planning and performance of other measured effort.
	Architecture	The underlying structure of a system.
	Architecture Baseline	The underlying structure of a system associated with a particular product or release.
	Artifact	A product of human effort.
	Attribute	A characteristic of a requirement that is useful in sorting, classifying, and/or managing requirements.
3.1	Baseline	A specification or product that has been formally reviewed and agreed upon, and thereafter serves as the basis for further development. It is changed only through formal change control procedures.
evms	Budget at Completion	The total authorized budget for accomplishing the project scope of work. The total planned value for that work.
EVP	Budgeted Cost of Work Performed (BCWP)	The budgeted cost for work that has been performed or earned value.
EVP	Budgeted Cost of Work Scheduled (BCWS)	The authorized budget assigned to the scheduled work to be accomplished. Also called Planned Value.
	Commercial-Off-The-Shelf (COTS)	An item of hardware or software that has been produced by a contractor and is available for general purchase.
	Constraint	A necessary attribute of a system that specifies legislative, legal, political, policy, procedural, moral, technology, or interface limitations.

	Control Account	A management control point at which budgets (resource plans) and actual costs are accumulated and compared to earned value for management control purposes.
evms		
EVP, 1.4	Cost Performance Index	A measure of cost efficiency on a project. It is the ratio of EV to AV. CPI = EV/AC.
EVP	Cost Variance (CV)	CV = EV – AC.
	Decomposition	Breaking apart the attributes of a customer need (the requirements of a system) so that
	Defect	A variance from a desired product attribute.
	Derived Requirement	A requirement that is further refined from a primary source requirement or from a higher-level derived requirement, or a requirement that results from choosing a specific implementation or system element.
	Design	The process of defining the architecture, components, interfaces, and other characteristics of a system.
	Development	The process of transforming a design into hardware and software components.
evms	Discrete Effort	Work effort that is related to the completion of specific end products and can be directly planned and measured.
evp	Earned Value (EV)	The value of work performed expressed in terms of the budget assigned to that work.
evp	Estimate to Complete (ETC)	The estimated cost of completing the remaining work.
evms	Estimate at Completion (EAC)	The current, most likely estimated total cost for project authorized work. EAC = AC + ETC.
	Event	A change in a system's environment that creates a response/set of actions.
	Framework	A basic structure of ideas or frame of reference, for example, the Capability Maturity Model Integration (CMMI).
	Function	A useful capability provided by one or more components of a system.

Functional Architecture	The framework for developing applications and defining their interrelationships in support of an organization's information structure. It identifies the major functions or processes an organization performs and their operational interrelationships.
Functional Requirement	A Necessary attribute in a system that specifies *what* the system or one of its products must do.
Hardware	Physical equipment.
Integration and Test	The activity in which modules of a system are combined according to the technical specification and the interfaces between the modules are examined critically to ensure that expected results are achieved. The results of testing provide the basis for acceptance or rejection of the system.
Integrated Product Team (IPT)	A group that includes customers and developers that blends perspectives into a functioning or unified whole. The joint team recommended in this book is an example of an IPT.
Level of Effort (LOE) evms	Unmeasured effort of a general or supportive nature, usually without a deliverable end product.
Life Cycle	The period of time that begins when a system is conceived and ends when the system is no longer available.
Life cycle model	A framework of processes and activities concerned with evolving a system that also acts as a common reference for communication and understanding among the participants in the effort.
Major defect	A problem that precludes effective use of a work product, such as a design deficiency or discovery of conflicting requirements.
Measures of Effectiveness (MOEs) 2.5	The metrics by which a customer will measure satisfaction with products produced by the technical effort. Key MOEs may include performance, safety, operability, usability, reliability, maintainability, time and cost to train, workload, human performance requirements, and other factors. (IEEE 1220)

Term	Abbrev.	Definition
Measures o Performance (MOPs)		Engineering performance measures that provide design requirements that are necessary to satisfy a measure of effectiveness. There are generally several measures of performance for each measure of effectiveness. (IEEE 1220)
Method		A way, technique, process, plan, mechanism, body of skills or techniques, dis cipline, practice, system, model, framework, capability, or procedure for doing something.
Methodology		A body of methods, rules, and postulates employed by a discipline; a particular procedure or set of procedures.
Minor defect		A problem that doesn't preclude effective use of a work product, such as a formatting issue, spelling error, language usage problem, acronym or definition not provided or explained.
Non-functional Requirement		A necessary attribute in a system that specifies *how* functions are to be performed, often referred to in systems engineering as the "ilities," e.g., reliability, reusability, portability, maintainability, compatibility, verifiability, predictability, safety, information assurance, resource efficiency, completeness, and human factors.
Performance Measurement Baseline (PMB)	evp, evms	An approved, integrated scope-schedule-cost plan for the project work against which project execution is compared to measure and manage performance. Also, the total time-phased budget plan against which project performance is measured.
Performance Requirement	2.5	The measurable criteria that identifies a quality attribute of a function, or how well a functional requirement must be accomplished. (IEEE)
Planned Value (PV)	EVP	The authorized budget assigned to the scheduled work to be accomplished.
Planning Package	evms	A logical aggregation of work, usually future efforts that can be identified and budgeted, but which is not yet planned in detail at the work package or task level.
Practice		The performance of work activities repeatedly so as to become proficient; the usual way of doing something so as to produce a good result.

Term	Ref	Definition
Process		A set of activities that results in accomplishment of a task or achieving of an outcome.
Process Flow Chart		A diagram that shows a step-by-step series of actions through a procedure using connecting lines and a set of standard symbols adopted by an organization.
Product Requirement	5.5	A statement that identifies a product operational, functional, or design characteristic or constraint, which is unambiguous, testable or measurable, and necessary for product or process acceptability (by consumers or internal quality assurance guidelines). (IEEE)
Product requirements baseline	3.1	See requirements baseline.
Product Scope	A.3	The features and functions that characterize a product, service, or result. The product scope includes the quality baseline. (PMBOK Guide)
Project Scope	A-3	The work that needs to be accomplished to deliver a product, service, or result with the specified features and functions. (PMBOK Guide)
Prototyping		A technique for building a quick and rough version of a desired system or parts of that system. The prototype illustrates the capabilities of the system to users and designers. It serves as a communications mechanism to allow reviewers to understand interactions with the system. It enables them to identify problems and consider ways to improve a system. It sometimes gives an impression that developers are further along than is actually the case, giving users an overly optimistic impression of completion possibilities!
Quality	2.5	The degree to which a set of inherent characteristics of a product or product component fulfills requirements of customers. (Derived from CMMI and PMBOK)
Quality Baseline		The basis for measuring and reporting quality performance as part of the PMB. (PMBOK Guide)

2.5	Requirement	A statement that identifies a product or process operational, functional, or design characteristic or constraint, which is unambiguous, testable, measurable, and necessary for product or process acceptability (by consumers or internal quality assurance guidelines). (IEEE 1220)
3.1	Requirements baseline	The set of requirements associated with a particular release of a product or system. Also, called the product requirements baseline when used in the context of a particular product.
2.5	Requirement	A statement that identifies a product or process operational, functional, or design characteristic or constraint, which is unambiguous, testable, measurable, and necessary for product or process acceptability (by assurance guidelines). (IEEE)
3.1	Requirement	A necessary attribute in a system; also a statement which identifies a capability, characteristic, or quality factor of a system in order for it to have value and utility to a user.
	Requirements Allocation	Assignment of requirements to architectural components of a system (e.g. a hardware or software configuration item, training, or documentation) sometimes referred to as flowdown.
	Requirements Analysis	A structured (organized) method to understand the attributes which will satisfy a customer need.
3.1	Requirements Baseline	The set of requirements associated with a particular release of a product or system.
	Requirements Derivation	To obtain requirements for a system from sources provided by the customer.
	Requirements Definition	A detailed description in general rather than functional terms of the attributes needed in a system.
	Requirements Elicitation	The process of drawing forth and bringing out requirements based upon information provided by the customer.
	Requirements Management	Tracking requirements status and change activity, and tracing requirements to the various phases and products of the development effort.

	Term	Definition
	Requirements Process	A full system life-cycle set of actions concerning the necessary attributes of systems. The requirements process involves understanding customer needs and expectations (requirements elicitation), requirements analysis and specification, requirements prioritization, requirements derivation, partitioning and allocation, requirements tracing, requirements management, requirements verification, and requirements validation.
	Requirements Traceability	The ability to determine the customer need to requirement relationship or connectivity, or of a parent requirement to a child and vice versa. The ability to trace a requirement throughout the system development process, from requirements specification to design, to system component through testing and system documentation. Absolutely critical for ALL systems.
2.6	Requirements Traceability	The evidence of an association between a requirement and its source requirement, its implementation, and its verification.
	Requirements Verification	Independent assurance that requirements are addressed and met in a system.
	Requirements Verification Matrix	An analysis that shows the verification method for each requirement.
	Risk	The possibility of suffering loss.
	Scalability	The capability to grow to accommodate increased work loads.
1.4	Schedule Performance Index (SPI)	The ratio of schedule progress against the plan based on budgeted resources, not time. SPI = EV / PV.
evp	Schedule Variance (SV)	SV = EV − PV.
	Specification	A document that describes technical requirements and verification procedures for items, materials, and services. An output of the requirements analysis process.
	Stakeholder	Anyone who has an interest in a system or in its possessing qualities that meet particular needs.
evms	Statement of Work	The document that defines the work scope requirements for a project.
	Supplier	An organization that contracts with a buyer to provide a system.

	System	An integrated set of people, products and processes that provide a capability to satisfy a customer need.
	System-level Requirements	A description of a system that provides the set of real stakeholder needs in terms of the general capabilities that are to be provided by the system and its products.
	System Life Cycle	The set of activities involved in understanding a customer need, defining and analyzing requirements, preparing a design, developing a system, testing, implementing, operating, and maintaining it, ending in its retirement.
	Systems Engineering (SE)	A technical and management discipline which translates a customer need into a system that meets the customer need. Another source states system engineering is the iterative but controlled process in which real user needs are understood and evolved into a operational system. The role of systems engineering is: technical authority on a project; single interface to customer and project architecture and system design; and requirements derivation, allocation and interpretation.
	Tailoring	The activity of modifying, elaborating, or adapting a process or document for another use. Reuse of tailored artifacts saves time and money and is an advantage of a process-oriented approach.
2.9	Technical Performance Measurement	Technical performance measurement compares technical accomplishments during project execution to the project management plan's schedule of technical achievement. Deviation, such as demonstrating more or less functionality than planned at a milestone, can help to forecast the degree of success in achieving the project's scope. (PMBOK Guide).
	Technical Performance Measures (TPMs)	Key indicators of system performance. Selection of TPMs should be limited to critical measures of performance (MOPs) that, if not met, put the project at cost, schedule, or performance risk. Specific TPM activities are integrated into the systems engineering master schedule (SEMS) to periodically determine achievement to date and to measure progress against a planned value profile. (IEEE 1220, 6.1.1.3).

	Term	Definition
evp	To-Complete Performance Index (TCPI)	The calculated projection of cost performance that must be achieved on remaining work to meet a specified goal, such as the BAC or the EAC. TCPI = (remaining work) / (budget remaining) = (BAC − EV) / (BAC − AV)
	Trade Study	An analysis of alternative courses of action in which a balancing of factors, all of which are not obtainable at the same time, is performed.
	Validation	A process for confirming that the real requirements are implemented in the delivered system
	Verification	A process for assuring that the design solution satisfies the requirements.
	Verification Methods	The approaches used to perform verification: test, inspection, demonstration, analysis.
	Work Package	A project work component at the lowest level of each branch of the work breakdown structure. It includes the scheduled activities and schedule milestones, or other objective indicators of schedule progress, required to complete the project work component.
	Work Product	A work product is an artifact that is the output of a work package. It need not be engineered or part of the end product.
evp	Work Scope	What work must be done.

About the Authors

Paul Solomon PMP is the principal and founder of the consulting firm, Performance-Based Earned Value® (PBEV℠). He is internationally recognized as a leader, teacher, and advisor on Earned Value Management (EVM). Mr. Solomon published articles on the use of PBEV to manage software and systems development projects. These articles have become standard, widely used references. He was the first EVM consultant in India, where he is called the Guru of Earned Value.

Mr. Solomon led the use of EVM at the Northrop Grumman Corporation on the B-2 Stealth Bomber, Global Hawk, and F-35 Joint Strike Fighter programs. He has taught thousands of professionals and led numerous independent assessment reviews, Integrated Baseline Reviews, and process improvement teams. He was a Visiting Scientist at the Carnegie Mellon University Software Engineering Institute where he developed training, participated in independent reviews, and authored the paper, "Using CMMI® to Improve Earned Value Management."

Mr. Solomon is a co-author of national and international standards for earned value management. He received the U.S. Department of Defense David Packard Excellence in Acquisition Award for his contribution to the standard, *Earned Value Management Systems* (ANSI/EIA-748-A-1998). He was also on the project core team that wrote the Project Management Institute (PMI) *Practice Standard for Earned Value Management.*

Mr. Solomon is a frequent speaker and tutor at conferences on project management, systems engineering, and software engineering

---

processes in the U.S. and India. He maintains a web site that is a source of guidance and best practices for Performance-Based Earned Value, www.PB-EV.com.

Mr. Solomon received his B.A. degree from Dartmouth College and his M.B.A. degree from the Amos Tuck School of Business Administration at Dartmouth College.

Dr. Ralph R. Young is an active leader and contributor in systems, software, and process engineering. His primary interest is to bring a sound working knowledge of the best practices to a wide professional and academic community. In this pursuit, he teaches requirements and process engineering courses and workshops, is a frequent speaker at meetings and conferences, and maintains regular contact with industry experts. He has conceived of a several-text series that covers the full spectrum of achieving his vision of requirements engineering. This is the fourth book in the series that draws heavily on his coauthor's expertise and experience in earned value techniques and his service mark in Performance-Based Earned Value. Ralph's first book, *Effective Requirements Practices* (Addison-Wesley, 2001), found a receptive audience with project managers and requirements analysts in computing and engineering. His second book, The *Requirements Engineering Handbook* (Artech House, 2004), is a desk guide for practicing requirements analysts that has become very popular with practitioners. His most recent book, *Project Requirements: A Guide to Best Practices* (Management Concepts, 2006), is targeted for project managers.

Dr. Young is the Director of Process Improvement, Systems and Process Engineering, Defense Group, at Northrop Grumman Information Technology, a leading provider of systems-based solutions. Dr. Young helped lead his former business unit (Litton PRC) to CMM Level 5 and another business unit Defense Enterprise Solutions (DES) to CMMI Level 5. DES was the first organization in the world to be evaluated a second time at CMMI Level 5. Ralph supports internal and external projects to improve their capabilities to utilize process improvement techniques, implement effective requirements practices, and develop innovations to facilitate project management. He leads a "Requirements Working Group" that involves over 50 requirements engineers from projects in his business unit.

Ralph is a graduate of the University of New Hampshire and earned a Master of Arts in economics and a Doctorate in Business Administration at The George Washington University in Washington D.C. He has been involved in systems and software development activities for 37 years. In 1972, he was appointed Director of the Systems Development Branch for Fairfax County, Virginia, where a group of 45 highly qualified developers provided state-of-the-art systems for local government functions. Subsequently, he was involved in and managed systems and software activities at Martin Marietta Corporation, TRW, PRC, Inc., Litton PRC, and Northrop Grumman Information Technology.

Ralph and his wife Judy have been married 40 years. Judy is an association executive and leader in sport and physical activity, and so has Ralph out walking at an early hour every day! Ralph enjoys family activities with children and grandchildren, music, singing, nature, the outdoors, and the wilderness. A priority in his life is active involvement in the faith communities of local churches. After retirement, Judy and Ralph have a dream of living aboard a trawler and traveling extensively.

Index

LaVergne, TN USA
17 December 2009
167397LV00002B/13/P